2000

ASSESSING
STUDENTS
WITH
SPECIAL
NEEDS

Contributors

WESLEY BROWN
College of Education
East Tennessee State University

SHARON S. COBEN
Department of Teaching and Learning
University of Miami

DOUG FUCHS
Department of Special Education
George Peabody College of
    Vanderbilt University

LYNN S. FUCHS
Department of Special Education
George Peabody College of
    Vanderbilt University

TED S. HASSELBRING
Department of Special Education
George Peabody College of
    Vanderbilt University

B. KEITH LENZ
Institute for Research in Learning
    Disabilities
The University of Kansas

DARYL MELLARD
Institute for Research in Learning
    Disabilities
The University of Kansas

PRISCA MOORE
Department of Special Education
George Peabody College of
    Vanderbilt University

CATHERINE V. MORSINK
Department of Special Education
University of Florida

MARILYN K. ROUSSEAU
School of Education
The City College of the City University of New York

CAROLE E. STOWITSCHEK
Title VI-B Grants Coordinator
Office of Superintendent of Public
    Instruction
Olympia, Washington

JOSEPH J. STOWITSCHEK
Department of Policy, Governance, and
Administration
University of Washington

ASSESSING STUDENTS WITH SPECIAL NEEDS

A SOURCEBOOK FOR ANALYZING AND
CORRECTING ERRORS IN ACADEMICS

Edited by

ROBERT A. GABLE
Old Dominion University

JO M. HENDRICKSON
University of Iowa

Longman
New York & London

Assessing Students with Special Needs:
A Sourcebook for Analyzing and Correcting Errors in Academics

Longman, 95 Church Street, White Plains, N.Y. 10601

Associated companies:
Longman Group Ltd., London
Longman Cheshire Pty., Melbourne
Longman Paul Pty., Auckland
Copp Clark Pitman, Toronto

Executive editor: Naomi Silverman
Production editor: Ann P. Kearns
Cover design: Susan J. Moore
Production supervisor: Kathleen M. Ryan

Library of Congress Cataloging in Publication Data

Assessing students with special needs: a sourcebook for analyzing and correcting errors
in academics / [edited by] Robert A. Gable, Jo M. Hendrickson.

    p. cm.
    Bibliography: p.
    Includes index.
    ISBN 0-8013-0177-7
    1. Remedial teaching.   2. Educational tests and measurements.
I. Gable, Robert A.   II. Hendrickson, Jo Mary.
LB1029.R4A5 1990
371.2'7—dc20
                                             89-35184
                                             CIP

ABCDEFGHIJ-ML-99 98 97 96 95 94 93 92 91 90

To
Karen, Melissa and Rebecca
—Bob
Marian and Otto
—Jo

Contents

Preface

Most teachers readily acknowledge that quality assessment is essential to successful instruction. Traditionally, academic achievement has been evaluated by means of periodic administration of various norm-referenced, standardized tests. However, there is growing dissatisfaction with the majority of these tests. Educational assessment is no longer viewed as a singular isolated act that takes place outside of the classroom. Increased importance is being given to forging a closer alignment between pupil assessment and instructional decision-making.

We recognize that a number of textbooks already provide teachers useful information on assessment. Even so, we are convinced that skill in uncovering *what* to teach should be linked to knowledge of *how* to teach it. With few exceptions, many otherwise excellent textbooks fail to establish this connection. This book arose, therefore, out of the recognition that many practitioners may lack skills to obtain classroom performance measures sensitive enough to make wise instructional decisions. Our decision was to focus on specific aspects of informal assessment. Our research and experience tells us that teachers will profit most from content that offers a clear set of proven strategies for identifying *and* remediating mistakes students make in reading, spelling, arithmetic, handwriting, and written language, combined with assessing skills in the content areas. Accordingly, we solicited contributions from colleagues who share the same conviction.

In the succeeding chapters, we provide regular and special education classroom teachers, psychologists, and other diagnosticians step-by-step procedures for strengthening the analytic-remedial process. The practical solutions discussed and illustrated through numerous tables and charts are drawn from a growing body of literature on educational assessment. We have pointed out many of these sources for those readers interested in a fuller discussion of various aspects of assessment. In that being a "good diagnostician" is comparable to being a "good detective," we encourage practitioners to constantly search for clues that may serve to further refine the teaching-learning process in all classrooms. We believe that this textbook will contribute to that effort.

We would like to express appreciation to our colleagues for their extraordinary effort in making this textbook a reality. In addition, we wish to give special thanks to Naomi Silverman for her technical assistance, encouragement, and support. Finally, we are indebted to Denise Huffman, Susan Hoebeke, and Crystal Tanner for their contribution to the preparation of the book.

R.A.G.
J.M.H.

CHAPTER 1

Traditional Academic Assessment: An Overview

Lynn S. Fuchs
Douglas Fuchs
Peabody College of Vanderbilt University

CHAPTER OBJECTIVES

After reading this chapter you should be able to:

1. Discuss a historical context of assessment practices in this country.
2. Discuss essential features of traditional testing and potential problems in traditional testing.
3. Provide an overview of alternative assessment practices.
4. Delineate several major types of nontraditional testing strategies.
5. Summarize the role of error analysis within assessment.

KEY TERMS

bias	psychometric characteristics
criterion-referenced test	referral
curriculum-based measurement	reliability
error analysis	selection response format
norm-referenced test	systematic error
precision teaching	test procedure error
production response format	validity

INTRODUCTION

Academic assessment involves measurement of pupil performance for the purpose of specifying and verifying students' instructional problems and formulating decisions about (a) screening and referral (i.e., identifying students in need of further assessment), (b) classification (i.e., determining who requires special educational services), (c) instructional planning, and (d) program modification (i.e., modifying instructional programs in response to student progress) (Salvia & Ysseldyke, 1988). Decisions in the first two assessment phases constitute the identification process, where comparisons among pupils are made to judge whether students' scores show sufficient discrepancy from those of their peers to require special intervention (L. S. Fuchs, 1986). These comparisons are called *norm-referenced*. During most of the twentieth century, such identification activity has dominated assessment practice in the public schools.

The purpose of this introductory chapter is to provide an overview of traditional academic assessment and provide examples of how alternative assessment procedures differ from and potentially enhance traditional assessment. First, we present a brief historical context for assessment practice in this country, followed by a discussion of essential features of and potential problems inherent in traditional testing. Next, we review the necessity for alternative assessment devices, with a delineation of several major types of nontraditional testing strategies. Finally, we summarize the role of error analysis within assessment.

HISTORICAL CONTEXT FOR ASSESSMENT PRACTICE

In the early part of this century, intelligence and achievement testing was the predominant assessment strategy in the schools. Such testing was employed primarily for sorting children into functional instructional groups (de Lone, 1979; Hendrick & MacMillan, 1984). Two forces emerged to create the context for which such testing was essential. First, urban growth, immigration, and compulsory attendance and child labor laws created a precipitous increase in school attendance, especially in major cities on the Eastern seaboard. As the school population grew, diversity of the student population increased, and the schools were faced with the task of teaching English to large numbers of pupils and motivating older students whose attendance was required by law. Intelligence and achievement testing was believed to represent an objective method for sorting the diverse student population into manageable instructional groups.

Concomitant with the increase in student diversity, pressure was applied by the business and academic communities to enhance the efficiency of schools (see Callahan, 1962). Efficiency was operationalized as regular class attendance, reduction in school dropout rates, and steady progression through the grades (Hendrick & MacMillan, 1984). Aptitude and achievement testing facilitated this goal by identifying lower ability students for special classes. In these special classes, practitioners were largely unaccountable for student progress; efficiency was not a criterion of the success of these classes.

In fact, many special classes rapidly became dumping grounds and holding tanks in which scant teaching or learning occurred (see Johnson, 1969). Consequently, children with the greatest need for effective instruction were frequently assigned to classes with inferior teaching. In recent years, of course, litigation (e.g., *Pennsylvania Association for Retarded Children v. the Commonwealth of Pennsylvania*) and legislation (e.g., Education for All Handicapped Children Act of 1975, or P.L. 94-142) have helped to transform previously ineffective and exclusionary special classes into more effective instructional environments in which a recognized goal is to reintegrate pupils into the mainstream of education. With the increase in accountability provided by legislation and litigation and with the simultaneous need to enhance the effectiveness of special programs, a selective educational enterprise has evolved into one that emphasizes the development of an educated society. The current focus is on an instructional environment as the important determinant of achievement, rather than on the inherent abilities of the individual (Glaser, 1981).

These recent developments have begun to shift attention away from classification decisions, which are based on descriptions of student abilities, to instructional programming decisions, which involve delineation of effective instructional environments. This transformation has created the need for alternative assessment strategies, which allow practitioners to plan sound instructional programs. Consequently, although traditional testing continues to dominate assessment practice in schools (e.g., Graden et al., 1984; Goh, Tesler, & Fuller, 1981; Winikur & Daniels, 1982), a stronger link between assessment and instruction is beginning to emerge (e.g., L. S. Fuchs & D. Fuchs, 1986c). Before describing developments in alternative assessment strategies that strengthen the link with effective instruction, we review essential features of and potential problems inherent in traditional assessment.

ESSENTIAL FEATURES OF TRADITIONAL ASSESSMENT

In everyday usage, the word *testing* denotes probing or sampling on a small scale in order to make broader generalizations (Jensen, 1981). So, for example, we taste or *test* a spoonful of the stew to decide whether the entire pot has enough salt. Educational tests are similar to such everyday tests: A small sample of behavior, based on limited observations, is examined to predict the general behavior or capabilities of an individual (Jensen, 1981). This definition of testing applies to all forms of educational and psychological measurement, including both traditional and alternative testing procedures.

Traditional tests are based on the common notion that most people are pretty much the same. For example, most people are relatively similar in height, and only occasionally do we notice an unusually tall or short person. In the same manner, most students within a classroom progress at a relatively consistent rate, with only a few pupils achieving at an uncommonly quick or slow pace. Traditional tests rely on this notion that most individuals cluster around the middle of any distribution and that increasingly fewer people fall at progressively extreme scores. Such an idea is represented in the bell-shaped, or normal, curve.

Given the assumption that achievement, like height, conforms to a bell-shaped distribution, traditional educational tests are designed to *produce* normal-shaped distributions. This means that traditional test items are selected specifically so that most students earn a "middle" score on a test, with fewer students achieving increasingly extreme scores.

Such tests are useful for making norm-referenced comparisons. Thus the primary purpose of these norm-referenced tests is to help determine how a particular student compares to other pupils of common background and experience. Consequently, if a multidisciplinary team were interested in determining whether a student required special intervention, an examiner might administer a traditional norm-referenced test. The resulting score would indicate how discrepantly the pupil tested from his or her peers and, consequently, how easy or difficult it might be to accommodate the pupil within a regular classroom. If the student's apparent capacity or achievement were notably lower than that of other pupils in the classroom, special educational placement, where a pupil could be grouped with similarly low achieving students, might be required. Such a decision constitutes a special education placement or eligibility determination. In a similar way, norm-referenced tests can be used to decide whether a pupil requires additional assessment (i.e., screening referral decisions) or whether a student currently being served within a special education program can be reintegrated into mainstream settings (i.e., certification or exit decisions).

At least two advantages of traditional norm-referenced achievement tests are frequently cited (e.g., Jensen, 1981). First, such published assessment instruments often are constructed carefully, with adequate attention to development of reliable measurements. This too frequently is *not* the case with teacher-made tests or commercially available criterion-referenced instruments (Tindal et al., 1985). Usually, during development of traditional tests, items are developed, revised, and selected on the basis of technical procedures known as "item analysis," based on tryouts of the items with samples of the test's population. Moreover, the technical features of traditional tests typically are documented and available to the public. Consequently, test users can judge the accuracy and meaningfulness of these instruments. A second advantage of traditional norm-referenced tests frequently cited is their norm group. Such tests are often standardized on large groups of children of diverse backgrounds. This can facilitate broad-based applications of findings.

POTENTIAL PROBLEMS WITH TRADITIONAL ASSESSMENT

Despite the (a) potential usefulness of traditional tests in formulating norm-referenced decisions, including screening, eligibility, and existing determinations, as well as (b) certain technical advantages of these instruments, serious problems exist in the use of traditional assessment instruments. First, whereas research generally supports the usefulness of traditional test content for predicting general achievement patterns in classrooms (e.g., Anastasi, 1976; Wigdor & Garner, 1982), bias sometimes appears to be inherent in the manner in which traditional tests are administered. For example, our research indicates that certain handicapped children obtain higher scores when tested by familiar, rather than by unfamiliar, examiners. Moreover, this pattern of performance appears in many different ways. For example, differential performance in favor of the familiar examiner was obtained (a) when examiners were inexperienced and when they were highly trained and practiced professionals, (b) across studies employing experimentally induced and long-term acquaintance definitions of examiner familiarity, (c) over various levels of test item difficulty and response modes, (d) irrespective of the sex of examinees, (e) for both preschool and school-age language-impaired students, (f) among language-impaired and learning disabled populations, and (g) regardless of whether examinees' performance was scored by the examiner or by a different rater who was responding to a videotaped replay of the testing (e.g., D. Fuchs, Featherstone, Garwick,

& L. S. Fuchs, 1984; L. S. Fuchs & D. Fuchs, 1984; D. Fuchs, L. S. Fuchs, Dailey, & Power, 1985; D. Fuchs, L. S. Fuchs, Garwick, & Featherstone, 1983; D. Fuchs, L. S. Fuchs, Power, & Dailey, 1983; D. Fuchs, L. S. Fuchs, & Power, 1987). An additional investigation has indicated that unfamiliar examiners depress the performance of language-handicapped, but not nonhandicapped, children (D. Fuchs, L. S. Fuchs, Power, & Dailey, 1983). This suggests that examiner unfamiliarity is a source of systematic error or bias in the assessment of language-handicapped children. Since this program of research has involved primarily language-handicapped children, and so few others are conducting research in this area, it is unknown whether findings are generalizable to students with other handicapping conditions, such as behavior disorders, mental retardation, and visual impairment.

Findings from this research appear to have important practical implications because of two salient features of normative tests. First, an average score on most norm-referenced tests reflects the mean performance of nonhandicapped children. This occurs because developers of norm-referenced tests appear to exclude handicapped children from their standardization populations (D. Fuchs, L. S. Fuchs, Benowitz, & Barringer, 1987). Second, during development of the norms, tests typically are administered by unfamiliar examiners (D. Fuchs, 1981). Experimental work (D. Fuchs, L. S. Fuchs, Power, & Dailey, 1983) suggests the use of such examiners in the development of norms does not depress the performance of the nonhandicapped standardization. In such comparisons, then, examiner unfamiliarity is a source of systematic error or bias that invalidates test-related diagnostic, classification, and program-placement decisions.

If studies demonstrate that examiner unfamiliarity depresses performance on the test but not on the criterion task, similar unrealistic teacher pessimism and unfair educational practice may unfold. Furthermore, the apparent bias caused by the use of unfamiliar examiners may be an explicit violation of the Education for All Handicapped Children Act of 1975 (P.L. 94-142) and Section 504 of the Rehabilitation Act of 1973 (P.L. 93-112), which stipulate that, for handicapped students, test instruments must be selected and administered to "accurately reflect the student's aptitude or achievement level or whatever other factors the test purports to measure" (34 C.F.R. 104.35 [b] [3] and 300.532 [c] [3]).

A second problem with traditional tests is that their nature typically requires objective, prescriptive scoring methods, which permit few decisions or judgments on the part of the scorer. This means that tests frequently are limited to multiple-choice (selection) response formats. For example, a selection response format might consist of a stem (the question or problem) followed by alternative responses from which the examinee tries to select the correct answer. Compared to production response test formats, where pupils are required to produce information in response to a structured task, these traditional selection test formats fail to assess students' skills in organizing knowledge in a manner similar to that required in natural contexts.

The selection format of traditional tests is also problematic because multiple choice responses reveal little about student strategies in problem solution. Therefore, such tests limit, if not preclude, detailed analyses of patterns of pupil errors, which may be useful for making instructional planning decisions. This problem is exacerbated by the fact that traditional norm-referenced achievement tests assess across multiple grade levels, with relatively few items at any one level or within any particular skill. Without multiple trials on a level/skill, it is extremely difficult for the teacher to identify the patterns of strategies students employ to execute skills and solve problems. This severely limits the process of identifying appropriate instructional strategies.

A fourth problem with traditional achievement tests concerns the lack of relationship between (a) traditional test content and (b) the instructional and curricular focus of particular classrooms. As Jenkins and Pany (1978) demonstrated and Shapiro and Derr (1987) recently replicated, different commercial reading achievement tests differentially sample the content of reading programs. Examination of these studies should alert special educators to the possibility that measurement of student achievement with commercial tests may better reflect performance on the specific test used than true levels of performance within classroom programs.

Together these problems are serious. They indicate the necessity for alternative assessment strategies that are more promising for the assessment purpose of instructional program planning and evaluation. Accordingly, we review several alternative assessment strategies. As each is discussed, we point out their advantages and disadvantages.

REVIEW OF ALTERNATIVE ASSESSMENT DEVICES

To summarize, various problems associated with traditional assessment instruments limit their usefulness for instructional program planning. These include the following: (a) bias emanating from the way in which tests are administered, which may be inherent in one-shot tests administered by unfamiliar examiners, (b) selection response formats, (c) insufficient number of responses for each skill, (d) poor match with program content, (e) limited use in designing interventions, and (f) poor utility for evaluation and program revision.

In light of these problems, Carver (1974) argued that alternatives to norm-referenced psychometric methods must be developed to enhance the usefulness of assessment for program planning. He labeled a new type of assessment as *edumetric* and emphasized the need for technically adequate procedures to evaluate individual performance and progress. Recognizing the need for an *edumetric* approach, Jenkins, Deno, and Mirkin (1979) outlined desirable characteristics of instructionally useful measurement systems: They must be reliable, valid with respect to criterion achievement measures, repeatedly and easily administrable, and sensitive to student growth.

Together, (a) the cited weaknesses of traditional tests and (b) the criteria for useful measurement procedures for instructional planning create a structure for evaluating alternative assessment instruments. Table 1.1 lists the considerations that alternative assessment strategies must address. These considerations provide the organization for the evaluation of the four alternative assessment procedures discussed below.

Precision Teaching

Precision teaching is a specialized measurement system, used within the past 15 years in special education programs. Typically, precision teaching incorporates several key elements (see White & Haring, 1980). First, the curriculum is segmented into a hier-

TABLE 1.1. How Alternative Assessment Procedures Address Basic Considerations

Considerations	Alternative Assessment Procedures			
	Precision Teaching	Teacher Tests	Basal Tests	CBM
Weaknesses of Traditional Tests				
Procedural bias	A	P	P	A
Selection response format	A	S	N	A
Few responses per skill	A	A	S	A
Poor match with program	A	A	A	A
Poor utility for designing interventions	P	P	P	P
Poor utility for program evaluation	P	P	A	Y
Criteria of Acceptability				
Reliable	?	?	?	A
Valid with respect to criterion achievement tests	?	?	?	A
Repeatedly/easily administrable	?	N	N	A
Sensitive to growth	A	?	?	A

NOTES: CBM is curriculum-based measurement. A = addressed; P = partially addressed; S = sometimes addressed; N = not addressed; and ? = unknown.

archy of behaviors, and a corresponding measurement procedure is designed to index student mastery of each successive behavior. Second, for each behavior within the hierarchy, student proficiency on the behavior is measured frequently, if not daily, as acquisition, mastery, and transfer of the skill is taught. Third, student scores are charted on semi-logarithmic graph paper and analyzed according to decision rules, typically referenced to so-called "aimlines" that show the anticipated student rate of progress toward an objective. These decisions address (a) when to modify the instructional program, (b) when to change the goal, and (c) how to modify the instructional program. Fourth, behavior modification principles are incorporated within instructional strategies, with a focus on direct teacher reinforcement of student behaviors.

So, for example, the target curriculum might comprise the following behaviors: saying sounds when presented with letters, reading consonant-vowel-consonant words (e.g., *cat, men, fit*), and reading final *e* words (e.g., *bite, mate*). For each of the three behaviors within this curriculum, the practitioner would design a measurement procedure. So, to test for saying letter sounds, the teacher might shuffle a deck of 26 letter cards and show each card until the student says the letter sounds or until 1 second passes, for a total of 60 seconds; the score would be the number of letter sounds said correctly per minute. For the second behavior in the hierarchy, the teacher might shuffle a deck of word cards, all of which conform to the consonant-vowel-consonant pattern, and show each card until the student says the word or until 3 seconds pass, for a total of 60 seconds; the score would be the number of words read correctly per minute. For the last behavior, the practitioner might shuffle a deck of word cards with words that conform to the final *e* rule and show each card until the student says the word or until 3 seconds pass, for a total of 60 seconds; the score would be the number of words read correctly per minute.

Having established the series of measurement procedures for the skills in the curricular hierarchy, the teacher would begin instruction on letter–sound correspondence. On an ongoing basis, the teacher would also administer the corresponding measurement task, graph scores, and inspect student performance on this skill to determine whether (a) the student's progress is adequate or inadequate according to the teacher's judgment, (b) a new goal and/or instructional program needs to be introduced, and (c) the goal has been met. If the student's progress were adequate, the teacher would continue the instructional program. If progress were inadequate, the teacher would inspect the database and lower the goal and/or change the instructional program to stimulate better growth; the pattern of student performance would determine the nature of the instructional change (see White & Haring, 1980). If the student had mastered the goal, the teacher would begin instruction on the next step of the curriculum (i.e., reading consonant-vowel-consonant words) and simultaneously begin to assess and graph student performance on the corresponding measure.

From the criteria in Table 1.1, we see that precision teaching addresses many of the considerations in designing an effective alternative assessment strategy. It eliminates test procedure bias, because familiar teachers administer the assessments across time. It incorporates a production, rather than selection, response format. This allows practitioners to observe patterns of behavior that might provide information for instructional planning, and it allows multiple responses per skill. Additionally, precision teaching corresponds extremely well with curricular content, mirroring the instructional focus, and it is likely to produce data that are sensitive to student growth.

Nevertheless, certain limitations are inherent in precision teaching procedures. First, instructional choices within precision teaching can be viewed as limited; the data are analyzed for instructional changes within a relatively narrow behavioral framework that emphasizes the breaking down of tasks into smaller units for initial teaching and the reinforcement of behavior for later skill development. Second, the assessment information may be limited for program evaluation purposes, because it summarizes pupil growth across time. As skills are mastered, the focus of the assessment changes so that assessments taken at different times of the year cannot be compared. Third, the accuracy or reliability of the assessment information is generally unknown, because the particular assessment methods are selected and designed by the teacher to conform with the particular skill to be addressed. Unfortunately, the technical features of teacher-constructed tests may be questionable. Similarly, the extent to which these measurement procedures relate to other important criteria of achievement is unknown. Therefore, for example, as students become more proficient on the series of subskills, it remains unclear whether their overall reading ability has improved. Research indicates that measurement of such subskills may relate poorly with global indicators of reading proficiency (L. S. Fuchs & D. Fuchs, 1986a). Finally, given that teachers must design a new assessment procedure and modify the measurement task each time a new skill is mastered, the practicality of the measurement process may be questionable.

Overall, precision teaching enhances the link between assessment and instruction in several important ways. Even so, key problems include the following: the instructional framework is limited to behavioral strategies; assessments taken at different times of the year are not comparable; and the technical features of the measurement are unknown. These limiting factors need to be considered as practitioners select alternative assessment strategies for designing effective interventions.

Teacher-constructed Tests

In most classrooms, teachers routinely design tests to assess student performance on instructional material. One reason for such testing is evaluation, that is, to assign students grades. However, a second, perhaps more important, reason for administration of teacher-made tests is to improve the quality of instruction delivered in classrooms or to evaluate the extent to which (and/or how) pupils have mastered the curriculum. Instructional decisions based on teacher-made tests can include determining what a student needs to learn next, how the study of the next instructional unit might best be accomplished, whether/when a student has mastered a particular objective, and whether to cycle back to reteach information (Nitko, 1983).

As we see in Table 1.1, as alternatives to traditional assessment, teacher-made tests exhibit certain strengths. They frequently assess multiple responses per skill and, if well designed, match the curricular focus nicely. Despite these strengths, however, important limitations are inherent in teacher-designed tests. First, they only partly address potential problems with test procedure bias: Although they are administered by familiar testers, they typically are completed in a single testing, a procedure which is prone to error due to transient student states (Stanley, 1971). Second and relatedly, because tests on a single topic are not typically administered on an ongoing, but rather on a one-shot, basis, the information frequently is not helpful for designing interventions. This is so because the only instructionally useful information usually addresses whether, but not how, a topic needs to be retaught, and this information is available only at the end of instructional units. Third, teacher-made tests frequently incorporate selection response formats, such as multiple choice or matching items, which do not permit detailed analyses of response patterns. Fourth, given that constructing tests is time consuming and that these tests are usually lengthy, repeated testing on alternate forms is not feasible. Additionally, because teachers rarely have the resources to investigate the technical characteristics of tests they create, information on the tests' reliability, validity, and sensitivity to student growth is rarely, if ever, known. Without such information, it is impossible to judge the accuracy and meaningfulness of test scores. Consequently, although the content of teacher-made tests frequently relates very closely to programmatic content, serious problems with the usefulness of such databases remain for effective instructional program planning.

Basal Series Tests

Basal series end-of-unit and end-of-book tests, as well as other published mastery tests, are examples of commercial criterion-referenced tests. As defined by Glaser and Nitko (1971), the criterion-referenced test is a sample of items yielding information that can be interpretable directly with respect to a well-defined set of tasks and to specific performance standards. In the past two decades, as an alternative to traditional measurement, these criterion-referenced tests have received increasing attention from measurement theorists, test developers, and school personnel.

As practiced in the schools, basal series and other commercial criterion-referenced testing frequently is designed to match prespecified objectives: Each unit of instruction encompasses a set of objectives and the content of the end-of-unit tests relates to these objectives. Following the delivery of a unit of instruction within the basal series, the teacher administers the corresponding test. Based on mastery/nonmastery determinations, instructional decisions typically address the need to reteach skills.

Given that such tests frequently match the content with respect to reading curricula, they do address certain weaknesses of traditional tests. Nevertheless, critical problems with end-of-unit and book basal series tests appear to exist; these problems limit the usefulness of these tests for instructional planning. First, research indicates that, when students receive nonmastery scores on these tests, teachers typically fail to actually reteach related skills (L. S. Fuchs, Tindal, & D. Fuchs, 1986). This, of course, limits the utility of the tests. Second, as with teacher-constructed tests, test procedure is only partially addressed. Whereas tests are administered by familiar examiners, one-shot administrations do not address sources of error due to fluctuating student conditions. Third, basal series tests usually incorporate a selection response format, as well as only a few items per skill. This limits the extent to which teachers can derive qualitative information for more effective instructional programming. Fourth, given that only one, or at most two, form of each test is available and that administration times are lengthy, repeated administrations are not feasible. Finally, as with teacher-made tests, the reliability, validity, and sensitivity of the measures to student growth is unknown. Research investigating the reliability and validity of basal series tests reveals that the technical adequacy of such tests is uneven, with some measures falling far below traditionally accepted criteria for reliability and validity (Tindal et al., 1985). Typically no information on reliability and validity is offered in test manuals of published criterion-referenced tests. Hence, the accuracy and meaningfulness of basal series and other commercial criterion-referenced tests is questionable, and this in and of itself reduces the potential usefulness of the information for instructional programming.

Curriculum-based Measurement

As employed in this chapter, curriculum-based measurement (CBM) refers to a set of measurement and evaluation procedures developed by Deno and colleagues (e.g., Deno, 1985, 1986, 1987; Deno & Fuchs, 1987) for the purpose of evaluating student progress in reading, spelling, written expression, and math. These procedures (see description below) incorporate the following dimensions: (a) selection of one long-term goal, instead of a series of short-term curricular steps, for monitoring student growth; (b) measurement of standard behaviors, which have documented reliability, validity, and sensitivity to student growth (see L. S. Fuchs, 1986); (c) use of prescribed measurement methods (e.g., test duration, frequency, administration, and scoring) that have acceptable reliability, validity, and sensitivity to student change (see L. S. Fuchs, 1986); (d) incorporation of rules that prescribe systematic procedures for summarizing and evaluating the assessment information, and (e) accommodation of any instructional paradigm (e.g., behavioral, cognitive).

Using CBM in the area of reading, a teacher might determine that, by the year's end, he or she wants the student to be proficient on grade level 3 material and that proficiency is reading at least 90 words per minute correctly with no more than five errors. This constitutes the long-term goal. Given the prescribed parameters of CBM, the teacher would assess the student at least twice weekly, each time on a different passage randomly sampled from the third-grade curricular text. Each time, the teacher would test in the exact same way: The teacher would state a standard set of directions, have the student read orally for one minute from the text, and score the number of correctly and incorrectly read words. This score would be charted on traditional graph paper, and the performance criterion of 90 words per minute for the year's end would be placed on the graph, at the intersection of the goal date and criterion level. Then, a goal line, connecting the baseline level and date and the goal criterion and date, would be drawn onto the graph. As the teacher provided an instructional program, she or he would continue to assess the student's performance on the goal task (i.e., reading aloud from the third-grade text) and would graph the scores.

Whenever at least eight scores had been collected in no less than three weeks, the practitioner would analyze the adequacy of the student's progress and then draw a line of best fit through the student's data, comparing the steepness of this line to that of the goal line. If the student's actual progress were steeper than the goal line, the teacher would increase the goal. If the actual progress were less steep than the goal line, the teacher would modify the instructional program in an attempt to stimulate better progress. (These procedures can be facilitated by use of computers for data collection, scoring, and analysis. See L. S. Fuchs, Hamlett, D. Fuchs, Stecker, & Ferguson, in press.)

CBM provides several important advantages over traditional assessment procedures. As shown in Table 1.1, CBM eliminates key sources of test procedure bias, by having tests administered by familiar examiners and by having information summarized across time and tests (L. S. Fuchs, Deno, & Marston, 1983). Additionally, a selection response format is employed in all academic areas (i.e., reading text, spelling words, computing problems, writing stories), and multiple responses are available within any measurement trial. Third, the match between CBM and programmatic goals is strong. The goals determine the measurement focus. Fourth, CBM is useful for program evaluation. With CBM, different assessment portions of graphs are always comparable; thus, one can summarize progress across school years. Moreover, since the data across students is the same, this facilitates program evaluation across students and program dimensions. Additionally, the criteria for acceptability as shown in Table 1.1, which so often are stumbling blocks for other forms of alternative assessments, are well met with CBM. The measurement procedures are reliable, valid with respect to other achievement tests, repeatedly and easily administrable, and sensitive to student growth. A program of research has addressed these issues, with CBM procedures developed in line with those research results.

Perhaps the one dimension on which CBM procedures may fall short of acceptability is in their usefulness for designing interventions. Although standard CBM procedures can be used to indicate *when* a program change is warranted, they do not provide systematic information for determining the *nature* of an effective program. Nevertheless, the database, in the form of student responses, is available with CBM. That is, one can analyze the tests completed by students to determine the nature of student errors and to formulate decisions about what instructional strategies and content might be use-ful. In fact, recent work (L. S. Fuchs, D. Fuchs, Hamlett, & Hasselbring, 1987) has employed computers to systematically analyze student responses within CBM. The computer automatically provides information concerning patterns of student errors and makes recommendations to teachers about instructional focus based on those patterns. Some of our recent work indicates that with this supplementary information teachers can plan more effective instructional programs and effect superior student achievement.

ROLE OF ERROR ANALYSIS WITHIN ASSESSMENT

Error analysis focuses on the student's academic response patterns as the "unit of analysis," which is critical for making instructional decisions (Gable, Hendrickson, Tenenbaum, & Morsink, 1986). Within error analysis, practitioners systematically observe correct and incorrect responses. However, they also conduct a detailed analysis of student responses that goes beyond the simple categorization of errors into right and wrong groupings. This analysis incorporates a reasonably large sample of behavior, where the student has produced, rather than selected, responses. Mistakes are systematically grouped so that information about students' patterns of responses and strategies for problem solution becomes apparent. This information constitutes the database for determining what *content* and *strategies* the teacher should incorporate into instruction (Howell, 1986).

Within the framework of the alternative assessment strategies described above, certain procedures generate superior databases for conducting error analyses. Useful databases for error analysis must: (a) incorporate a response format; (b) control testing conditions across time to yield standard formats (i.e., number of test items, administration procedures, length of testing, and type of pupil responses—Stowitschek, Gable, & Hendrickson, 1980), and (c) involve adequate numbers of responses. As you might suspect from the foregoing discussion, traditional assessment procedures fail to provide appropriate information for successful error analysis. Promising alternative assessment strategies include precision teaching and curriculum-based measurement. Within the framework of these approaches to instructional assessment, practitioners can inspect errors carefully, analyze patterns of responses, and make predictions about useful instructional strategies. The remainder of this book deals with promising strategies for conducting error analysis and for utilizing the derived information to enhance instructional program planning, especially for students experiencing academic difficulties.

DISCUSSION QUESTIONS AND ACTIVITIES

1. What has been the predominant assessment strategy in the schools during the twentieth century? What forces created the context for this assessment focus?
2. What factors have created the need for an alternative assessment approach? What is the focus of this alternative assessment?
3. Identify the basic notion underlying the normal curve.
4. Explain five key problems with traditional testing.

5. Describe four criteria for judging the adequacy of testing procedures to formulate instructional programs.
6. Identify four alternative assessment practices. Define each and discuss how each strategy satisfies the requirements for useful measurement procedures for instructional planning.
7. What is error analysis? Explain its function within assessment.

CHAPTER 2

Enhancing the Learning of Preschoolers with Handicaps

Wesley Brown
East Tennessee State University

Jo M. Hendrickson
University of Iowa

CHAPTER OBJECTIVES

After reading this chapter you should be able to:

1. Discuss the major components of PL 99-457 and its potential impact on special education services for young children.
2. Describe an interactional perspective on assessment and intervention with the preschool learner.
3. Discuss the importance of play and interactive learning in the life of the preschooler.
4. Identify five basic response-building strategies that are appropriate for teaching skills in various developmental domains.
5. Identify adult interaction strategies and environmental manipulation strategies for enhancing social, language, and other readiness skills.

KEY TERMS

developmentally at risk	IFSP
developmentally delayed	PL 99-457
developmental stage	preacademics
errorless learning	

INTRODUCTION

This book emphasizes error assessment and intervention strategies for teachers of elementary and secondary students. Here we focus on the learning needs of a special subset of students—preschool children who are handicapped, developmentally delayed, or at risk of becoming developmentally delayed. Therefore, the content and format of this chapter does not strictly parallel chapters dealing with error analysis in the academic arena. We wish to convey to the reader that we fully acknowledge the importance of applying the principles of learning to addressing the educational needs of young children; however, our goal is not to identify specific error patterns and related remediation strategies. Rather, our intent is to supply pertinent information, guidelines, and practical suggestions to help the teacher better conceptualize the overall learning process and learning needs of the young student. We believe that, through such an approach, mislearning may be prevented and efficient learning promoted.

In working with young children we recommend that teachers carefully assess the general and specific antecedents to and the consequences of behavior. We recommend that the environmental milieu which surrounds the child's learning experiences be systematically evaluated. We support an eco-behavioral approach to behavior analysis and endorse the use of a broad cognitive-developmental framework for establishing learning objectives. Teachers are encouraged to focus on child strengths and approach instruction as a response-building endeavor.

The chapter is divided into several sections. First, recent federal legislation that will have an unprecedented impact on education for developmentally at-risk and handicapped preschoolers is discussed. Next, we introduce an interactional perspective on teaching/learning, followed by guidelines adults should incorporate into their interactions with young children. Play contexts are recommended for adult–child, child–child, and child–material interactions designed to enhance learning. Five basic strategies teachers can use to promote initial skill acquisition are presented. Finally, we offer relatively detailed information and suggestions regarding preacademic skills, social skills, and expressive language.

LEGISLATION FOR PRESCHOOLERS WITH HANDICAPS

Public Law 99-457, entitled Education of the Handicapped Act Amendments of 1986, currently is having a broad impact on the planning of early intervention services for preschool children. This legislation departs from previous education mandates by creating incentives for states to develop new interdisciplinary services for young students with special needs. There are two major parts of P.L. 99-457 that affect preschoolers. First, state education agencies are strongly encouraged to extend special education services, as they are currently provided to school-aged students under P.L. 94-142, to students as young as 3 years old. If states have not done so by the 1991 school year, they will forfeit their existing federal funds for preschool children and also lose eligibility for certain other discretionary funds. Second, a new program known as *Part H* was created for infants and toddlers with handicaps.

Part H—An Interagency Approach

Part H encourages states to develop a policy requiring comprehensive services to children who are developmentally delayed. States also may serve, at their option, children who are at risk of becoming developmentally delayed. Rather than extending the edu-

TABLE 2.1. Minimum Components of a Statewide System of Early Intervention Services for Children with Handicaps from Birth through Age 2

1. A definition of "developmentally delayed" to be used by the state.
2. Timetables for serving eligible children by October 1991.
3. Multidisciplinary evaluations of the needs of eligible children and their families.
4. Individual Family Service Plans (IFSP) and case management services.
5. Comprehensive child find and referral system.
6. A public awareness program on early identification.
7. A central directory containing services and other resources.
8. A comprehensive system of personnel development.
9. A single line of authority in a lead agency designated by the governor.
10. A policy related to contracting or making other arrangements with local providers.
11. A procedure for timely reimbursement of funds.
12. Procedural safeguards.
13. Policies and procedures for personnel standards.
14. A system for compiling data on early intervention programs.

cational model already in place, states are expected to develop new coordinated, inter-disciplinary, interagency approaches to serving these children *and* families. Early intervention developed under Part H must coordinate the services of multiple state agencies including those directed toward health, human services, education, mental health, and mental retardation. Furthermore, each state must include 14 components (see Table 2.1) in its statewide system of early intervention.

Part H—A Family-oriented Approach

Departing from the traditional focus of providing special education services directly to the handicapped individual, Part H makes provision for comprehensive services to the families of infants and toddlers with developmental delays. Previous attention to the Individual Education Plan (IEP) is shifted to the Individual Family Service Plan (IFSP). The IFSP extends the IEP by including an assessment of family strengths and needs and the provision of services to families. All 50 states have participated in planning for Part H programs. States that continue to participate will be required to provide all 14 of the components in Table 2.1 to all eligible children and families.

PRESCHOOL LEARNERS WITH HANDICAPS

Early childhood special education represents an approach to preschool education that integrates the early childhood education focus on the whole child with the special education attention to the unique needs of individual learners. For handicapped and non-handicapped preschoolers, greater emphasis is placed on the process of learning than on the product. Two major perspectives toward learning are useful as a framework for structuring preschool education—cognitive-developmental and eco-behavioral theories. Together, they guide us in determining *what* and *how* to teach.

Cognitive-developmental Theory

The views of Jean Piaget (1952) form the cornerstone of the cognitive-developmental perspective that conceptualizes preschooler learning as both biological maturation and experience with the environment. Children's learning proceeds in a gradual manner and is related to the equilibrium achieved between two adaption processes. Through *assimilation,* children take in new information from the world but use this information within their current understanding of their environment; that is, the world is adjusted to fit their views. Through *accommodation,* children change their ideas to include new experiences; that is, their behaviors change because of their environment. The balanced dynamic of modifying one's knowledge of the world and the nature of one's actions allows children to interact and learn.

An Eco-behavioral Perspective

Taken as a unit, a modified behavioral and ecological paradigm provides an excellent framework for the assessment of environmental variables that may impinge on the young child's performance and learning. First, applied behavior analysis (ABA) tactics have been demonstrated empirically to be extremely powerful in aiding teachers in the instruction and management of children (Hendrickson, Gable, & Shores, 1987). Within an ABA framework, assessment focuses on the antecedent and consequent stimuli within the immediate environment that most directly influence behavior. Traditionally, an ABA assessment involves careful analysis of three events—the stimulus (S), the response (R), and the consequence (C). On the other hand, an ecological perspective encompasses a broader view of the factors influencing the learner and traditionally has included assessment of three primary ecosystems—the home, the school, and the community (Hobbs, 1966). By expanding the S-R-C paradigm to include other factors called *setting events,* we achieve a melding of the ecological and behavioral perspectives. Setting events comprise the milieu that surrounds the child. Setting events are those environmental events that determine which of the potential stimulus–response relationships appear at a given moment. Physical/social setting events within a classroom ecology might include the lighting, the noise level, the teaching/learning arrangements, the number of children and adults present, and the types of toys and materials accessible.

An Interactional View

Both the cognitive-developmental and eco-behavioral perspectives contribute to understanding the learning process of preschoolers. On one hand, preschoolers advance cognitively and developmentally as a result of the influences of interacting with their world. At the same time, they are influenced behaviorally because of how the world responds to them. Teachers must be sensitive to antecedent conditions and environmental consequences of child behavior because of the power of such events on learning. We can promote growth through establishing interactions that are sensitive to the child's cognitive level and maturation.

Adult-Child Interactions

Many researchers have studied the interactions of young children and their parents, caregivers, and teachers. Mahoney and Powell (1986) in *The Transactional Interaction Program* (TRIP) have researched such interactions extensively. Their analysis has yielded two particularly critical findings. First, adults often select content (or topics) for a trans-action that is at a level too advanced for the child, thus, limiting the child's capacity to learn and benefit from the interaction. Second, adults' rate of transactions generally are too rapid to allow sufficient time for child learning. Mahoney and Powell (1984) de-signed two instructional paradigms to help adults be more responsive (and less directive) to children: the turn-taking paradigm and the interactional match paradigm. The objec-tive of turn taking is to create an exchange that is characterized by balance (in number and length of turns) and that enables each person to have an equal opportunity to control the focus of the interaction. The instructional match paradigm is grounded on several conditions that must exist for the child to benefit optimally from an interaction. These factors are: (1) the adult's interactional style must be compatible with the child's, (2) the focus of the interaction must coincide with the child's present interests, (3) the

TABLE 2.2. Developing Play Environments

A. The physical environment
   1. Provide adequate, uncrowded space indoors and outdoors.
   2. Prepare small, separate play spaces for solitary activity.
   3. Prepare larger spaces for cooperative activities.
      a. Block and building materials.
      b. Housekeeping.
   4. Maintain the physical arrangement, but store and rotate play materials.
   5. Include clay and easels and monitor their use.
   6. Have puppets, animals, dolls, doll houses, and barns available to be set up.
   7. Relocate materials that encourage incompatible activities or noises.
   8. Have safe areas and structures for running, climbing, crawling, and riding.
   9. Provide special equipment for children with special needs.
B. Coordinating play activities
   1. Alternate use of indoor and outdoor spaces.
   2. Have limited, simple rules.
   3. Children need to learn the rules through observation and experience.
   4. Rules should support positive social behavior and respect individual play.
   5. Teachers need to model positive interactions.
   6. Play items should be returned before new items are chosen.
   7. Facilitate the observations of a child who wants to watch, not participate.
   8. Adults, like children, should not barge into an established group.
C. Guidelines for careproviders
   1. Respect student choices of activities.
   2. Anticipate and prevent problems, rather than punishing.
   3. Interfere only when absolutely necessary and avoid overprotectiveness.
   4. Constantly monitor all that is happening in the room to develop consistency.
   5. Find ways to allow children to be noisy and very active when necessary.
   6. Avoid comparisons and making children self-conscious.

SOURCE: Adapted from R. E. Cook, A. Tessier, and V. B. Armbruster, *Adapting Early Childhood Curricula for Children with Special Needs*, 2nd Ed. © Merrill Publishing Company, Columbus, OH: 1987, pp. 149–50. Reprinted with permission.

complexity of adult behavior must not exceed the child's capacity to process information, and (4) the difficulty of the activity should not exceed the child's competence.

Play as Transactional Interaction

Sameroff (1981) noted that the child's total development is the sum of the actions to and reactions from the environment. While early childhood educators always have stressed the value of play, we can see that play also may meet Mahoney and Powell's guidelines for positive transactions. During play, children select activities that match their interests and transact at their own rates of turn taking, motivated through their successful interactions with other children. Their successful play experiences provide positive practice of multiple skills with feedback and behavior alterations a natural part of adjusting to the play activities.

Structuring Playful Interactions

Piaget (1963) postulated three categories of play—practice play, symbolic play, and rule-governed games. *Practice play* allows the exploration and repetition needed to be successful with the activity. Later, *symbolic play* emerges as play objects come to represent other objects with which the children are familiar. Finally, play becomes complex, expressing itself in the form of *games with rules*. Such play requires coordinated activity and communication. Teachers are admonished to select materials and toys to correspond with each level of play. Table 2.2 provides guidelines to assist the teacher in arranging play environments for enhanced learning.

LEARNING THEORY APPROACHES FOR PRESCHOOLERS

Preschoolers are in a nearly constant state of learning from their environmental interactions. They continue learning by practicing what they have learned in order to master the new information. Teachers actively facilitate this acquisition of new learning by structuring antecedent conditions. Establishing a set of environmental conditions that will not allow the child to make errors or incorrect responses has become known as *errorless* learning. Wolery, Bailey, and Sugai (1988) present several reasons for using errorless learning procedures. First, errorless learning tactics are *effective* ways of teaching a wide range of behaviors. Second, they promote *positive social interactions* while avoiding inappropriate social behaviors associated with errors. Finally, errorless learning strategies are based on the belief that students learn little from errors under most conditions. We can promote errorless learning by presenting tasks to match the learner's capabilities and teaching these tasks in appropriate steps with the use of prompts, cues, models, and contingent reinforcement.

Promoting Initial Learning

A variety of teaching strategies can be used to promote new learning by preschoolers. Table 2.3 identifies five strategies—prompting, modeling, shaping, chaining, and discrimination training—known to be appropriate for minimizing errors and promoting

TABLE 2.3. Learning Strategies and Related Learner and Task Characteristics

Learning Strategies	Learner Characteristics	Task Characteristics
Prompting	Learners who do not easily attempt new behaviors Learners who have difficulty focusing on critical stimuli Learners with problems with attention	Tasks where shaping alone would be too time consuming Tasks where it is important to start, stop, and change behavior in response to signals
Modeling	Learners who can imitate Learners who enjoy identifying with others Learners with good attention and observation skills	Tasks where unique performances are not required Behaviors where the environment provides many models
Shaping	Learners who cannot imitate Learners who are resistant to performing the behavior Learners who require immediate reinforcement	Tasks involving improving skills, e.g., speed, accuracy Tasks involving fine motor coordination
Chaining	Learners who cannot imitate sequences Learners who cannot follow sequenced verbal directions	Tasks involving several steps or complicated activities Tasks where behavior must be in a quick or precise sequence
Discrimination training	Learners who confuse two stimuli Learners who overgeneralize	Tasks involving attaching labels to concepts Tasks where multiple stimuli are similar

SOURCE: Adapted from *Individualized Education for Preschool Exceptional Children* by J. T. Neisworth et al., p. 99, with permission of Aspen Publishers, Inc., © 1980.

learning in youngsters exhibiting difficulties. Table 2.3 depicts both the characteristics of the learner and the tasks for which a given strategy is recommended. Teacher activity that comes *before* a student responds often consists of prompts and models. Such instructional strategies assist the student by providing information about task demands and teacher expectations. Antecedent strategies typically include pictures, gestures, physical assistance, and verbal statements.

Wolery, Bailey, and Sugai (1988) provide the following guidelines for selecting and using prompts: (1) use the least intrusive, simplest prompt that will be effective (e.g., a gesture is preferable to physical assistance); (2) use several prompts in combination; (3) select natural prompts (i.e., use conventional gestures) that are consistent with the student's response capabilities; (4) obtain the student's attention before providing the prompt; (5) use prompts in an instructive manner prior to the student response; and (6) gradually eliminate the prompt(s) as the behavior is learned. As the child progresses, offer less and less guidance.

When it happens that learning is not most efficiently facilitated through prompts and modeling, other applied behavior analysis strategies—shaping, chaining, and discrimination training—are suggested. Wolery, Bailey, and Sugai (1988) have developed extensive supportive materials to illustrate these strategies.

CURRICULAR APPROACHES FOR PRESCHOOLERS

Young students are prepared for learning academic information through preacademic curricular experiences. To enhance the likelihood of a successful transition to academic learning, all preschoolers must be assisted in developing the competencies expected in the next educational environment (e.g., kindergarten). Hoyson, Jamieson, and Strain (1984) doubled the normal rate of development for both normal and autistic-like students with a combination of an individualized curriculum, daily lessons and review of goals, revised objectives, frequent assessment of the curriculum's impact, and effective group behavior management. Additionally they found independent work and task performance skills to be the most critical transitional skills. Following directions and routine, concentration and persistence, observation and communication skills, and problem-solving skills are necessary to teach in preparation for the next level of schooling. Curricular approaches must maximize the amount of *engaged* or on-task time of preschool learners. Thus while play and interactive contexts are viewed as ideal teaching milieus, early educators increasingly are aware that precious time can be spent nonproductively if careful instructional planning has not taken place.

Developmental Domains

Developmental and other preschool curricula traditionally have been organized by skill domains. The most commonly designated developmental domains are: gross motor, fine motor, self-care, social, cognitive, and language. Successful skill mastery within these domains provides a basis for later academic learning and social skill development. However, care must be taken not to view these domains too discretely. These domains are so intimately related that they are often inseparable for educational purposes (Bricker, 1986). Instructional activities may cross developmental domains. As skills are developing, the young student will show evidence of progression from simple to more complex forms of behavior within and across domains.

Preacademics and Readiness

The developmental activities that prepare young students for later academic learning are referred to commonly as preacademic or readiness skills. Preacademic skills include but are not limited to reading readiness, the alphabet, and understanding of the concept of a word; understanding of quantitative concepts, number recognition, and counting; listening and auditory discrimination skills; visual memory and visual discrimination skills; social skills; speech and language abilities; and fine motor abilities such as drawing, copying, and printing. For most children, preacademic skills can be taught effectively by maximizing the learning that transpires in naturally occurring, daily events. With preschoolers, the daily activities and interactions involved with self-care, feeding, music and art, and play are excellent for providing incidental learning experiences (Hart & Risley, 1975; Mudd & Wolery, 1987). (See the section on language and the preschool learner for more detail on incidental teaching strategies.) Conversation, or language, is a critical medium for developing readiness. In the course of conversing, children develop listening skills that help them recognize, interpret, and understand their environment. They learn through matching, grouping, perceiving common elements, understanding cause and effect, ordering, seriation, and conservation during their play experiences (Hendrix, 1988). Eventually, preschoolers need to work/play independently as well as in a group. They must attend to tasks and interact constructively with materials.

SOCIAL SKILLS TRAINING

Communicative competence, affective development, and cognitive skills are acquired and enhanced in the context of social exchange. Infants and young children learn to initiate and respond in the course of social dialogue. Indeed, a wide variety of vocal-verbal and motor-gestural behaviors of young children may be viewed as social or precursory to the development of the complex array of behaviors that together comprise successful social discourse in older children and adults. As the majority of children reach primary age, their social competence opens the door to a multitude of learning opportunities. Conversely, handicapped children and children with social skill deficits or behavioral excesses are likely to become increasingly rejected by and segregated from the common social interactions most young children experience. Reduced opportunities to practice the give and take of social encounters place these children at great risk for acquiring and mastering more complex social skills. Simply stated, the development of positive social behavior in young children has an unquestionably significant effect on their overall development (Ainsworth, 1970; Blurton-Jones, 1972) as well as their future academic progress, social acceptance, and emotional adjustment.

Social Skill Assessment

Parent and teacher rating scales, behavior checklists, teacher nomination, and direct observation techniques may be employed to identify high-risk children and pinpoint specific behaviors needing intervention. Direct observation of the type, frequency, and/or intensity of more than one behavior may be preliminary to modifying the social skills of children with markedly deviant, developmentally deficient, or socially unacceptable behaviors. Data on facial expressions, gestures, gaze, vocalizations and verbalizations, approach and withdrawal, offering and receiving, toy and material use, social activity contexts, and physical contact with others often constitute the basis for intervention decisions.

However, caution must be exercised in collecting assessment data that reflect only the behavior of the target child. Challenging behavioral excesses (e.g., aggression) and/or deficits (e.g., social isolation) are more fully assessed by examining both the behavior of the child and those with whom he or she interacts (i.e., a dyadic measurement system). Thus, examination of persisting social difficulties should include the manner and frequency with which the target child *and* others initiate and respond to one another. Dyadic systems of measurement enable examination of the antecedent and consequent events that are the immediate determinants of behavior (Hops, 1982). A dyadic system of measurement is an excellent tool for daily monitoring of behavior change and intervention effect.

Figure 2.1 contains an example of a dyadic measurement system. Data entries are

	Minute 1			Minute 2		
Child Behavior						
Initiates	V−		M+		V+	M−
Responds		V−		M+		
Peer/Adult Behavior						
Initiates		V+		M+		
Responds	V−		M+		V+	V−
Activity Context						
Isolate						
Observer						
Parallel	/	/	/			
Cooperative				/	/	/
Fantasy						
Material/Equipment						

20 Second Intervals		Minute 1	Minute 2
	1	*blocks*	*sand box*
	2	*blocks*	*sand box*
	3	*sand box*	*sand box*

Figure 2.1. Sample Dyadic Behavior Data Collection System

NOTE: V = vocal/verbal;   M = motor/gestural;   X = no interaction.

23

made at the end of each of three 20-second intervals per minute. In this system, the observer places a plus sign ($+$)—positive behavior, minus sign ($-$)—negative behavior, or slash (/)—type of activity context to mark each relevant category of the behavior sequence in progress. A tape-recorded sound is recommended to denote the beginning of each 20-second interval. Codes are used to designate the behavior categories of interest. Specific behaviors such as shares, assists, play organizers, greetings, affection, and rough and tumble play can be substituted for the general categories of vocal-verbal (V) and motor-gestural (M) behaviors coded in Figure 2.1. Teachers usually collect data from 5-minute to 10-minute segments.

Figure 2.2 contains an alternative dyadic recording system. When using the dyadic system in Figure 2.2, teachers simply circle codes that describe the behavior sequence in progress at each 20-second beep. In this example shares (sh), affection (af), and verbalizations (v) are the behaviors of interest. No interaction is again indicated with a large X. The activity context is circled, I = isolate, O = observer, P = parallel, C = cooperative, and F = fantasy play. Again, the teacher notes the materials in use at the moment of observation.

Once baseline data are collected on the child's interactions, behavior priorities, teaching contexts, and materials to be used for intervention are selected. Generally speaking, intervention strategies are based on whether the child (1) has acquired a behavior, but is not exhibiting it, (2) must develop/learn the behavior, or (3) is exhibiting negative behaviors. Several approaches known to promote the social competency of young children are presented below.

Teacher-mediated Strategies

Most often teachers choose to directly intervene in building prosocial behavior or extinguishing undesirable behavior. Teacher-mediated strategies include providing clear, simple instructions, using simple advance organizers, modeling the behavior, rehearsing the behavior, and providing prompts and praise (McEvoy & Odom, 1987). Shaping successive approximations of a desired behavior (e.g., approaching others) and chaining behavior sequences (e.g., turn taking) are generally accomplished through teacher-mediated strategies.

Public praise by teachers and the award of special privileges (e.g., line leader) may increase a child's popularity and encourage others to interact with the child to gain adult approval. Group contingencies in which the target child earns a reward for all children may be employed with higher functioning children. If the teacher or parent wishes to extinguish a behavior through the use of ignoring or mild verbal aversives, care must be taken to ensure that the child can access attention and reinforcers with more acceptable behaviors.

Peer-Initiation Strategies

Children who are socially competent or more competent than the target child are taught to initiate positive interactions with the target child. Teachers must take care to train peers to continue initiating even if the target child does not respond.

	Minute 1			Minute 2		
Target Child		X	X			
Initiates	+ - sh af v	+ - sh af v	+ - sh af v	+ - sh af v	+ - sh af v	+ - sh af v
Responds	+ - sh af v	+ - sh af v	+ - sh af v	+ - sh af v	+ - sh af v	+ - sh af v
Peer						
Initiates	+ - sh af v	+ - sh af v	+ - sh af v	+ - sh af v	+ - sh af v	+ - sh af v
Responds	+ - sh af v	+ - sh af v	+ - sh af v	+ - sh af v	+ - sh af v	+ - sh af v
Activity Context	I O P C F	I O P C F	I O P C F	I O P C F	I O P C F	I O P C F
Material/Equipment 1	ball			book		
Material/Equipment 2	ball / book			feather scarf		
Material/Equipment 3	book			feather scarf		

Figure 2.2. Sample Alternative Dyadic Behavior Data Collection System

NOTE: Sh = shares; af = affection; v = verbalizations; I = isolate; O = observer; P = parallel; C = cooperative; F = fantasy play; X = no interaction.

Peer-Tutoring Strategies

The peer is taught to prompt and reinforce the target child for exhibiting specific behaviors such as sharing and turn taking. Initally, the peer is praised and reinforced by the teacher for successful interactive trials. Teacher support is gradually withdrawn.

Peer-Association Strategies

The target child is paired with popular and/or socially competent children in different activities. Praise and attention is given to the peer and the popular child as a unit. Pairing may lead the other children to view the target child in a more positive manner.

Proximity Intervention Strategies

Adults may decrease inappropriate behaviors and increase compliance by regulating their proximity to the child before and after an instruction is given. Usually, no additional verbal cues are provided; instead the adult physically moves close to the child and waits for the desired behavior. A gesture (e.g., pointed finger) may be issued to prompt a desired response. Verbal praise follows compliance.

Closer physical proximity of the children to each other may be established by using a visual marker of a play space in which the children are expected to remain. Observational learning, parallel play, and cooperative play may result by placing one to three socially competent peers in a designated play area with the target child.

Material/Toy Control Strategies

Classroom materials identified by the teacher as facilitative of social interaction and as being popular with all children may be given to the target child, who then has the option of sharing or of not sharing. Materials facilitative of play styles slightly above the daily functional level of the target child may be introduced. For instance, the child who primarily engages in isolate or observer behavior may be given the choice of using some materials associated with parallel play (e.g., paint and easel) or with cooperative play (e.g., housekeeping items).

Time Extension Strategies

Children can be required to interact positively for very short periods (e.g., 30 sec.) to receive a desired object or reinforcer. A timer is used to mark the end of the interval. Once children are consistently successful for the desired number of seconds or minutes, the length of time is increased or the materials involved are exchanged for others.

Problem-solving Strategies

Role playing and rehearsal can be used to demonstrate and practice appropriate ways to solve problems and express feelings. Young children with language can be taught positive self-verbalizations as a way of monitoring and regulating their own behavior.

Family-mediated Strategies

Parents and teachers can and should collaborate to set intervention priorities as well as reinforce and ignore the same behaviors. Children can earn rewards (e.g., stickers) at home for behavior at school. Siblings can be taught and reinforced for initiating and responding in positive ways to the social bids of their brother or sister with a handicap. Parent–teacher collaboration can be very useful in promoting skill generalization across settings and people.

Behavior Selection Strategies

Teachers should attempt carefully to target and intervene upon those behaviors that have a high probability of eventually being maintained without any intervention. Behaviors that are likely to be valued in other settings (e.g., greeting behavior) should have priority over less functional behaviors. Behaviors that are similar in topography and function to the behaviors of socially competent peers should be taught.

LANGUAGE AND THE PRESCHOOL LEARNER

Language learning occurs in the course of social exchange and typically involves reciprocal interaction between the caregiver and the child. The development of language generally is considered in terms of three basic features—its form (syntax), content (semantics), and use (pragmatics). Difficulties in language acquisition may arise in one or all of these categories. Often preschoolers with language difficulties exhibit low levels of communicative behavior and decreased spontaneous language. Frequently these children avoid situations that require language use.

As in the assessment of social behavior, an eco-behavioral perspective and direct observation system similar to those in Figures 2.1 and 2.2 may be essential for identifying the frequency and function of specific language behaviors. The reader is encouraged to adapt the observation systems presented earlier to incorporate targeted language features. The remainder of this section presents strategies to facilitate language development in the preschool child.

Social Play as a Context for Building Communication

MacDonald and Gillette (1988) provide convincing argument for the importance of social play in the building of communicative behavior in young children. Several strategies adults should employ include: (1) using play routines that allow the child to predict sequences and learn new behavior in the context of old, safe interactions; (2) turn taking or the development of the give-and-take habit across settings; (3) increasing the wait time you allow for the child to respond; (4) imitating the child's actions and sounds; (5) entering the child's world by acting as the child acts; (6) being animated and interesting; and (7) responding acceptingly of the child's contacts. These authors believe that one unifying principle, the "progressively matched turn-taking" principle, may govern all successful interactions. During turn taking the give and take is balanced in terms of who is modeling and who is responding or waiting for feedback. The adult continues to perform as the child does but moves to a slightly higher model or "progressive match" in which something the child is capable of doing is modeled.

Adults, professionals and paraprofessionals, may fall prey to using language that is counterproductive with the young child. MacDonald and Gillette (1988) describe language habits that may interfere with the child's language learning and conversation building. These include: (1) the use of adult language (syntax and semantics), which cannot be performed by the child and often leads to learning not to listen; (2) the use of academic or school language, which has little interest to the preschooler; (3) adult control of the topic of conversation, which reduces child motivation; (4) adult lack of responsiveness to opportunities for conversation; (5) overuse of questions and commands; (6) the use of rhetorical language, which may result in the child's learning not to respond to "talk"; and (7) the use of excessively directive language, which precludes the child's influencing and controlling the conversation.

Milieu Language Teaching

Milieu teaching is a naturalistic intervention strategy that uses everyday instances of social communicative exchange to teach elaborated language (Kaiser, Hendrickson, & Alpert, in press). Milieu teaching is based on the instructional technology of behavior analysis and relies on the systematic presentation of antecedent events (e.g., prompts) and consequent events (e.g., delivery of the desired object). For example, following a child initiation, a specific verbal prompt (a command or model) or nonverbal prompt (a time delay) is presented. If the child's response is at the appropriate level and suited to the communicative context, positive consequences are provided. A response that is incorrect, incomplete, or less complex than desired is followed by another prompt. A maximum of three prompts is offered, and the interaction is always terminated positively by the child's accessing the object of interest and/or the adult's delivering an expansion or other topic-affirming comment.

During milieu teaching, language with an immediate function for the child is taught. Numerous environmental arrangements may be set up to facilitate milieu teaching. Specific setting conditions the teacher may employ to encourage functional communication include: (a) involving objects and activities likely to interest the child, (b) creating a need for the child to communicate by putting a desirable object in view but out of reach, (c) creating a situation where the child wishes *more* of something, (d) not giving the child all the materials required to carry out a task she wishes to perform, (e) providing the child with materials that require assistance, (f) creating a situation where the child wants the adult to stop doing something, and (g) setting up a sequence of events where the child develops an expectancy, but the teacher then does something unexpected.

SUMMARY

The present chapter introduced PL 99-457 and briefly discussed its implications for early childhood special education services. The learning characteristics of young children were presented and an argument made for focusing on building the preschooler's repertoire of functional behavior by using the daily interaction contexts of the child as opportunities for teaching. Play and social communicative contexts are described as particularly rich milieus for enhancing development. Five specific strategies for promoting learning were described in relation to learner and task characteristics. Numerous examples of ways adults may modulate their own behavior and regulate aspects of the environment to promote the acquisition of school readiness skills are provided.

DISCUSSION QUESTIONS AND ACTIVITIES

1. Use both of the sample dyadic data collection forms on two separate occasions to observe the same child for 10 minutes. Discuss their advantages/disadvantages. How would you modify the systems to gather information more pertinent to the child you observed?
2. Audio or video tape a conversation that you or another have with a young child. List the kind and number of facilitative and nonfacilitative behaviors emitted by the adult.
3. Discuss learner and task characteristics that may call for prompting, modeling, shaping, chaining, and discrimination training.

CHAPTER 3

Errors in Arithmetic

Robert A. Gable
Old Dominion University
Sharon S. Coben
University of Miami

CHAPTER OBJECTIVES

After reading this chapter you should be able to:

1. Define error analysis and describe a system for classifying errors in arithmetic.
2. Outline a strategy for conducting error analysis.
3. Identify approaches to remediating arithmetic errors, according to learning stages.
4. Apply error analysis techniques to problem solving activities.

KEY TERMS

algorithm	criterion-referenced test
arithmetic operation	error analysis
computation skill	norm-referenced test

INTRODUCTION

Arithmetic is a branch of mathematics that deals with computational procedures for working with addition, subtraction, multiplication and division of whole numbers and fractions (McLoughlin & Lewis, 1986). Its importance rests with the fact that other curricular areas rely on arithmetic skills, for example, bookkeeping and science (e.g., Choate, 1987). Also, basic computational skills are fundamental to coping with everyday living—eating at fast food chains, operating vending machines, using public transportation. Finally, arithmetic computation is a prerequisite for persons seeking employment in a service-oriented occupation.

Assessment is facilitated by the fact that arithmetic is based on a limited number of operations and is governed by a set of rules that have no exceptions (Zigmond, Vallecorsa, & Silverman, 1983). Arithmetic assessment usually relies on paper-and-pencil tests of computational skills, problem solving, and basic applications of measurement, money, and geometry (McLoughlin & Lewis, 1986). The bulk of standardized tests survey a wide range of skills. Also available are various criterion-referenced tests and informal inventories. For an excellent review of standardized arithmetic tests, we recommend Compton's *Guide to 75 Tests for Special Education* (1984) and Salvia and Ysseldyke's *Assessment in Special and Remedial Education* (1988). Our discussion begins with a brief description of traditional assessment practices, which is followed by an examination of error analysis strategies that hold promise for directly linking assessment and remediation.

TRADITIONAL ARITHMETIC ASSESSMENT

Traditionally, the assessment of a student's arithmetic skills was accomplished by the administration of various norm-referenced, standardized tests. One or more tests were usually given by the psychologist or an educational diagnostician. General information often was gleaned from group administration of standardized achievement tests that contained a section on arithmetic. If the results suggested that a student was having difficulty performing certain arithmetic operations then the examiner would administer an individualized diagnostic test. Test interpretation often included the clinical observations of the examiner along with actual student scores on the test(s). Unfortunately, many of these tests lack sensitivity to daily instruction and contain too little of what usually comprises the content of the arithmetic curriculum.

The criterion-referenced test is a relatively recent tool that has gained acceptance over more conventional instruments for evaluating student academic performance. Sometimes known as an objective-referenced test, this measure more directly relates to the sequence of daily instruction than do the majority of norm-referenced instruments. Criterion-referenced tests are usually developed by the teacher to measure a student's ability to perform specific academic tasks at a preselected proficiency standard (or criterion). Accordingly, criterion-referenced tests place importance on teacher knowledge of student performance.

There are several advantages to using criterion-referenced tests. First, test items are usually linked to actual instructional objectives. This can be particularly useful to the teacher, not only for planning programs, but also for monitoring student progress. A second advantage is that the student is judged on the basis of his or her performance alone. A major disadvantage of criterion-referenced tests is that, although they can include specific instructional objectives that are helpful to the teacher, they may be invalid if they fail to accurately reflect the content of instruction. A second disadvantage to the use of criterion-referenced tests is that the performance criteria imposed by the teacher constructing the test is usually arbitrary (e.g., 80% correct) and not always conducive to promoting student gains across time (Howell & Morehead, 1987).

Summary

For those practitioners who recognize the importance of the linkage between quality assessment, daily classroom instruction and specific corrective strategies, many of the available assessment tools fail to offer a complete picture of students' needs. Today teachers realize that arithmetic assessment is not a singular, isolated event; and that only by uncovering precisely what students are doing wrong can a quality plan of instruction be established (Gable, Hendrickson, Tenenbaum, & Morsink, 1986). Finally, in eschewing the common practice of simply scoring student responses as "right" or "wrong," a growing number of teachers recognize that there is more than one way for a student to make a mistake (Howell & Kaplan, 1980). Analysis of the mistakes students make in arithmetic is seen as a useful means for strengthening the diagnostic-remedial process (Enright, Gable, & Hendrickson, 1987).

ERRORS IN ARITHMETIC— GROUPING FOR INSTRUCTION

As Howell and Kaplan (1980) assert, some mistakes students make in arithmetic occur in "recognizable and correctable patterns." As an aspect of arithmetic assessment, error analysis has enjoyed a long history, dating back to the work of Osborn (1925) and Buswell and John (1925). Since that time, numerous articles and books have been written on the subject (e.g., Ashlock, 1982; Bachor, 1979; Cox, 1975; Reisman, 1982). Simply put, error or "miscue" analysis is the examination of mistakes made by a student on problem(s), to determine how the student arrived at the incorrect answer. In conducting error analysis, the teacher is usually able to collect the information that is required to plan an appropriate program of remedial instruction.

Categorizing Errors in Arithmetic

Several strategies for classifying arithmetic errors—particularly computation errors, have been developed. These range from the relatively simple to the more complex. For example, Cox (1975) classified computation errors into three types: systematic, random, and careless mistakes. Systematic errors reflect a pattern of incorrect responses (i.e., the student consistently employs an incorrect operation, number fact, or algorithm). Table 3.1 presents several examples of systematic errors evidenced in addition, subtraction, multiplication and division. While systematic errors clearly present an identifiable pattern, random errors do not. According to Cox (1975), random errors occur in three out of five problems; whereas, careless mistakes occur in only one or two out of five problems and do not follow any pattern.

Roberts (1968) proposed four error types: wrong operation, obvious computational errors, defective algorithm (i.e., failure to follow specific steps), and random errors (i.e., no apparent relationship between students' problem solving and actual problem). Zigmond, Vallecorsa, and Silverman (1983) elaborated on Roberts' classification system

TABLE 3.1. Systematic Errors in Addition, Subtraction, Multiplication, and Division

	Addition	Subtraction	Multiplication	Division
1. Wrong operation	454 +187 267 (Subtracts instead of adding)	242 −171 413 (Adds instead of subtracting)	15 ×2 13 (Subtracts instead of multiplying)	216 3)72 (Multiplies instead of dividing)
2. Computational error	41 +3 45	254 −129 113	34 ×4 132	71 4)288
	(Student performs correct operation but makes mistakes in calculating)			
3. Defective algorithm	67 +7 614 (Adds but does not carry)	622 −244 422 (Subtracts lowest digit from highest regardless of position)	33 ×9 342 (Multiplies but carries wrong digit)	121 4)484 4 80 8 40 4 (Divides in reverse order)
4. Grouping error	67 +7 614 (Adds but does not carry correctly)	375 −227 158 (Subtracts but does not regroup correctly)	514 ×24 2056 (Multiplies correctly but does not place digits in correct column)	13 2)206 2 006 6 (Divides but does not observe rule of zero)
5. Random error	354 +627 22	124 −63 34	28 ×3 45	3 4)24
	(These errors show no identifiable pattern)			
6. Other	62 +34 32 (Involves more than one type of mistake. Student subtracts instead of adding, and when doing so subtracts lowest digit from highest digit regardless of position.)	64 −23 12 (Cannot be easily classified. When asked the student explained that: $6-4=2$ and $3-2=1$.)		

and suggested that error categories include: wrong operation, computation error, faulty algorithm, random response, carelessness, and not understanding the concept. Enright (1986) identified seven error clusters: regrouping, process substitution (i.e., changing 1 or more of the steps in process), omissions (i.e., leaving out 1 or more steps), directional (i.e., performing steps in the wrong direction), placement (i.e., recording answer in the wrong place), attention to sign, and guessing errors. Finally, Reisman (1982) offered an extensive system which lists 46 common math errors covering facts, operations, and algorithms. Regardless of the exact system employed, by becoming familiar with common error patterns, teachers are better able to: (a) develop an understanding of student error patterns, (b) develop an ability to look for error patterns in daily assignments, and (c) prescribe programs to meet individual student needs (Hopkins, 1987). In the next section, we will describe strategies for conducting error analysis in arithmetic.

Step I: Gather Multiple Work Samples.   Accurate classification of arithmetic errors depends on gathering multiple samples of a student's work. To be valid, samples must accurately reflect the content of the arithmetic curriculum; and, to be reliable, they must be collected by means of uniform procedures. Furthermore, several authorities recommend that at least three problems of each subskill should be collected in order to make an accurate diagnosis (Hopkins, 1986; Stowitschek, Gable & Hendrickson, 1980). Grossnickle and Reckazch (1973) assert that three samples of the same mistake are needed in order to reliably distinguish between chance and consistent errors. According to Cox (1975), however, at least five errors of a specific subskill must be evident for a pattern to emerge. It follows that if you are going to obtain a reliable indication of a student's error patterns, repeated testing with at least 3–5 items from each subskill area should be obtained. By gathering multiple samples that each contain enough student errors, the teacher diminishes the likelihood that he or she will misclassify a mistake.

Step II: Score, Analyze, and Identify Possible Error Patterns.   Once the arithmetic samples are gathered, the next step is to score the responses. Although teachers routinely score arithmetic responses as correct or incorrect, little knowledge is gained about the student's instructional needs by stopping at this point. First, examining correct responses can help in determining why the student arrived at other incorrect answers (e.g., a careless error). Then the teacher is ready to analyze the incorrects and identify any possible error patterns. Table 3.2 provides definitions of error patterns discussed previously: wrong operation, computational error, defective algorithm, grouping error, plus random error and other error types (see Table 3.1). We singled out these categories because they represent the most frequently cited mistakes students make in arithmetic. However, it may be necessary for you to add to this list in order to make the classification process more precise. For example, a separate category for grouping errors may be added even though such errors could fall under the broader category of Defective Algorithm. Through the creation of an individual category for grouping errors, the range of problems included in the algorithm section is reduced. One category that should routinely be listed is Other. An Other category is a place for those errors that cannot be easily classified or that involve more than one type of student mistake.

TABLE 3.2. Common Error Patterns in Arithmetic

Error Type	Definition
1. Wrong operation	Student uses an operation other than the one required to solve the problem.
2. Computational error	Mistake in calculating basic number facts; number fact is incorrect.
3. Defective algorithm	Use of correct operation—but incorrect or incomplete procedure is used to solve the problem.
4. Grouping error	Mistake in placing digits in proper column for regrouping.
5. Random error	Nonpattern mistake. Attributable to chance.
6. Other	Error in computation that cannot be identified by type.

SOURCE: Based on How Do Students Get Answers Like These? by B. E Enright, R. A. Gable, and J. M. Hendrickson, 1987. Unpublished manuscript. Old Dominion University, Norfolk, VA. Reprinted by permission.

Problem

Example: 62 (faulty
(wrong operator) $+18$ algorithm)
                    56

Explanation

The student not only employed an incorrect operation but also a faulty algorithm.

Instead of trying to decide in which category to place this error, the teacher might record it in the Other category. However, when a large number of errors fall under this category, the examiner needs to create a more comprehensive list of errors. Readers interested in discussion of additional categories are referred to the work of Ashlock (1982) and Reisman (1982).

Step III: Interview the Student.   Once the errors are scored and analyzed, the student should be interviewed to determine *how* the incorrect answers were obtained. In conducting a diagnostic interview, the teacher asks the student to talk through the problem from beginning to end and explain the calculations. Students should be encouraged to explain the step-by-step solution of each problem aloud (Fennell, 1981). Hammill and Bartel (1982) suggest that teachers adhere to the following: (1) select only one type of problem at a time; (2) begin with an easy problem first; (3) tape or keep a written record of the interview; (4) ask the student to solve the problem orally; (5) avoid offering hints; and (6) do not hurry the student. They recommend that the interview be conducted while the student is actually solving the problems. In contrast, Cawley (1978) suggests conducting the interview after the student has completed the activity and after it is scored. At that time, the student can describe the procedure used to solve each problem—both corrects and incorrects. Those who advocate conducting the interview during the computational activity assert that if it takes place afterward the student may forget the steps followed in solving the problems. One possible solution to these conflicting recommendations is to try both. That is, a teacher can conduct an interview during one arithmetic activity and after another (Ashlock, 1982). In addition to having the student "talk through" the arithmetic problems, it is useful to ask questions about related matters that may affect student performance, for example, study or homework routines, the family situation.

Teacher-conducted interviews have been used extensively primarily because of the valuable information they provide regarding conceptual misunderstandings. By conducting a diagnostic interview, insight can be gained in five possible areas: (a) the process a student uses to solve problems, (b) factors that may be interfering with a student's performance, (c) verification of findings of the error analysis, (d) attitudes and feelings of the student toward arithmetic, and (e) arithmetic study habits.

Step IV: Record Findings regarding Errors.   Figure 3.1 contains an Error Analysis Chart that illustrates one way that errors in arithmetic can be grouped and recorded. As can be seen, the teacher is able to match specific problems with proven remedial strategies. In all, the procedures necessary to accurately analyze a student's errors in arithmetic are four-fold:

1. Gather multiple work samples
2. Score, analyze and identify possible error patterns
3. Interview the student
4. Record findings regarding error patterns

REMEDIATING ERRORS IN ARITHMETIC

Once error analysis is completed, the diagnostic interview conducted, and error pattern(s) identified, the teacher then devises a plan of remediation. A description of some of the corrective strategies that have proven successful follows. We also discuss quantitative and qualitative aspects of arithmetic assessment and instruction.

Corrective Strategies in Arithmetic

Certain corrective strategies have been demonstrated to be successful in remedying students' problems in arithmetic. It is important to point out that accumulated evidence indicates that so-called stages of learning influence the impact of most instructional tactics (e.g., Smith, 1981). That is, a growing body of literature has borne out the fact that the effectiveness of a corrective strategy depends on the skill level of the student. Some strategies work best at the acquisition stage when a skill is first being introduced; once a student demonstrates a basic grasp of the skill, other strategies facilitate performing it with greater fluency, that is, both more correctly and faster. Still other procedures have been shown to be useful in maintaining a previously mastered skill and facilitating its generalization to new situations. Figure 3.2 illustrates the stages of learning concept. As we discuss later in the chapter, learning stages are linked not only to specific interventions but also to performance measures.

Acquisition Stage Strategies.   For students performing at the acquisition stage of learning, Lovitt and Curtiss (1968) report that verbal mediation is an effective strategy for teachers to use to improve accuracy and response rates for computation problems. That

Student _____ Date _____

Problem Class _____ No. of problems/digits _____

	Error Type/Number	Corrective Strategy
Wrong operation		
Computational error		
Defective algorithm		
Grouping error		
Random error		
Other		

Time beginning _____ Ending _____

Correct rate _____ Error _____

Peer-referenced standard _____

Figure 3.1. Error Analysis Chart

SOURCE: Adapted from *Analysis of the Academic Errors of Students with Learning Difficulties* (Monograph No. 14), by R. A. Gable, J. M. Hendrickson, H. Tenenbaum, and C. V. Morsink, 1986, Gainesville, FL: University of Florida, Multidisciplinary Diagnostic and Training Program. Reprinted by permission.

37

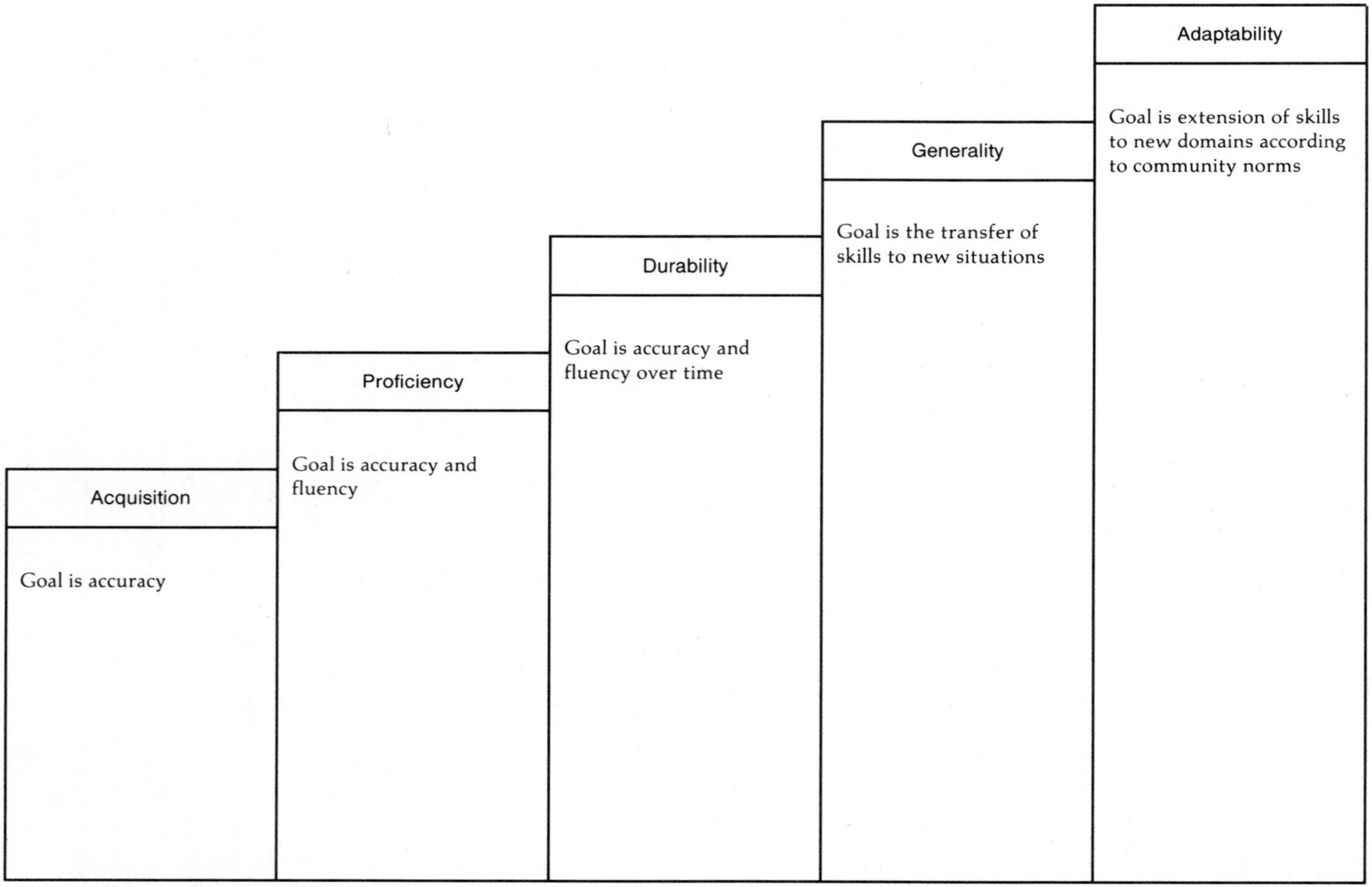

Figure 3.2. Stages of Learning

The diagram shows a series of overlapping boxes, each representing a stage of learning:

- **Acquisition** — Goal is accuracy
- **Proficiency** — Goal is accuracy and fluency
- **Durability** — Goal is accuracy and fluency over time
- **Generality** — Goal is the transfer of skills to new situations
- **Adaptability** — Goal is extension of skills to new domains according to community norms

is, while the teacher listens, students are required to verbalize each problem and its solution before they write an answer. Specifying the operation—for example, the teacher identifies the operation as "plussing"—also decreases mistakes associated with applying the wrong operation. Since some students attempt to find "short cuts" to completing arithmetic problems, teacher modeling or demonstration of the proper step-by-step operation is a simple but effective intervention (Smith & Lovitt, 1975). The teacher "shows and tells" the student how to solve the problem by computing and recording the solution to a sample arithmetic problem on the student's paper. The student then proceeds to compute a series of similar problems and is permitted to refer to the original sample problem. Teacher "show and tell" combined with verbal feedback to the student on steps that are troublesome is especially useful for dealing with procedural mistakes (e.g., a defective algorithm).

Transition Stage Strategies.   At the transition or "fluency building" stage of learning, a number of different tactics have been used. For example, students' correct rate scores have been improved as a result of daily drill and practice exercises, use of answer keys for self-correction, teacher praise for accuracy and/or punishment for mistakes (e.g., loss of free time), public postings of student scores, or simply the announcement that a student's performance is being timed (e.g., Cullinan, Lloyd & Epstein, 1981; Smith, 1981; Van Houten, Morrison, Barrow, & Wenaus, 1974). Random mistakes on the part of the student can usually be corrected easily if the teacher introduces either contingent rewards or a response cost (e.g., and extra assignment) (Lovitt & Esveldt, 1970). Other strategies for increasing fluency in arithmetic include having students decide "on their own" about exact contingencies of reinforcement; and teaching them to graph their own scores (Cullinan et al., 1981).

Mastery Stage Strategies.   Only a modest number of procedures have been shown to be effective in producing sustained mastery of arithmetic skills. One of these pertains to what is called strategy training. First, a task analysis is conducted on prerequisite skills as well as on the skills and the strategy as it is applied by a student capable of solving a particular type of problem. Second, a strategy for attacking any problem of that type is identified. Finally, the teacher trains students to apply a system for solving the problems: engage repeatedly in the proper order of steps; and thus get the correct answer to the problem. For a more complete description of strategy training, readers are referred to Cullinan et al. (1981). Another proven strategy relies on a combination of procedures. The teacher demonstrates the solution, gives verbal feedback on multiple problems completed by the student, and couples to these teacher reinforcement (e.g., "Good adding"). Finally, changing the material itself—from worksheets, to oral presentation of arithmetic problems, to computer software, and so on—is a promising way to promote mastery and generalization. In Table 3.3, we provide a summary of strategies for remedying computation problems. As you can see, the strategies are organized according to both temporality (i.e., events that precede or follow a student response) and stages of learning (i.e., acquisition, transition, mastery). The following case study shows how the error-analysis procedure we have discussed can be applied.

TABLE 3.3. Corrective Strategies in Arithmetic

Acquisition Stage	Transition Stage	Mastery Stage
Antecedent Events		
Teacher uses flashcards and antecedent models	Teacher tells student to "go faster"	Teacher moves to more difficult material
Teacher models computation process	Teacher uses drill and practice sheets	Teacher shifts from direct instruction to independent assignments
Teacher records cues on applying procedures; then fades cues	Teacher introduces computation games	Student taught to select performance standards
Teacher "highlights" operations—plussing	Student taught verbal mediation—"say it before you do it"	
Subsequent Events		
Teacher gives specific written feedback	Teacher praises gains in fluency	Student self-scores with answer key
Teacher increases the amount of reinforcement	Teacher imposes penalty for 'slippage'/careless mistakes	Student determines contingency arrangement
Teacher introduces contingent modeling to correct mistakes	Teacher provides reinforcement contingent on corrects	Teacher reviews student performance and provides periodic feedback
	Student taught to self-record, graph	

CASE STUDY NO. 1

While most classmates are progressing at a satisfactory pace, Bill appears to be struggling and is unable to correctly calculate some double-digit addition facts. In an attempt to uncover the exact nature of the problem, Mr. Collins compiles a folder of worksheets Bill has completed in class. Because he is reluctant to rely on a limited sample, Mr. Collins constructs a two-part probe containing 20 single and double-digit addition facts, some with carrying. Administering a 10 problem probe on consecutive days, Mr. Collins scores the problems and adds these samples to the work folder.

To facilitate error analysis, Mr. Collins "plots" the incorrect answers on a chart (see Figure 3.3). As can be seen, Bill had 7 mistakes, 6 of which involved carrying. Although he is being somewhat speculative, based on his experience with Bill, Mr. Collins attributes one error to chance (i.e., random error), perhaps a result of Bill's having been distracted. Further analysis suggests that the remaining mistakes are an outcome of a defective procedure (i.e., defective algorithm). In comparing corrects and errors, Mr. Collins notices that Bill seems to repeatedly have difficulty when carrying is required. Next, Mr. Collins arranges to set aside time to ask Bill to review and "say aloud" his step-by-step solutions to selected problems. On a separate sheet, Mr. Collins has recorded each of the problems, allowing space to record a narrative account of Bill's calculations.

Supported by information gleaned from the diagnostic interview, Mr. Collins is reasonably certain that the intervention called for should be one that will remedy the misconception(s) Bill has about "carrying." Mr. Collins selects to apply an acquisition stage strategy, namely, teacher modeling of the operation combined with specific feedback on Bill's ability to emulate the model shown him by the teacher.

Student __Bill__   Date __Oct. 15__

Problem Class __single & double digit add facts__   No. of problems/digits __30__

	Error Type/Number	Corrective Strategy
Wrong operation		
Computation error		
Defective algorithm		
Grouping error	THL I	interview supports misconception about use of columns in regrouping
Random error	I	distracted? model process w/ feedback
Other		

Time beginning _____   Ending _____

Correct rate _____   Error _____

Peer-referenced standard _____

Figure 3.3. Sample Error Analysis Chart on Bill

SOURCE: Adapted from *Analysis of the Academic Errors of Students with Learning Difficulties* (Monograph No. 14), by R. A. Gable, J. M. Hendrickson, H. Tenenbaum, and C. V. Morsink, 1986, Gainesville, FL: University of FL, Multidisiplinary Diagnostic and Training Program. Reprinted by permission.

ERROR ANALYSIS AND PROBLEM SOLVING

Although the bulk of the work with error analysis has focused on computational skills, similar procedures can be applied to problem solving activities. As with errors in arithmetic, error analysis in problem solving begins with collecting samples of student's work. What is recommended is the collection of multiple samples with at least three to five items covering each type of computation skill in which the student has demonstrated competence. Otherwise, it becomes difficult to pinpoint the error and distinguish between faulty computational versus faulty problem-solving skills. Once the samples are gathered, they are scored and then analyzed to determine why the student made mistakes in solving the problem(s). In conducting an analysis of problem-solving activities, Goodstein (1981) recommends that the examiner follow these three steps:

1. Check to determine the magnitude of the discrepancy between the incorrect and correct response. Small discrepancies for large numbers will often indicate carelessness in the computational aspect of the task.
2. Check to determine if the magnitude of the response indicates selection of the proper operation. This will more typically be a probable source of error for problem sets, including indirect action-sequence problems, problems that require various operations, or problems indicating less common algorithms.
3. Check to determine if the response could have been generated by the inappropriate combination of numerical data in the problem. (Obviously, this step is only used when extraneous information is present (pp. 42–43).

If the error appears to be in either step 2 or 3, then interview the student. As with errors in computation, the purpose of the diagnostic interview is to uncover exactly what steps the student followed to solve the story problem. In order to accurately analyze the procedure used by a student to solve word problems, it is essential to be aware of the steps involved. Zigmond et al. (1983) identify five steps to solving a single-step problem:

1. Reading the problem and understanding the language.
2. Choosing the correct operation.
3. Writing the correct number sentence.
4. Applying the computation algorithm.
5. Supplying the correct answer.

For a multi-step problem, you will repeat steps 2 to 5. The primary goal of the diagnostic interview is to determine at which step the error occurred. Then the teacher is able to introduce the most appropriate corrective strategy. For example, a teacher asks a student to complete five single-step word problems. Upon completion, the teacher notices that the student has consistently employed the wrong operation. If the teacher suspects that the student either has a reading problem or difficulty understanding the language, the teacher might: (a) read the problems to the student to determine if a reading problem exists or (b) have the student read the problems aloud and verbally identify the correct operation. In this way the teacher may uncover a language problem. The teacher would then initiate remediation based on a somewhat complete understanding of the specific type of error(s) the student is making.

Remediating Mistakes in Problem Solving

Compared to arithmetic computation, our knowledge regarding remedies for deficits in problem solving skills is somewhat limited. As we know, some story problems require students to discriminate relevant from irrelevant information; some to recognize that not enough information is provided in the problem. In one study that examined a technique for teaching these skills, Lydra and Church (1964) began with the assertion that problem solving activities should be as "real" (rather than hypothetical) as possible. They found that having students solve real classroom- and home-related problems was highly effective for developing recognition skills. In a related investigation, Blankenship and Lovitt (1976) analyzed story problems and found little consistency in their organization. As a result, they developed categories or classes of word problems. They also controlled for such variables as word difficulty, sentence complexity, relevance of information, and so on. They began with the careful organization of the material, and then systematically taught the students methods of solving word problems. Percentage scores improved on each type of word problem. Another strategy used in teaching students to deal with story problems involves four steps: S Survey—reading the problem to obtain a general understanding; Q_1 Question—deciding what exactly to do; C Compute—actually completing the operation; and finally Q_2 Question—problem review to decide if the answer fits the question. As in similar reading-related strategies, each step is taught independently on simple story problems before the training is repeated on more complex material. It is apparent that more studies need to be conducted, especially in the area of problem solving, to provide teachers greater numbers of proven corrective strategies. Future efforts will likely contribute to this important area of instruction. We conclude this section with a second case study that illustrates the stepwise application of error analysis to problem solving in arithmetic.

CASE STUDY NO. 2

Sheila is a fifth-grade student who is experiencing some difficulty in arithmetic. During class, she is attentive and is an active participant in the instruction. She appears to enjoy the computational aspects of arithmetic but "wanders" when it is time to solve story problems.

Mr. Jones, her mathematics teacher, is concerned and has gathered several samples of Sheila's work. These samples consist of both story problems and computation problems that involved the same computational skills. This was done in order to determine if Sheila's difficulty is related to computation and/or to problem solving.

After reviewing the work samples, Mr. Jones is able to determine that Sheila's difficulty was not due to an inability to compute the problems correctly but instead directly related to solving word problems.

Next, Mr. Jones interviewed Sheila in an attempt to determine the specific problem area. Prior to this interview, he put together 10 story problems so he could observe Sheila "work out" and "talk through" each problem. Sheila fluently read the first problem aloud. However, shortly after reading the problem, she gave up, saying, "I don't like to do these." Using the structured interview, Mr. Jones was able to determine that although she was able to read the problem and choose the correct operation, Sheila had difficulty in writing the correct number sentence. Based on this analysis, Mr. Jones incorporated instruction that emphasized effective questioning strategies with feedback into Sheila's individualized program of arithmetic instruction.

Measurement of Arithmetic Performance

The concept of stages of learning that we have discussed also relates to the measurement of student performance in arithmetic. In the early stages of learning (i.e., from acquisition to beginning proficiency), teachers ordinarily measure pupil performance in a way that reflects a concern for accuracy alone (i.e., percent). However, once a student demonstrates the ability to correctly calculate the arithmetic problems, a shift in interest from the measuring of accuracy alone to that of both accuracy and fluency should take place. Fluency may pertain to the number of digits manipulated, to the steps in a problem completed, or simply to the number of whole problems completed in a specified time period. Later at maintenance stages, measurement can be conducted less often, but should still occur and should still take fluency into account. Table 3.4 contains quantitative standards in the form of rate figures suggested by Deno and Mirkin (1977). It is important to emphasize that these figures pertain to the number of digits; however, the number of operations necessary to answer correctly a particular problem may be worth measuring, too. Just to mark an answer right or wrong is to ignore the fact that some problems may be more difficult than others (e.g., single-digit addition versus double-digit subtraction with borrowing). Therefore, the complexity of an arithmetic facts problem can be accounted for by counting and summing the number of operations and scoring students according to each subskill operation.

Use of Regular Student Standards.   Today the majority of exceptional learners receive a portion of their daily instruction in regular classrooms. It follows that special students should be able to compute arithmetic problems at a rate that compares to their regular class counterparts. To find the accuracy and rate scores of the local school district, teachers can collect from regular education personnel samples of the work of successful students. Analysis of these quantitative measures will provide you with the information

TABLE 3.4. Rate Figures That Define Mastery in Arithmetic Computation

Grades 1, 2, and 3
20 or more digits per minute correct *and* 2 or fewer digits per minute incorrect

Grade 4 and above
40 or more digits per minute correct *and* 2 or fewer digits per minute incorrect

on a special student's skills in comparison to normal agemates and can serve as a standard against which to make grouping and instruction decisions as well as reintegration decisions (i.e., mainstreaming).

SUMMARY

In the area of arithmetic—in which problems progress from simple to complex—the question is not if but when a student will experience difficulty in completing a problem correctly (Bereiter, 1968). It is not surprising, therefore, that the use of error analysis holds promise for teachers interested in identifying specific error types and choosing a proven corrective strategy. Error analysis is by no means foolproof, and it is susceptible to the same questions regarding validity and reliability that other assessment procedures are. Even so, the various steps we have discussed can provide effective guidance to those responsible for carrying out arithmetic assessment and remediation.

DISCUSSION QUESTIONS AND ACTIVITIES

1. Interview a school psychologist or diagnostician to learn about the selection, administration and interpretation of standardized arithmetic tests.
2. List the advantages of conducting error analysis, and the steps you would need to take to ensure that the procedure is valid and reliable.
3. Gather timed samples of students' written work in arithmetic. Establish a set of standards for one or more grade levels.
4. Practice classifying mistakes in arithmetic that have been collected from students at various grade levels.

CHAPTER 4

Errors in Reading

Catherine V. Morsink
University of Florida

Robert A. Gable
Old Dominion University

CHAPTER OBJECTIVES

After reading this chapter you should be able to:

1. Define error analysis and discuss classifying mistakes in oral reading and comprehension.
2. Outline a strategy for carrying out error analysis in reading.
3. Describe strategies that have proven successful in remediating oral reading and comprehension errors.

KEY TERMS

automaticity	phonetic approach
basal reader	previewing
cloze procedure	sight words
Informal Reading Inventory (IRI)	word analysis
miscue	word recognition

INTRODUCTION

By most accounts, learning to read is the most difficult of all of the academic skills. Accordingly, the growing number of students who perform poorly and the increasing rate of illiteracy, particularly among students from urban and minority groups, is of major concern to both educators and the public alike (e.g., Anderson, Hiebert, Scott, &

Portions of this chapter that deal with error analysis in word recognition were developed by Gable, Hendrickson, and Meeks (1987) and are used here by permission of the authors.

Wilkinson, 1985; Stedman & Kaestle, 1987). Among the obstacles to reducing reading deficits are ones regarding placement of students and selection of teaching strategies and materials (e.g., Pink & Liebert, 1986). These obstacles appear to be related to current thinking about diagnosing and treating reading difficulties. While it is generally recognized that reading assessment should facilitate instruction, there is little evidence that diagnosis and remediation have ordinarily been related (Weinshank & Vinsonhaler, 1983). One possible solution that holds promise and is a logical extension of standardized test administration is the use of error analysis—the assessment of mistakes students make in oral reading and those they make in response to comprehension questions.

We begin this chapter with a brief review of reading assessment procedures. Next we examine some strategies that have been shown to be effective for teaching reading to students with special needs. We present charts for plotting student errors and ones for making instructional decisions. Also, we offer some cautions regarding the use of error analysis. In discussing reading assessment and remediation, we present word recognition and reading comprehension separately. We proceed according to the stages of learning, from acquisition to proficiency. In a real sense, however, reading comprehension (i.e., the comprehension of written as opposed to oral language) for students with learning difficulties may begin at the stage of oral reading proficiency, which follows the acquisition of word recognition skills and the development of automaticity in decoding (Samuels, 1980; Snider & Tarver, 1987).

TRADITIONAL ASSESSMENT IN READING

In conducting traditional assessment of reading problems, usually a psychologist or reading specialist administers a series of special tests to the student, in an effort to pinpoint the nature of the difficulty. First, the student is given a group standardized test of reading achievement as a gross measure of reading ability. This test typically consists of "vocabulary"—a series of words at a particular grade level, to be matched with a choice of pictures or written definitions; and "comprehension"—a series of written paragraphs, followed by questions related to the paragraph content. If the student appears to have difficulty with this group test, if there is a discrepancy between the grade level score and daily reading performance, or if the test appears to overestimate the student's reading ability, the diagnostician might administer an individualized oral reading test. The diagnostician would observe the student's reading performance during testing (e.g., greater ability to recognize words in context than in isolation; finger pointing, the appearance of inefficient eye movement, and so forth). Additional tests to determine specific difficulties in word attack (word beginnings or endings, specific vowel sounds, and so forth) or in comprehension (recall of facts, ability to draw conclusions, and so forth) would be administered. As this sequence of events shows, traditional reading assessment was designed to pinpoint the student's reading grade level and to provide the teacher with information about the student's reading abilities and specific skill deficits. Even so, it is time consuming and does not always relate directly to the student's instructional needs.

There are other traditional procedures by which teachers themselves have conducted assessment in reading. The most widely employed is the Informal Reading Inventory (Johnson & Kress, 1965). Using a series of graded paragraphs taken directly from the classroom's basal series, the teacher asks the student to read aloud until his or her performance matches the "instructional level"—defined as approximately 95 percent accuracy in word recognition and 75 percent accuracy in comprehension. The teacher might also select words from the basal reader to design a graded list of sight vocabulary, administered individually as a means of observing further a student's word recognition skills.

In summarizing the criteria for accuracy in oral reading of paragraphs used by eight different specialists, G. Spache and E. Spache (1986) report that there are many discrepancies in the traditional informal inventory criteria (e.g., 95 percent accuracy, 75 percent comprehension). However, Powell (1968, 1978) has shown that students can tolerate more word recognition errors in easier material, while still maintaining their ability to comprehend. In short, although the informal inventory procedure for matching the student with an appropriate level in reading material is logical, its application is often inaccurate.

Miscue Analysis.   The use of miscue analysis has grown in popularity during the past ten years. Based on the work of Goodman (1965), its emergence was based on the assumption that teachers could accurately diagnose student's oral reading skills by analysing the types of errors they made. The errors were assumed to be so-called "windows" into the reading process that reflected the student's efforts to make sense out of written language. While the use of miscue analysis has heightened the clinician's sensitivity to the reading proccess, it has not been shown to relate to those aspects of reading which were indicative of proficiency (Wixson, 1979).

Cloze Procedure.   The cloze procedure has been widely advocated as a method of establishing a student's comprehension of written text. In applying the cloze procedure, every nth (5th, for example) word was deleted from a written passage. As the student reads, he or she has to supply the missing word(s) on the basis of context cues. Some specialists indicate that the cloze procedure was equivalent to traditional measures of comprehension in determining a student's ability to comprehend (G. Spache & E. Spache, 1986). However, others found through more extensive analysis that, for the special needs student, the cloze procedure was not as accurate as the simple measurement of oral reading proficiency (Deno, Mirkin, & Chiang, 1982).

Use of Direct Assessment in Reading

As you can see by the previous discussion, reading assessment can be time consuming, difficult to conduct, and often relates only indirectly to daily classroom instruction. As a result, efforts have been made to find a more effective and efficient method, one that directly relates the instructional material to the student's stage of learning. Lovitt and Hansen (1976a) were among the first to use direct measurement for placement of students in the correct instructional level of a basal series. To do so, they asked the student to read aloud a five-hundred word sample from the first story in each of several books in the series. They used as criteria for instructional placement a correct response rate of 45–65 words per minute with four to eight errors in word recognition and a comprehension score of 50–75 percent, based on responses to six questions ranging from recall to interpretation.

Other reading authorities have outlined procedures for reading assessment which include the use of direct assessment as a supplement to diagnostic tests and informal checklists. The steps include the use of direct measurement, the identification of appropriate learning conditions, the initiation of individual testing and teaching, and the selection of appropriate curricular material (e.g., Elliott & Piersel, 1982). In adhering to these recommendations, there is less speculation about a student's performance than with traditional assessment, since the predictions are made from a representative sample of the behavior which is the focus of assessment, namely reading.

Information on a student's reading performance should be gathered repeatedly over time in order to obtain a large enough and representative sample for making valid instructional decisions. Also, the same administration procedures must be followed each time. After the initial reading assessment, it may not be necessary to repeat steps 2 and 3 of the procedure that follows (rereading and interviewing). However, it is important for the teacher to collect in a uniform manner additional samples of the student's reading performance. The likelihood that certain errors will occur is obviously related to the presence (or absence) of particular types of words in the sample passage. Finally, evaluating both corrects and errors allows the teacher to compare and contrast the ability of students to apply reading skills (Deno et al., 1982). This combined picture should contribute to decisions about possible remediation.

Categorizing Errors in Word Recognition

Information on the types, or qualitative aspects, and the number, or quantitative aspects, of student errors is potentially useful for formulating an initial plan for the remediation of word recognition problems. Specialists have proposed various systems for classifying types of errors in reading. Generally, substitutions, omissions and insertions have been singled out for attention. In other systems, hesitations have been treated as actual mistakes or time-limited nonresponses. Repetitions, self-corrections and "I don't know" responses may or may not be construed as being meaningful depending on the student's level of reading proficiency (e.g., Gable & Shores, 1980). In some systems (e.g., Gray, 1967), self corrections are not counted as errors, since they reflect attempts by the reader to make sense of written language. Because of their diagnostic utility, they are, however, classified under the system we propose. In the next section we will discuss a step-by-step application of the entire error analysis procedure.

Step I: Initiate a Procedure for Sampling Errors.   In initiating the error analysis procedure, we suggest that you listen to the student reading orally from graded material from a basal series or other instructional material used in the classroom. Although the sample may be drawn from several grade levels, the most useful information is usually obtained from passages in which the student comprehends about 60 percent (Howell & Kaplan, 1980). During the oral reading session(s) the teacher should note, but not correct, errors. The number of words or sentences, the administration procedures, and the length of the reading session should remain constant across sessions. This increases the likelihood that you will make valid conclusions regarding pupil instructional needs (Stowitschek, Gable, & Hendrickson, 1980).

Qualitative Information. According to G. Spache and E. Spache (1986), the types of qualitative errors in reading may each hold particular meanings. For example, insertions of words that do not appear in the passage may indicate a superficial reading, a reliance on context for assistance, and a lack of interest in accuracy. Omissions may suggest speed with inattention, or the skipping of unknown words. Both insertions and omissions are more characteristic of older students. Repetitions may indicate a reader who is tense and nervous; or one who rereads words as a strategy for delay, that is, as a way to gain time to attack the next unknown word. Reversals are common at the primary age level, and infrequent thereafter. They may also be found in students for whom English is a second language.

    There are various types and levels of severity in substitutions. In a pattern of gross substitutions, the student may substitute words which bear no resemblance in either form or context, for example, "house" for "there." In a pattern of minor substitutions, the reader most often substitutes for similar form: "house" for "horse" or similar contextual meaning: "can" for "will." Mispronunciations are common among beginning students who rely heavily on phonics and try to sound out every word without knowing the exceptions to the phonetic rules. But they may also occur in students who have low levels of listening vocabulary and are thus unable to use context clues. Self-corrections are indicative of a more mature reader who is attempting to read more accurately and to rely upon the additional information available from the context of the sentence. Conversely, the aid, in which the teacher supplies the word because the student makes no attempt at decoding, is suggestive of an exceptionally dependent reader. Although somewhat speculative, it is potentially useful to identify the exact nature of the problem to facilitate the selection of an appropriate strategy.

Quantitative Information. The actual amount of quantitative data required to carry out a thorough reading analysis is not yet known. Some authors recommend that a series of one to two minute samples that contain at least one hundred to two hundred words is acceptable (see Gable, Fleming, & Smith, 1980; Smith, 1981; Starlin, 1982). To guide curricular placement decisions, Starlin (1982) offers the following figures: 70–149 words correct and/or 6–10 incorrect per minute. Others propose standards that call for 50–99 words correct per minute and/or 3–7 incorrect per minute (Deno & Mirkin, 1977). As you may recall, Lovitt and Hansen (1976a) advocate 45–65 words correct with 4–8 errors per minute. Regardless of the exact standards, scoring pupil reading is easier if you prepare copies of the reading selections or make audiotape recordings for scoring and (rescoring) students' reading.

Step II: Identify Possible Error Patterns: Confirm by Retesting. Retesting will help the teacher determine whether the student is simply tense and careless, or whether he skips, repeats, and otherwise conceals an inability to decode the words in a passage. Although it is more likely that the student who requires a lot of teacher assistance has no basic skills and is performing at the acquisition stage, it is also possible that the student has been told "not to guess" at words, and finds it safer not to make a mistake.

After the student has finished reading the selected passages, the teacher should ask the student to attempt to reread the passage, allowing an unlimited amount of time. According to G. Spache and E. Spache (1986), word recognition accuracy may increase by as much as 50 percent during rereading. Only those errors which are missed on the second attempt should be counted as errors for the purpose of analysis.

During retesting, the examiner should state clearly the behavior the student is expected to exhibit. For example, if initial reading has been careless, you should ask the student to read more carefully, even if this means reading more slowly. Conversely, if the student failed to attempt certain words, the examiner should request that he or she "try every word," even if the student isn't sure about some. If, given this second opportunity, the student reads correctly, then the examiner knows the errors are probably due to factors other than lack of skill (e.g., lack of directions, failure to attend, or lack of reinforcement).

Step III: Interview the Student.   The next step in the error analysis process is to conduct a structured interview. A number of authors advocate the use of a structured interview as a valuable source of diagnostic data (Howell & Kaplan, 1980; McLoughlin & Lewis, 1986; Zigmond, Vallecorsa, & Silverman, 1983). Having students verbally describe faulty approaches to word recognition or analysis can yield clues to remediation not otherwise available. Specifically, the teacher asks the student to explain how he or she tried to figure out each error word during reading. If the student is unresponsive, it may be necessary to provide verbal prompts, such as: "Did you read the whole sentence, paying special attention to the other words that may help you figure out the unknown word?" or "Did you look carefully at the ending of this word? It ends in 'ing,' like sing." If the student has appropriate decoding strategies but uses them inconsistently, then the remedial plan should focus on techniques used during the transition stage: prestructuring and repeated practice with teacher feedback. For the student who has no appropriate decoding strategy, you will need to design a program that corresponds to the acquisition stage: direct instruction with teacher modeling of correct reading; prompting and cueing; closely supervised practice with immediate reinforcement of corrects (e.g., "good reading") or corrective feedback (e.g., "try that word again").

Some Limitations of Error Analysis.   In classifying errors in reading, the teacher should be aware of the distinction between reading errors and dialect differences. The student who is not a native speaker of English, or who is from an area of the country different from that from which the examiner originates, may pronounce words differently. Such errors in pronunciation are not reading errors. The most common dialect differences are specified by G. Spache and E. Spache (1986). In Black English, these dialect differences include omissions of *r* or *l*, of final consonants or consonant clusters, as well as additions of plurals to words ending in "*st*," and certain word-order and syntax changes. For the native speaker of Spanish, confusions of the vowels used in English are prevalent, as are consonant substitutions, such as *s* for *th* or *sh, ch* for *j, b* for *v,* or *j* for *y.* The teacher who is uncertain about whether reading "errors" are true errors or simply dialect differences should ask for assistance from a linguist or a teacher of limited English proficiency (LEP) students.

You should also be aware that sometimes the need exists for further diagnosis or for highly specialized remediation. This would be indicated by the student's total lack of ability to use any type of word recognition techniques. The difference between those students with mild disabilities who can be assisted in the regular reading group and those with severe disabilities who require long-term remedial assistance, has been discussed in detail in an earlier work (see Morsink, 1984).

Step IV: Record Findings regarding Errors.   In Figure 4.1, we show an Error Analysis Chart for recording and analyzing mistakes students make during the oral reading exercises. The case study that follows illustrates its actual application.

Case Study in Word Recognition

The case study is designed to clarify the use of the error analysis process. As in the discussion of arithmetic, we recommend a stages of learning perspective. Figure 4.2 shows the results of an analysis of one student's oral reading errors plotted on a chart. In this case, Bill's error pattern seems fairly clear. He is self-correcting miscalled words and occasionally inserting words. The layout of the Error Analysis Chart assists the teacher in: (a) categorizing errors in relation to reading stage, (b) visually identifying error types, and (c) specifying an intervention approach appropriate to the student's instructional level.

The chart shown in Figure 4.2 covers both quantitative (i.e., data on number of words and on rate) and qualitative (i.e., the exact type of incorrects) aspects of reading. As we previously suggested, the teacher should zero-in on specific errors and correct and error rates. If previously cited rate figures are used as a standard, Bill's performance indicates that the material employed for obtaining samples is appropriate for beginning instruction (see Figure 4.2). If, on the other hand, Bill made a large number of errors and if these were clustered at the acquisition stage of reading with a low correct rate and high error rate, this would suggest a need for the teacher to try lower-level instructional material.

Learning Stages and Instructional Decisions in Reading

As introduced in Chapter 3, the concept of learning stages can be applied to decisions on reading instruction. Specialized instruction based on your knowledge of a student's oral reading can be viewed according to: (a) stages of learning and (b) order of instructional events (i.e., stimulus presented immediately before and following a student response). As we illustrate in Table 4.1, the stages of learning—acquisition, transition, proficiency and generalization—are presented in three vertical columns. Antecedent and subsequent events, those which you can adjust before, during or after the student reads, are presented along the left hand side of the table.

Acquisition Stage Strategies.   If students are experiencing difficulty during the acquisition stage, an initial option is to make changes in the antecedent events, such as the format of instruction, the difficulty level of the reading material, the teaching strategy, and whether partial or full models (e.g., ''sounds like _____'') are provided.

Student _____ Dates _____

Material/Level _____

	Error Type/Number	Prioritized Instruction	
Ignore Punctuation			Proficiency
Hesitation			
Repetition			
Insertion			Transition
Self-Correct			
Substitution			Acquisition
Teacher Aid			
Mispronounce			

Number of readings _____

Average number of words _____

Average time of readings _____

Correct rate _____ Error rate _____

Figure 4.1. Error Analysis Chart for Oral Reading

Student ___Bill___ Dates ___9/21___

Material/Level ___Ginn Reading Series (H)___

	Error Type/Number	Prioritized Instruction	
Ignore Punctuation	/		Proficiency
Hesitation			
Repetition			
Insertion	//	Work on fluency with tapes and repeated readings with intermittent praise.	Transition
Self-Correct	⊞ //		
Substitution			Acquisition
Teacher Aid			
Mispronounce			

Number of readings ___2___

Average number of words ___122___

Average time of readings ___2 min.___

Correct rate ___61___ Error rate ___5___

Figure 4.2. Bill's Error Analysis Chart for Oral Reading

TABLE 4.1 Developing Oral Reading Proficiency through Stages of Learning

Stage I (Acquisition Phase)	Stage II (Transition Phase)	Stage III (Proficiency/Generalization Phase)
Antecedent Events		
Change format (e.g., signal, model) of reading instruction	Teacher-directed previewing	Promote silent/critical reading
Adjust difficulty of reading materials	Repeated oral or silent reading, individual or group	Move to more difficult reading materials
Change teaching strategy (e.g., pace: wait-time) Present word families, component parts	Teacher modeling of word-recognition strategies	Vary type/complexity of reading materials
	Modify format of instruction	Shift direct instruction to independent assignments
	Instruct student to "go faster"	
Subsequent Events		
Give specific academic praise	Reduce frequency of reinforcement	Adjust schedule of reinforcement
Enrich frequency of reinforcement for corrects	Introduce corrective feedback on oral reading	Review and periodically provide feedback on reading performance
Increase immediacy of feedback on oral reading	Introduce contingent "skip and drill" exercises	Provide for naturally occurring reinforcers
Flash card drill on words	Introduce self-assessment/correction	Provide for student assessment of reading proficiency
Focused practice on skill	Repeated readings, with timings	
Repeated readings, with timings		

SOURCES: Adapted from "Data Decisions for Instructing Behaviorally Disordered Students," by R. A. Gable, J. M. Hendrickson, S. S. Evans, and W. H. Evans, in R. Rutherford, Jr., C. M. Nelson, and S. Forness (Eds.) *Bases of Severe Behavioral Disorders in Children and Youth* (pp. 75–88), 1987. San Diego, CA: College-Hill Press. *Teaching the Learning Disabled,* by D. D. Smith, 1981. Englewood Cliffs, NJ: Prentice Hall.

Increasing the frequency of the verbal praise given by a teacher, bolstering the power of the reinforcers (e.g., adding something to teacher praise) or introducing drill on misread words are recommended as subsequent events.

Transition Stage Strategies. During the transition stage, changes in antecedent events might consist of the following: providing teacher previewing before student recitation; reading exercises, whether individual or group, repeated oral, or silent; teacher modeling of word-recognition strategies; modifying the format of instruction; or simply telling students to "read faster" (Gable et al., 1987). Modification of subsequent events typically includes lessening the frequency of teacher praise, increasing the amount of work required for reinforcement, introducing corrective feedback on errors, using contingent skipping and drill (students either read additional selections, or advance to more difficult material, depending on their performance), or instructing students in self-assessment and correction (see Gable et al., 1986; Lovitt & Hansen, 1976b).

Proficiency Stage Strategies. During the proficiency-generalization stage, we suggest antecedent events that include promoting extended periods of silent and critical reading, encouraging more independent performance, or placing the student in more demanding material. Subsequent events may consist of further adjusting the frequency of teacher-administered reinforcement and of periodic teacher feedback to students on performance. We may emphasize, as well, student self-assessment of their own reading performance. It is generally advisable to adjust the subsequent events first. Such changes are usually less time-consuming than when we make changes in antecedent events (Stowitschek et al., 1980).

Now we return to our analysis of Bill's chart. Decisions regarding curricular placement should relate to the transition stage of oral reading. Teaching strategies linked to transitional instruction include teacher corrective feedback; or silent, oral student previewing; or a teacher's previewing passages before student recitation and practice (Gable et al., 1986; Lovitt, 1975; Samuels, 1979; Skougie, 1987). Generally speaking, we should probably remediate errors of substitution and omission during the acquisition stage. Errors consisting of hesitations, repetitions, or disregard for punctuation appear to be of concern during transition or proficiency stages of reading instruction (see Table 4.1).

Errors in Comprehension

The procedure for identifying errors in reading comprehension is similar to the four steps followed in identifying errors in word recognition. Therefore, our discussion on errors in comprehension will be more succinct. At the start, we identify the types of errors through direct observation of the student's performance in reading material used in the curriculum. Then we retest these errors, by means of questions and the analysis of written work samples. Next, we interview the student, using minimal prompting, to obtain a verbal description of the way in which this student attempts to comprehend written language. Finally, we make a summary of the findings. As in the analysis of word recognition errors, the procedure will help assessment to remediation.

Types of Errors.   The types of comprehension errors have been classified most often according to an analysis of the skills used in comprehension of printed language. Adapted from Ingram (1980), these skills include: recall of factual details, comprehension and summary of main ideas; understanding of sequence; making inferences; and, critical reading and evaluation. Since comprehension cannot occcur in the absence of word recognition, the analysis of errors in reading comprehension is more difficult than in word recognition (Chall, 1983; Snider & Tarver, 1987).

Schreiner (1983) suggests that a student's success with reading comprehension is influenced by several factors: (a) the difficulty and complexity of the text, (b) the reader's interest, (c) the reader's knowledge and intellect, and (d) the type of text used, whether narrative or expository. An expository text is generally more logically organized and straightforward. A narrative text, combining the elements of setting, plot and problem solution, is less linear in its organization. It makes more sense for teachers to focus on the analysis and subsequent teaching of comprehension through use of the material which comprises the reading curriculum. At the elementary level, these are basal readers. In these, most material is in story form, as narrative (Flood & Lapp, 1987). In narrative, most of the actual practice with comprehension—even at the sixth-grade level, up to half—focuses on the recall of questions which could be classified as literal comprehension (G. Spache & E. Spache, 1986). This is not to suggest that we recommend that teachers avoid developing students' abilities in the area of inference or critical reading. Indeed, the lack of these skills is becoming an increasing problem in our schools. However, for elementary-level students with reading difficulties, it is more realistic to zero-in initially on those basic skills most closely related to the demands of the curriculum. This means that the teacher should focus error analysis and related instruction on the mastery of increasingly larger units. When the student experiences difficulty, the teacher should then revert to the analysis of smaller units (Carnine & Silbert, 1977).

Step I: Initiate Procedures for Identification.   We suggest a two-step procedure, adapted from the work of Schreiner (1983), C. Mercer and A. Mercer (1985), and Carnine and Silbert (1977), to identify a student's comprehension problems. First, the teacher asks the student to read aloud from a premarked passage. If it meets the criteria both in error rate and in words read correctly per minute, then the passage is at the student's instructional level and may be used for the identification of word recognition errors (Deno et al., 1982) as well as comprehension.

After the student has completed reading the passage: (1) the examiner says, "Tell me what this story (passage) was about." As the student answers, the examiner checks off on a copy of the passage the key thought units that are recalled. Then (2) the examiner looks over the information recalled and completes an initial tally of the types of thought units reported: main ideas, factual details, sequential events, inferences, and so forth.

Step II: Identify Possible Errors: Confirm by Retesting.   When you notice that a student appears to have difficulty with a particular aspect of comprehension, you should attempt to confirm the student's problems. Ask specific questions to probe that difficulty. If, for example, the student has related the main idea but omitted factual details, you may want to test for detail comprehension by asking "who," "what," "when," "why" questions. Or, if the student's description of directions given in the passage are out of sequence, you might focus on "What is the first step in. . . ?"

If narrative rather than expository text is being used to evaluate reading comprehension, you may find it useful to evaluate the student's understanding by use of a story grammar (Schmitt & O'Brien, 1986). That is, questions would center around the story's setting, its plot, and the attempts of the main character to resolve problem(s).

We also suggest that confirmation of a reading problem during retesting focus on the student's understanding of the key vocabulary. For each key word on which the student made a word recognition error during initial reading, you should point to the word in the text and say, "This word is. . . ." Then ask, "What does . . . mean?" Similarly, you should point to any other key words in the passage and ascertain the student's understanding of those words.

As part of this step in the diagnostic procedure, the teacher collects multiple samples of the student's comprehension skills. This is done most easily by marking the student's reading comprehension work daily. Use the same kind of workbook or worksheet assignment as is used during the independent work period. Determine if (1) the teacher has provided instruction on how to complete the practice exercises, (2) these are related to the skill being taught, (3) the teacher has modeled the completion of at least one of the examples and has been available to provide feedback as students complete their work (see Rupley & Blair, 1987). If so, students should score at least 90 percent correct on the assigned tasks. You should mark these exercises daily (or guide students in marking them). Record the type(s) of errors, for example, in literal comprehension, story retelling, summary or main ideas, sequence, inference, critical reading and evaluation (Carnine & Silbert, 1977).

Step III: Interview the Student.   If the teacher notes that a particular student consistently has difficulty with any of the types of comprehension skills, then this is what should be done: The teacher should observe the student individually for a short time period during the reworking of the exercise page on which the student scored less than 90 percent. Before deciding that the student lacks the strategy for comprehending the materials, you should eliminate the following factors (abstracted from Carnine & Silbert, 1977):

- *lack of effort*—the student is not attending to the task, or has no motivation to complete it correctly;
- *decoding problem*—the student can complete the task correctly when the teacher reads the examples out loud to him;
- *not knowing critical vocabulary*—when the teacher selects several key words from the passage or examples and asks the student to tell what they mean, the student answers incorrectly;
- *not following directions*—when the teacher asks the student what work is required on the page, the student answers incorrectly or says he or she does not know.

The next step is to identify the comprehension problem by examining the comprehension strategy used by the student. Carnine and Silbert (1977) suggest that students with comprehension difficulties may lack appropriate strategies for comprehending written language. The best way to determine whether this problem exists is to observe the student and to ask the student to describe the strategy being used to complete the comprehension exercise. For example, the student with difficulty in simple, literal comprehension may say, ''I just try to remember what it says. But when there are so many things, I can't remember them all.'' This type of response indicates the absence of a workable strategy for recall.

Step IV: Record Findings for Analysis.   Finally, it is recommended that you write down the mistakes on a chart. As with word recognition, the recording of the exact nature of the comprehension error facilitates the selection of a corrective strategy (see Figure 4.3).

Some Limitations of the Procedure.   The previous discussion should be viewed as a surface-level analysis of comprehension errors. It does not take into account the student's ability to apply logic and use reasoning; nor does it account for the complexities of syntax or semantics. In addition, this procedure does not include a detailed analysis of the environment within which the student is placed for reading instruction (Elliott &

Error Type/Number		Prioritized Instruction	
Critical reading	*n/a*		Proficiency
Making inferences	*I*		
Sequence of events	*I*		Transition
Main idea/summary	*II*		
Recall: factual detail	*HH I*	*Teach use of "who, what, when, where" in factual questions, model scanning of text for answers using these questions; give specific academic praise and frequent reinforcement.*	Acquisition

Figure 4.3. Bill's Comprehension-Error Analysis

*This skill may be more difficult in narrative than in expository text.

Piersel, 1982). It may be, for example, that the student is not being given adequate instruction before being asked to complete a reading assignment (Rupley & Blair, 1987), or that the teaching procedures used in the "higher" groups are superior to those used with lower functioning readers (G. Spache & E. Spache, 1986). Even so, the error analysis procedure we have discussed is directly related to the task of comprehension of the curriculum in which students must succeed, and is therefore a logical first step. After the teacher's best efforts along these lines have failed, it is time to seek further assistance from the reading diagnostician, a psychologist, or a language-learning specialist (see Carnine & Silbert, 1977; Morsink, 1984; Schreiner, 1983).

Case Study on Comprehension

The use of the error analysis procedure in teaching comprehension is dependent upon: (1) elimination of factors other than comprehension of printed language as the source of the problem; and, (2) identification of instructional procedures most closely related to the student's stage of learning: acquisition, transition, or proficiency. For the purpose of this description, the need for acquisition of the skill is indicated when the student cannot perform at all, even when heavy reinforcement is provided. The need for emphasizing transition learning exists when the student can, with teacher prompting and appropriate reinforcement, perform some of the time or make responses which are partially correct.

A representative sample of a student's comprehension error analysis is shown in Figure 4.3. Bill, the student described in the case study on word recognition, is shown again. The next section deals with stages of learning and corresponding corrective strategies.

Multistage Comprehension Strategies

At the beginning stages, the teacher needs to show the student how to use the comprehension strategy. First use modeling; then use prompting; and finally use self-questioning techniques. The specifics for developing the strategy differ slightly according to the subskill being taught. Procedures found to be effective in teaching comprehension are shown in Table 4.2. This summary is adapted from the work of Carnine and Silbert (1977), G. Spache and E. Spache (1986), and Rupley and Blair (1987).

There exists only limited knowledge of problem solving in some curricular areas (e.g., arithmetic). However, a number of researchers have investigated aspects of reading-comprehension strategies. They have offered guidelines for their use. These strategies include the development of word-recognition skills to the point of automaticity to permit disabled readers to concentrate on reading comprehension (Snider & Tarver, 1987), and the use of direct instruction and follow-up practice to enhance fluency and expression (Hoffman, 1987; Sindelar, Smith, Harriman, Hale, & Wilson, 1986). Other authorities suggest that comprehension of main ideas can be facilitated through direct instruction when this is paired with self-monitoring by the students themselves (Graves, 1986). Details and inference questions can be added to the students' use of self-questioning strategies (Sundbye, 1987). The cloze procedure has also been found to be effective in improving of students' inference skills (Dewitz, Carr, & Patberg, 1987).

Chan and Cole (1986) have shown how to teach disabled learners to use a meta-

TABLE 4.2. Developing Comprehension Proficiency Through Stages of Learning

Acquisition	Transition	Proficiency
Antecedent Events		
Explain directions, model words (circle, underline, and so forth)	Preview text	Provide advanced organizers
	Explain and model task, use examples	Teach key vocabulary
Label words by actions/ attributes	Review prior experiences, direct students to use context for meanings	Encourage students to use dictionary
Define words, use known words		Teach "how, why" explanatory questions
Teach "who, what, when, where" factual questions	Direct students to reread for answers	Teach prediction from past events
Model scanning for answers	Use structures such as "story trees"	Direct students to engage in self-questioning
Teach self-questioning following sentences	Direct students to cover text during recall	Show students how to distinguish fact/fiction
Use cloze procedure to train in use of context analysis	Demonstrate self-questioning following paragraphs	
	Teach sequence words, before, after	
	Model the numbering of sequential events	
Subsequent Events		
Give specific academic praise (brief feedback indicating why response is correct)	Give specific corrective feedback	Encourage students to elaborate on responses
Provide frequent reinforcement	Reduce frequency of reinforcement	Provide periodic reinforcement
Reward students by allowing them to question each other	Reinforce students for self-correction	Review reading performance on the basis of student's use of self-correction and questioning
Show picture after student answers related question correctly	Reinforce students for self-questioning	
	Show students how to chart responses	Encourage students to chart own responses
Demonstrate charting correct responses		

cognitive strategy of self-questioning. Students should imagine they were helping a toy robot with reading comprehension. The strategies of self-questioning; of underlining key points; and the combination of questioning and underlining were more effective than simple instructions to read and reread the passages. Varnhagen and Goldman (1986) were able to teach special students to understand logical connections between the goals of a story's characters and their attempts to satisfy these goals. They taught the skill through categories as "story trees." They sequenced instruction from the small parts of the task to the whole. First, students were asked to identify the antecedent and the consequence; then to find the relationship between them. Using the story tree, they asked students to employ certain beginning information and to make up different episodes about the characters. Later they asked students to generate the entire story, one based on the goal attempts. In this process, the instructor would remove a card from the tree. Then the instructor asked students to make up or to recall information to fill in the gaps in the story. Finally, students were encouraged to develop internal procedures for questioning that helped them to see causal relationships. The procedure did improve students' comprehension of ''why'' in complex but not simple stories. It also assisted them in memory, structure and story production. The authors cautioned that the procedures should match students' developmental levels. The technique appeared more effective for students with reading levels of 3.5 and above. Procedures drawn from the work of G. Spache and E. Spache (1986), Rupley and Blair (1987) and from the direct instructional procedures employed by Carnine and Silbert (1977) and others are presented in Table 4.2.

We have presented the process of reading comprehension as a sequence of skills that go from acquisition to proficiency. However, it should not be viewed as a separate process which precedes or parallels that of word recognition. In a real sense, all of reading comprehension may be said to begin at the stage of proficiency. This follows the acquisition of word recognition skills and the development of automaticity in decoding. Both of these occur during the transition stage. This view is consistent with the work of Chall (1983) and Snider and Tarver (1987) among others. Many students experiencing difficulty in reading are unable to comprehend written language because they have not yet developed to the point of automaticity these prerequisite level skills.

SUMMARY

Our discussion on error analysis in reading should not be viewed as rigid standards for improving classroom diagnosis and remediation. First, errors students make in reading are unlikely to conform exactly to the model we have introduced. Second, we urge you to use all available information when establishing a plan of reading instruction. Include the knowledge of possible variability in reading performance. This is linked to the difficulty of that material as well as to its motivational appeal. Third, since uniform criteria for acceptable levels of corrects and errors in oral reading have not yet been established, it is best to remain flexible in applying the figures we have offered. As in other subject areas, we encourage you to collect information on regular-class students performing acceptably. Use this data to develop local normative standards. Lastly, although the available literature is encouraging, a clear linkage between error types and remediation has yet to be firmly established. Even so, we are convinced that error analysis of both word recognition and reading comprehension skills can improve the quality of both assessment and remediation.

DISCUSSION QUESTIONS AND ACTIVITIES

1. Interview a school psychologist to learn about what tests are routinely administered in your school system.
2. Interview a reading specialist to learn about administration, scoring, and interpretation of various reading tests.
3. Practice classifying errors in oral reading collected on students at various grade levels.
4. Practice classifying errors in comprehension collected on students at various grade levels.

CHAPTER 5

Error Analysis in Handwriting Instruction

Carole E. Stowitschek
*State of Washington, Office of Superintendent
of Public Instruction, Olympia, Washington*

Joseph J. Stowitschek
University of Washington

CHAPTER OBJECTIVES

After reading this chapter you should be able to:

1. Discuss a rationale for teaching students to write legibly.
2. Describe handwriting assessment procedures (both historical and current).
3. List the advantages and disadvantages of modeling procedures, both appropriate and inappropriate, used to teach handwriting.
4. Identify generalization issues regarding handwriting instruction.

KEY TERMS

copy	self-analysis
cursive	template overlay
handwriting	template underlay
legibility	tracing
manuscript	transfer/generalization

INTRODUCTION

Poor letter formation skills are evident in the handwriting of many students. This should not be surprising because the teaching of handwriting has not received much attention (e.g., Addy & Wylie, 1973). Even so, given adequate instruction, the majority of students have the ability to produce legible handwriting. The prerequisite perceptual, motor, and intellectual skills are in the repertoires of most students including those identified as eligible for special education services. Nonetheless, few of these students exhibit good handwriting skills. The best examples of good handwriting are found in classes where teachers expect, value and reinforce legible handwriting, and where they directly teach handwriting skills. Unfortunately, few special or general educators have been trained to teach handwriting. As a result, handwriting is the "neglected R" (Milone & Wasylyk, 1981).

The major purpose for legible handwriting is to record and to communicate information. This includes writing for your own personal use, writing to others, writing related to seeking employment and to job-related skills, and writing to obtain information from others. Recent technological advances, including the introduction of computers in the home and in the workplace, have helped circumvent some of the problems associated with poor writing. Still, the need exists for students to be able to proficiently form letters and words for the purpose of communicating (Naisbett, 1982). Students who do not learn to form letters well—either in isolation or within the context of written language—have a reduced ability to compete in the classroom.

Since comprehensive treatment of the topic of handwriting requires more attention than we can give it in a single chapter, our discussion focuses on priority instructional issues and the application of error analysis in handwriting. We begin with a brief overview of handwriting assessment to establish the place of error analysis as an evaluation tool. A procedure for analyzing handwriting errors in initial or remedial instruction is demonstrated. Finally, we conclude with an illustration of how error analysis can be integrated with a systematic contingency arrangement to improve the learner's everyday handwriting.

REVIEW OF RESEARCH ON HANDWRITING

How much instructional attention does handwriting receive? Addy and Wylie (1973) reported the results of an international survey on handwriting. They distributed four-hundred questionnaires to urban and rural teachers, kindergarten through third grade. Some of the results are summarized below:

1. Handwriting instruction is fairly uniform throughout the United States and Canada.
2. Manuscript writing is initiated in the first grade and cursive writing in the third grade. Formal classes in handwriting are given in kindergarten by 34 percent of the rural teachers and 15 percent of the urban teachers.
3. The entire class is taught at one time in most schools. The length of lessons ranges from eleven to twenty minutes per day.
4. Only 30 percent of all teachers use workbooks for instruction. Copying models, a common instructional practice, is accomplished through the use of chalkboards, overhead projectors, workbooks, and work sheets.
5. Left-handed children usually are given some special instruction in handwriting.
6. Grades are given for handwriting in 70 percent of the schools surveyed.
7. The evaluation of handwriting almost always is made by casual teacher observation (rather than through the use of criterion models and evaluation scales).

These results, and findings of other studies, suggest that handwriting instruction is not only minimally taught but is a low instructional priority. Nonetheless, poor handwriting can compound academic problems.

Handwriting educators have had varied opinions regarding what should be emphasized and how it should be taught. In the early years of special education, the best or most appropriate mode of initial handwriting instruction had been widely debated. For example, the development of associative processes, such as eye-hand coordination, figure-ground discrimination and proprioceptive feedback were touted as critical initial steps in handwriting instruction (Pomeroy, 1971; Stewart, 1973). As a result, young children spent many hours tracing letters in the sand, feeling the contours and texture of cut-out letters and numerals, and connecting dots. Regardless of the questionable merit of these activities, they can still be found in both initial and remedial handwriting instruction. Probably the most predominant form of initial handwriting instruction, as reflected in instructional materials and teaching practices, is tracing along dotted lines and over prepared samples of letters and numerals. Judging from years of research (cf. Askov & Greff, 1975; Stewart, 1973), the value of tracing as an initial instruction activity is grossly overrated. This is particularly true to the extent that it is prolonged for weeks, months, and even years beyond any demonstrated utility.

Since the 1940s, copying from a model consistently has been demonstrated to be superior to tracing or associative process building in the teaching of handwriting. Hirsh and Niedermeyer (1978) examined the effects of copying versus faded tracing on letter formation. They found that copying is the most effective procedure to promote correct letter formation. Similar outcomes were reported by Askov and Greff (1975) and Stewart (1973). It is unfortunate, therefore, that copying from a model has been given a lesser role in handwriting programs than tracing. Modeling is a documented successful strategy for teaching handwriting. When integrated with systematic instruction, copying from a model produces a rapid remediation of handwriting deficits (Stowitschek, 1978; C. Stowitschek & J. Stowitschek, 1979). In addition, it appears that students who show improved handwriting when models are used demonstrate improved production of letters and numerals once the model is removed (Stowitschek, 1978).

Techniques for Evaluating Handwriting

As in the teaching of handwriting, the evaluation of students' handwriting typically has been inconsistent and nonsystematic. Most teachers simply do not know how to adequately evaluate student performance and to relate the outcome of that evaluation to appropriate corrective strategies. Fortunately, both norm- and criterion-referenced alternatives are available to assist the teacher in making instructional decisions regarding the form and function of handwriting.

Normative Assessment.   Two of the first normative handwriting scales were developed by Thorndike (1910) and Ayres (1912). These scales consisted of a series of graded handwriting samples, as well as guidelines for comparing the samples to the student's handwriting products. Unfortunately, the reliability of procedures using graded samples has been poor and their utility questionable (Buros, 1965; Watts, 1971). Responding to these issues, Freeman (1959) used a set of letter formation criteria initially in his hand-writing scales. However, later versions focused on measuring general excellence. The scales devised by Thorndike, Ayre, and Freeman are used to compare a student's hand-writing performance to those of others, and not to a standard of letter formation. Thus, these scales have dubious utility in conducting quality assessment.

Criterion-referenced Assessment.   In recent years, attempts have been made to design objective, reliable procedures for measuring students' manuscript letter formation. Some efforts have focused on establishing measurable criteria for determining quality (accu-racy) and/or quantity (fluency) of performance (Hopkins, Schutte, & Gorton, 1971; E. Lewis & H. Lewis, 1965; Watts, 1971). In other studies, pre- and posttest samples (Hofmeister, 1969), transparent overlays (Helwig, Johns, Norman, & Cooper, 1976; Jones, Trap, & Cooper, 1977; Trap, Milner-Davis, Joseph, & Cooper, 1978), and tem-plate underlays (J. Stowitschek & C. Stowitschek, 1975; C. Stowitschek & J. Stowit-schek, 1979) have been used for assessment. In the later cases, measurable criteria and pre- and posttest comparisons were used in combination. The criterion-referenced as-sessment process appears to be more practical for diagnostic and remediation purposes than for the comprehensive assessment of handwriting achievement.

Form and Function.   Although handwriting itself yields a concrete permanent product, it has proven to be exceedingly difficult to measure objectively. Handwriting assessment procedures are based on both form and function. Form assessment pertains to general factors affecting letter formation itself. The form of letters may be affected by the three "Ps" of general handwriting assessment. These are: *posture, position,* and *pencil.* "Posture" pertains to correct alignment of the body and positioning in the chair in relation to the desk or writing surface. "Position" concerns placement of the writing paper so that the letter characters are not on a severe slant. "Pencil" refers to the manner in which the writer holds the pencil.

Assessment of Movement.   Another important factor in letter formation is continuity of movement. Assessment of movement in manuscript letter formation often focuses on the ability to place a pencil point at a prescribed starting point, produce circles in both clockwise and counterclockwise directions, and produce straight lines from top-to-bot-tom and left-to-right. For cursive handwriting, and intermediary approaches, such as the D'Nealian, an additional movement consideration is the uninterrupted flow of intercon-nected letters within a word through the use of leading and trailing lines. Continuity of movement is a major factor affecting the rate or quantitative aspect of handwriting.

Qualitative Aspects of Handwriting Assessment

Probably the most critical aspect of form assessment is evaluating the accuracy with which characters are produced. That is, the qualitative dimensions of handwriting must be evaluated carefully. Criteria used in inspecting handwriting samples are centered on specifying attributes of shape, spacing, size, connectedness, slant, and position. The function of handwriting pertains to the extent to which a written product communicates. Students may be able to produce correctly formed letters in isolation. However, in the process of writing rapidly to finish an assignment legibility often suffers. As noted, assessment of handwriting legibility typically has been based on subjective opinion. For example, Starlin (1982) divides legibility into four categories for judging accuracy: letter formation, letter size, slant, and spacing. Letter formation includes correctly connecting strokes, closing such letters as *o* and *a,* dotting such letters as *i,* crossing *t* and *x,* and forming the descending portion of such letters as *f* and *g.* Letter size is grouped into maximum, intermediate and minimum size letters. A sixty degree slant is recommended.

Starlin suggests these criteria for spacing: between letters, enough space for the oval of a *9;* between words, enough space for a lower case *o;* between sentences, enough space for two lower case *oo*s. These subjective criteria are similar to those recommended by numerous other authors and may be useful for assessing and teaching students who have a few difficulties. In the case of extreme illegibility, the ability of one or more readers to recognize written words may be the assessment index of choice.

Quantitative Aspects of Handwriting Assessment

In addition to the qualitative aspects of letter formation and its affect on legibility, the rate or quantitative nature of a student's handwriting influences school achievement. Students whose rate of letter and word production is very slow, are unable to communicate to their teachers the knowledge they have on a particular subject. The simple cycle of not finishing assignments, getting poor grades, and appearing less than competent may set the stage for progressive failure. To assist the student who painstakingly executes each letter, the teacher needs to set rate objectives and increase the student's performance to an acceptable level of proficiency (Gable, Hendrickson, Tenenbaum, & Morsink, 1986). Starlin (1982) suggests various proficiency rates for letters in words, for letters in sentences and paragraphs and for words in prose writing. They are as follows: (a) one hundred to two hundred correct *letters* in words, (b) one hundred to two hundred correct *letters* in sentences and paragraphs, and (c) twenty to forty correct *words* in prose if the prose composition itself is 99 percent correctly written. Starlin (1982) also suggests rates for prealphabetic and isolated alphabet writing. Right curves ()), left curves ((), under curves (◡), over curves (◠), and ovals (o ⊙ ⊙) are taught to a rate of one hundred to two hundred characters per minute. Single connected letters (e.g., *ℓℓ*) and double connected letters (e.g., *oa oa*) also have a recommended criterion of one hundred to two hundred minute. In summary, when assessing or remediating handwriting deficiencies, teachers must consider both the qualitative and quantitative dimensions of handwriting. Subsequent sections of this chapter address issues related to assessing and remediating students with more severe and persistent handwriting difficulties.

INSTRUCTIONAL ASSESSMENT— ITS VARIOUS PURPOSES

The purposes of assessment vary according to the stages of the instructional process. Decisions regarding each student become progressively more discrete as the teacher determines the focus of instruction and progressively more comprehensive as the teacher seeks to determine the impact of instruction. Stowitschek, Gable, and Hendrickson (1980) describe four levels of assessment relative to instructional decision-making: 1) initial selection, 2) specific skill assessment, 3) baseline performance and on-going monitoring, and 4) mastery assessment.

Typically, the initial step is to determine the kind and degree of a student's instructional needs in handwriting. A global assessment procedure (such as a normative handwriting scale) is appropriate for identifying students in need of handwriting instruction. Criterion-referenced assessments, such as the ®Brigance Diagnostic Inventory of Basic Skills (Brigance, 1977), may be useful for this general level of assessment as well as for the second step. Next, students identified as potential candidates for handwriting instruction should have their performance sampled on a variety of skills to pinpoint deficits. This more in-depth assessment of a specific handwriting skill (e.g., writing one's name, address, and phone number) is done by further sampling student performance. At this stage, either an informal or criterion-referenced test may be used to pinpoint skill deficits and to establish baseline levels of performance prior to beginning instruction. Curriculum-based or precision teaching probes (i.e., one minute samples of targeted handwriting skills) may be taken to determine student rate of performance. Once instruction is initiated, daily or weekly assessments are conducted to ascertain the rate of growth. Finally, the last type of assessment relates to mastery. Mastery of the specific skills must be assessed first. This is then followed by the application of the handwriting skills. Ultimately, the student should evidence generalized achievement. Handwriting programs such as the one described by C. Stowitschek and J. Stowitschek (1979) include procedures for pinpointing skills, for the daily monitoring of student handwriting, and for inspecting and evaluating mastery of handwriting skills. It is during this assessment-intervention process that error analysis has its greatest applicability.

As handwriting instruction progresses, the focus of assessment can involve: (a) developing or remediating individual letter-formation skills, (b) pinpointing problems as they occur, and (c) determining whether or not mastery of targeted skills constitutes a substantive improvement in overall handwriting. In the assessment plan we have just described, the analysis of handwriting errors becomes an integral part of the teaching of handwriting because it is embedded within the framework of an instructional program. The sections which follow describe two approaches to error analysis which have been used as part of the instructional program.

Analyzing Errors in Handwriting

Analysis of handwriting errors during initial or remedial instruction of letter and numeral production can be approached using the principles of "discrimination learning." Students struggling to improve their handwriting should be given ready access to appropriate models and taught to judge the adequacy of their writing in relation to these models or "objective standards." Faulty handwriting instruction, on the other hand, typically includes the use of massed practice (e.g., one and one-half hours on Tuesday), nondifferential teacher feedback (e.g., "That looks pretty good, Jill"), and inappropriate models which can hinder acquisition of handwriting (Hofmeister, 1973). Furthermore, in the absence of a standard criterion, the student's own writing efforts end up serving as models.

Since letter formation is associated closely with legibility, during initial instruction center error analysis around identifying discriminations that are relative to the formation of letter components (Buros, 1965; Quant, 1946). C. Stowitschek and J. Stowitschek (1979) began to explore the issue of teaching discrimination skills. They developed an error-analysis matrix to help teachers: (a) to identify letter formation attributes and (b) to communicate letter analysis to their students. The letter formation attributes they use to assess writing samples drawn from several subject areas are shown in Figure 5.1.

Samples of handwriting are taken from different subject area assignments and analyzed according to each of eleven attributes. The clustering of error types provides the teacher with specific targets for remediation.

However, there is more to error analysis than looking for error clusters. At least three approaches to analyzing handwriting errors using the error matrix and models have been discussed in the literature. In Hofmeister's early work (1973), the teacher relies on visual inspection. The teacher judges whether there is a match or mismatch between the model and the copied letter. A drawback of this approach is that daily visual inspection procedures were found to require considerable teacher time (C. Stowitschek & J. Stowitschek, 1979). In another approach, Cooper and his associates (Waggoner, LaNunziata, Hill, & Cooper, 1981) used transparent overlays to facilitate the comparisons. With overlays alone, students were able to reliably discriminate between correct letters and letters produced with errors. Additionally, teacher involvement was reduced.

In a third approach, C. Stowitschek and J. Stowitschek (1979) and Stowitschek, Ghezzi, and Safely (1987) used correction templates and translucent paper as part of a training procedure in which exceptional students analyzed and corrected their own handwriting errors. As you can see in Figure 5.2, the student was required to produce a row of letters. Then, before proceeding to the next row, the student used the template to correct the letters. This self-analysis and correction procedure is efficient in that one does not have to be at the student's side to provide feedback. In addition, the student relearns the letter while the correction procedure is taking place. The procedure is simple to teach because students are able to generalize the use of the templates across practice sets.

Using this procedure, the student corrects each incorrectly written letter, practices only those letters needing correction, and produces a correct model for successive practice rows. The teacher observes and assists the student until the student demonstrates reliable use of the evaluation and correction procedure.

In repeated field tests (C. Stowitschek & J. Stowitschek, 1979; Stowitschek, 1978; Stowitschek et al., 1987), students have rapidly acquired the use of these correction steps and generalized their use to handwriting worksheets for which no training was provided. Daily handwriting practice was relatively brief (one and one-half to three minutes per worksheet set of nine letters each). Yet, when teacher reinforcement and post-practice monitoring were combined with the self-analysis and correction procedure, the average rate of student improvement was 1.66 letters per day.

The use of models and carefully structured instructional procedures does not guarantee improved handwriting. As we mentioned, models may be used inappropriately. For instance, teachers who almost exclusively write large model letters on the board or refer to permanent models posted above the blackboard or bulletin board, make the assumption that students are able to transfer from blackboard to paper.

Hofmeister (1973) points out another example of inappropriate copying strategies.

DLM Handwriting Tally Sheet

Name J. Smith   Date 9/10

HANDWRITING PROBLEM	SUBJECT AREAS			TOTAL
	Spelling	English	History	
1. Letters omitted	||	|	|||	6
2. Letters added				
3. Letters too large				
4. Letters too small		|		1
5. Bottoms of letters not on line	ﷻ |	|||	||||	13
6. Tops of small letters not at midline	||	|	||	5
7. Letters too far apart	|	|		2
8. Letters too close together	||||	|	||||	9
9. Letters too slanted				
10. Letter lines not connected	|		|	2
11. Parts of letters missing				

Figure 5.1. Handwriting Error Analysis Guide

SOURCE: DLM [Developmental Learning Materials] Handwriting Tally Sheet, "DLM Handwriting Program," C. Stowitschek, Hofmeister, and J. Stowitschek, #763, *Handwriting Transfer Techniques,* © DLM, 1981. Reprinted with permission.

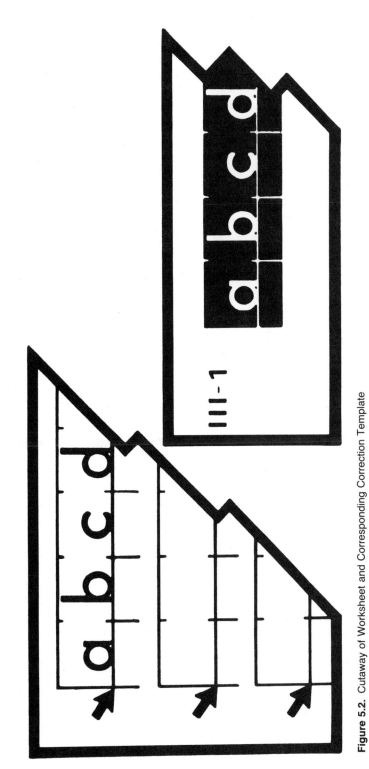

Figure 5.2. Cutaway of Worksheet and Corresponding Correction Template

SOURCE: " 'I'd rather do it myself': Self-evaluation and correction of handwriting" by J. J. Stowitschek, P. M. Ghezzi, and K. V. Safely, 1987, *Education and Treatment of Children, 10,* pp. 209–224. Reprinted by permission.

Many prepared worksheets have model letters printed on the left side of the page. Students are required to copy entire rows of letters from the single model. Teacher feedback is usually delayed at least a day or more. Not only is delayed feedback a problem, but because of the worksheet design students use their own previously produced letters as the model for the next response. A characteristic outcome is that letters become progressively worse as the student uses his or her own incorrectly produced models. This happens in left to right copying, as well as in instances where model letters are placed at the top of worksheets and students produce columns of copied letters. The problem is that these activities do not have a correction feature or that feedback is not provided until the page is finished, turned in, and checked by the teacher.

Other problems in handwriting instruction have to do with overestimating the transferability of letters produced from a model. That is, teachers frequently assume that practice at individual letter production is transferable to the production of letters in words. For many students, appropriate teacher modeling combined with corrective feedback is necessary for the acquisition of both letter-production and word-production skills. Another problem occurs when teachers assume that the production of copied letters or words is transferable to conditions in which students use handwriting in the absence of models. Although there is evidence of generalization and transfer from copied letters, the transfer process must be facilitated using intermediate modeling steps, corrective feedback, and appropriate contingencies.

The handwriting instruction problems and principles described above are not indigenous to a particular handwriting style or curriculum-sequencing approach. Whether the choice is D'Nealian or traditional approaches, the principles are generic.

Integrating Error Correction into Daily Instruction

The analysis of handwriting performance following the completion of initial handwriting instruction is integral to overall assessment and instruction. Teachers must be able to discern when skills mastered in one setting have not transferred to other settings or when handwriting has deteriorated and become nonfunctional. In these instances the teacher must determine the exact source(s) of the problem and design remediation activities accordingly.

As we have noted earlier, formal handwriting instruction and practice occurs during the early years of a student's primary education (grades K-3). After this point, the learner must transfer whatever skills he or she has developed to the contexts of everyday classroom use. Although this generalization is expected of students, there are numerous contextual variables which mitigate against the natural transfer of previously learned skills. Chief among the variables resulting in deficient handwriting are the following: (1) It is difficult to concentrate on handwriting when the focus of instruction is on learning and the demonstration of skill in another subject matter (e.g., arithmetic computation, history, and language arts); (2) time constraints are imposed on the completion of subject area assignments; (3) the controlling stimuli during handwriting drill and practice (e.g., copying from a model) are different from the stimuli expected to control handwriting quality in other contexts (e.g., "Answer the questions by filling in the blanks").

In many classroom situations, handwriting is largely ignored and becomes an issue only when the teacher cannot read a student's written work or when a student writes so slowly that assignments do not get completed. This is the point at which the student may be referred for handwriting remediation. As a result of the referral, the student may be pulled out of the class to "learn" handwriting skills. Remedial practice is provided out of context and the "real" problem may never be addressed. Although remedial practice may be appropriate when initial letter and numeral formation skills are lacking, remediation of illegible handwriting is best accomplished in the setting in which the problem originated. Consider the following case study:

CASE STUDY

Mr. Watts, the fifth-grade reading teacher, and Ms. Greene, a middle-school resource teacher, shared a morning break time in the teachers' lounge. Today's topic of discussion was Jeremia, an 11-year-old who had been mainstreamed into Del Watts' class. When asked how Jeremia was doing, Mr. Watts said, "Well, he seems to be able to handle the content, but I'm sure getting tired of trying to read his handwriting. Can't you do something about it?" Ms. Greene's response was, "He is fine when he comes to my room for reading and language arts, but I'll look into it." Subsequently, Ms. Greene had Jeremia complete a series of test sheets in which he copied upper and lower case letters of the alphabet, and completed words and numerals in both manuscript and cursive. Although Jeremia could form acceptable letters and numerals, Ms. Greene started him on a program of practice worksheets. Over time, Jeremia became a quite accomplished letter and numeral producer. However, Mr. Watts' complaints about Jeremia's legibility remained unchanged.

When a student may demonstrate the ability to adequately form characters and words, but not write legibly for regular classroom assignments, then, drill and practice are not appropriate intervention strategies. However, the resource teacher, serving as a consulting teacher in the regular classroom, can be an effective change agent. "Pullout" instruction on letter and number production typically is not effective because the skill is practiced in isolation from the natural writing context in which there was a problem. One effective approach is to use a diagnostic procedure wherein the teacher and student identify the problem area. Next, the targeted behaviors are monitored in relation to the student's classroom performance. This procedure could be accomplished with a student like Jeremia. Ms. Greene, serving as the consulting teacher, might work with Jeremia in the regular classroom in the following way:

Example: After assessing Jeremia's performance in an individual handwriting drill and practice session, Ms. Greene went back to Mr. Watts and asked to see some of Jeremia's science worksheets. Ms. Greene also collected written work samples from his language arts and history teachers. At the next session, Jeremia and Ms. Greene looked through the collected worksheet samples together. Ms. Greene explained that in order to improve his handwriting, they should determine exactly why Jeremia's handwriting was difficult to read. Here are the steps and the mutual diagnosis and monitoring process which Jeremia and Ms. Greene agreed upon:

1. *Identify words or phrases which are hard to read.* Jeremia and Ms. Greene went through the worksheets circling all words or phrases which were illegible or nearly illegible.

2. *Determine what makes the word or phrase difficult to read.* After illegible words and passages were identified, Ms. Greene asked Jeremia what he thought was different about each identified word or passage, and what made it hard to read.

3. *Designate a diagnostic indicator.* After Ms. Greene and Jeremia discussed each circled word and phrase, and identified the problem he was having with each, Ms. Greene said, "Now, let's go back and see if we can figure out the best way to keep track of what we said was different about each word. Look at *steam* again. Take a colored pencil and redraw the line that the word *steam* seems to follow so we can compare it to the actual line on the paper" (see Figure 5.3). "Now what would you do with those words where the letters are jammed together?" Jeremia, "I'd draw a line between them." Ms. Greene, "You mean like a slash? That's a good idea. Let's do that." Ms. Greene and Jeremia continued this discussion until they determined a mutually agreed upon diagnostic indicator for each problem type. Figure 5.3 contains a sample of words identified by Jeremia and Ms. Greene that fall into each of the eleven error categories.

4. *Prioritize diagnostic indicators.* Ms. Greene prepared a chart. She listed the diagnostic points pertaining to Jeremia's handwriting illegibilities. The most common errors contributing to illegibility were at the top of the list. Next to the diagnostic points, she listed the corresponding indicator marks. (See Figure 5.3).

5. *Involve teacher confederates.* Ms. Greene met with Mr. Watts and explained the mutual diagnosis process. She asked Mr. Watts to use the first diagnostic indicator (a line redrawn with a blue pencil) as he corrected Jeremia's assignments and tests. She arranged to collect the corrected assignments and record the results on her chart before the assignments were returned to Jeremia. Ms. Greene repeated the teacher confederate procedure with Jeremia's language arts and history teachers.

6. *Establish contingencies for handwriting improvement.* Ms. Greene established a contract with Jeremia as follows: for each assignment returned to Ms. Greene with no redrawn lines, Jeremia would be permitted to take a 10-minute-longer recess (as had been arranged with the principal). Figure 5.4 illustrates the contractual arrangement and record keeping system.

7. *Monitor the program.* After receiving three successive assignments from each teacher with no redrawn lines, Ms. Greene asked the teachers to add the next diagnostic check (e.g., a slash between letters that were jammed together). In addition, Ms. Greene began to shift the reinforcing contingencies to the regular teachers' classrooms. For instance, in Mr. Watts classroom Jeremia was given the opportunity to help set up science demonstrations following the successful completion of three successive assignments. This process continued until all teachers were satisfied that Jeremia's handwriting had become legible. Ms. Green continued to track Jeremia's performance with occasional checks and feedback to Jeremia.

These procedures have been refined into a consulting teacher package and published (C. Stowitschek, Hofmeister & J. Stowitschek, 1981). This type of assessment and remediation is likely to be successful because the confederate teachers can complete one step at a time. It is relatively simple system, and therefore teachers are likely to be more willing and able to participate. The focus on error reduction narrows the scope of work so that the additional analysis task is manageable for a busy teacher. This error analysis procedure can be tailored to the needs of individual students and is based on samples drawn from everyday handwriting assignments. It has a relatively broad range of application and has direct relevance to practical handwriting uses.

DLM Handwriting Marking Guide

Handwriting Problem	Problem Indicator	Manuscript Example	Cursive Example
1. Letters omitted	write the missing letter above where it should be	tru͡ck	steam
2. Letters added	draw a slash line through the extra letters	trucke	steam
3. Letters too large	draw rectangle on the too large letter	tr☐ck	Steam
4. Letters too small	draw a rectangle on the too small letter	tru☐k	steam
5. Bottoms of letters not on line	with a continuous line, underscore the bases of the letters	truck	steam
6. Tops of small letters not at midline	draw a line through the mid-point and across tops of lower-case letters	truck	steam
7. Letters too far apart	draw double slashes between the letters	t//ru//ck	steam
8. Letters too close together	draw single wavy line between letters	truck	steam
9. Letters too slanted	draw a dotted line through the center of the letters that are too slanted	truck	steam
10. Letter lines not connected	connect the lines	truck	steam
11. Parts of letters missing	draw in the missing letter part	truck	steam

Figure 5.3. Diagnostic Indicators Used in Mutual Diagnoses of Handwriting Samples

SOURCE: DLM [Developmental Learning Materials] Handwriting Marking Guide, "DLM Handwriting Program," C. E. Stowitschek, Hofmeister, and J. J. Stowitschek, #763, *Handwriting Transfer Techniques,* © DLM, 1981. Reprinted with permission.

DLM Handwriting Improvement Contract

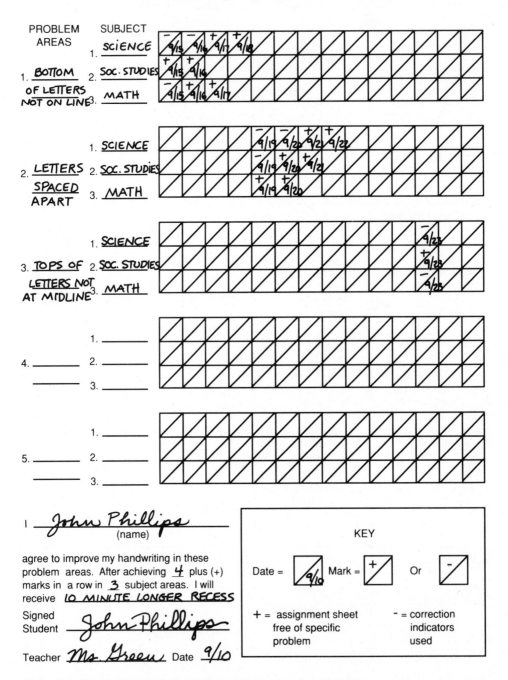

Figure 5.4. Combination Monitoring Chart and Contingency Contract

SOURCE: DLM [Developmental Learning Materials] Handwriting Improvement Contract, "DLM Handwriting Program," C. E. Stowitschek, Hofmeister, and J. J. Stowitschek, #763, *Handwriting Transfer Techniques,* © DLM, 1981. Reprinted with permission.

SUMMARY

In this chapter we have attempted to relate some appropriate uses of error analysis to handwriting. We have identified the relationship of error analysis to handwriting and instruction. The assessment and remediation approach recommended may focus on either initial skill development or correction of handwriting difficulties. Error analysis is not an intervention in and of itself. In fact, there are dangers inherent in focusing exclusively on performance errors when correct performance is the object of instruction. However, error analysis can be a useful tool when identifying and defining the problem. We must remember that although handwriting is an individual expression, it is also a communication tool. If one wishes to communicate (e.g., to gain recognition from those with whom we communicate), the recipient of handwritten materials must be able to easily read the communicative attempt. If the reader can easily decipher the written word, the writer will have a much greater chance of procuring reinforcers from school, community and employment settings.

DISCUSSION QUESTIONS AND ACTIVITIES

1. Differentiate between the form and function of handwriting skills as well as between the qualitative and quantitative dimensions of handwriting.
2. Name five possible positive outcomes for students who become proficient in handwriting.
3. Give a rationale for integrating handwriting error analysis and instruction or remediation.
4. Name steps you might take to set up a plan for assessing and remediating handwriting skills.

CHAPTER 6

Errors in Spelling

Jo M. Hendrickson
University of Iowa

Robert A. Gable
Old Dominion University

CHAPTER OBJECTIVES

After reading this chapter you should be able to:

1. Illustrate five procedures for scoring spelling errors.
2. Describe the five step spelling error analysis process.
3. Select and provide a rationale for selecting remediation strategies given diagnostic information on a student's error patterns.

KEY TERMS

derivational relationship	morpheme
free dictation format	phoneme
grapheme	prerequisite skills/concepts

INTRODUCTION

Research and classroom experience substantiate a positive correlation among reading, written expression, and spelling competency (Carpenter & Miller, 1982; Hammill & McNutt, 1981). Learning to spell is related closely to vocabulary development and reading. However, its functional context is writing. Spelling is a means to an end, not an end unto itself (Graham, 1985). In order for the chronically poor speller to improve, the student must not only learn spelling and memory strategies but come to value the importance of spelling correctly.

Similar to Graham (1985), we define spelling as a multifaceted process which involves the ability to recognize, reproduce, and put in writing the correct sequence of letters in a word. For many students and in particular those with learning, language, and reading difficulties, learning to spell is an ordeal.

The present chapter is designed to assist the teacher in helping students with severe spelling difficulties. We approach this task a two-fold manner: (a) by focusing on the properties of words and student error patterns, and (b) by suggesting instructional procedures for ameliorating spelling mistakes.

INFORMAL ASSESSMENT AND ERROR ANALYSES

In the course of daily instruction, most classroom teachers simply score spelling words as right or wrong (Howell & Kaplan, 1980). The number of correct and incorrect words provides a glimpse of possible learning problems. However, impressions gleaned from such a broad analysis can be misleading. More detailed information is needed on the student's errors before a remediation plan can be devised. This section describes five basic steps to improved spelling.* The steps consist of: (1) obtaining a sample of the spelling errors, (2) interviewing the student, (3) analyzing and classifying the errors, (4) selecting a corrective strategy, and (5) implementing the strategy and evaluating its effect.

To illustrate these five steps we will consider Albert, a 14-year-old seventh grader who attends a special education resource room for reading and language arts. Albert's mainstream teachers are not satisfied with his written performance or his attitude about spelling in his science and social studies work. They report that his handwriting is legible but his spelling "atrocious." Table 6.1 contains an entry of Albert's response to a dictated passage from a second grade Ginn reader (Clymer & Martin, 1976). This sample was collected by Mr. Wiltry as step 1 in analyzing Albert's spelling errors.

Step 1: Obtain a Sample of Spelling Errors

The minimum number of incorrectly spelled words needed for validly assessing error patterns is as yet unknown. Spache (1976) recommends a sample of at least 75 errors. Hasselbring and Owens (1981) suggest as few as 25 incorrect responses for initially classifying errors.

Samples of errors may be obtained by dictating word lists or paragraphs and stories (for student's achieving in the fourth- to fifth-grade range). Starlin (1982) recommends using this approach—free dictation. Once the student acclimates to free dictation, the student will spell at an optimal level. Research suggests that student errors are usually consistent across dictated word lists (DeMaster, Crossland, and Hasselbring, 1986). On the other hand, the free dictation method is beneficial in that contextual spelling closely parallels actual usage.

Turn to Albert's performance. (See Table 6.1). It can be seen that Albert mis-

---

*These steps are adapted with permission from " 'Pleez lit me pas splelin': Diagnosing and Remediating Errors in Spelling," by J. M. Hendrickson, R. A. Gable, and T. S. Hasselbring, *Education and Treatment of Children, 11,* pp. 166–178.

TABLE 6.1. Hypothetical Sample of Student's Response to Free Dictation

Passage from "Chipmunk Goes Hunting"

He followed his uncle along the trail. On and on they went, far into the forest. At last Chipmunk stopped to rest. But when he was ready to start again, he could not see his uncle. He looked for the trail, but he could not find it. There were trees on all sides, but he saw no knife marks on them.

He heard the sound of the brook, but the brook was far away, somewhere below him. . . .

Albert's Response

He *folled* his *unkle alone* the *trale*. On and on they *wint* far into the *forresst*. At last *chipmnk stoped too* rest. But *wen* he was *redy* to start *agin*, he *cood* not see his *unkle*. He looked *four* the trail, but he *cood* not *fined* it. *Their where treez* on all sides, but he saw no *kniv* marks on them.

He *hurd* the sound *ov* the brook, but the brook *waz* far *awey, sumwhere beelow* him.

SOURCE: "Chipmunk Goes Hunting," *The Dog Next Door and Other Stories* (Ginn and Company, 1976).

spelled 27 words, two of which were misspelled twice. As Albert wrote, Mr. Wiltry noted Albert's points of hesitancy and nonproductive body movement, his fluidity in spelling, and the amount of confidence Albert appeared to have. Mr. Wiltry writes down his observations and goes on to objectively assess Albert's performance.

Mr. Wiltry knows a student's spelling rate, that is, the number of letters correct per minute, is very relevant to success in spelling. Using Koening and Kunzelmann's (1980) recommendations for determining spelling proficiency rates, he examines Albert's spelling sample. Albert wrote 190 letters correctly and made 36 errors in a two minute probe—a rate of 95 letters correct per minute. According to Koening and Kunzelmann (1980), 90–100 correct letters per minute may be considered proficient for a third-grade student. The rate of 18 errors per minute, however, indicates Albert is not spelling proficiently. Instead, his error rate indicates that this passage is at the frustration level. Based on subjective and objective observations, Mr. Wiltry is in an excellent position to analyze error types, establish performance criteria, and prioritize instruction.

Step 2: Interview the Student

Structured interviews are advocated (Howell & Kaplan, 1980; McLoughlin & Lewis, 1981; Zigmond, Vallecorsa, & Silverman, 1983) as a source of diagnostic data. Interview questions may help identify faulty spelling strategies not uncovered by analyzing the spelling error sample. When students verbally describe why they spelled an erred word the way they did, inappropriate and incorrect problem-solving strategies may be discovered. The diagnostic interview also should focus on the positive. Questions such as, "What difficult words can you spell correctly?" and "How do you remember these words?" help the teacher identify remedial strategies that may work with the individual student. The one-to-one positively focused interview helps the teacher better understand and appreciate the student's strengths and struggles.

Albert gave Mr. Wiltry insight to his attitude about spelling when he proclaimed, "I don't need to spell every word right. My teachers always figure it out." This proclamation indicates that Albert has not developed a "spelling conscience." That is, he does not appear to recognize the importance of spelling correctly. Mr. Wiltry makes a note, "Albert needs illustrations and reminders of how correct spelling affects his life."

Step 3: Analyze and Classify Errors

After gathering a sample of the student's spelling, correct and incorrect words are charted and analyzed. Scoring spelling errors can be accomplished by using one of five approaches: (a) whole words, (b) syllables (P. Hanna, J. Hanna, Hodges, & Rudorf, 1966; Haring & Gentry, 1978), (c) sound clusters (Lessen, 1980), (d) letters-in-place (Starlin, 1982), and (e) letter sequencing (Hasselbring, 1986b; White & Haring, 1980). Whole-word errors can be identified easily by entering a slash next to or through each error. By comparison, recording the actual response should include a syllable, sound cluster, letters-in-place, or letter sequencing approach to error analysis. Identify the stimulus (word), and pinpoint the erred component of the response with a circle, caret (Hendrickson, Gable, & Hasselbring, 1988) or highlight marker.

For routine classroom usage, the whole word approach is most feasible. However, one of the other five methods is recommended for pinpointing persistent errors of poor spellers. Sound clusters, broadly speaking, may be thought of as consonant (c) and vowel (v) sounds formed by one or more letters. A word such as *f-o-ll-ow-ed* (see Table 6.2) can be scored in relation to its c-v-c-v-c pattern. Using the sound cluster scoring procedure, Albert's spelling, *f-o-ll-( )-ed,* would earn a score of 4 of 5 sound clusters correct (see Table 6.2). A letters-in-place procedure gives "credit" for the smallest of units of the word (i.e., the letters). The letter-in-place approach is much more sensitive to the complexity and difficulty of individual words than a whole-word approach. The letter-sequencing approach is a variation of the letters-in-place scoring procedure. In letter sequencing, students may earn $N + 1$ (N = number of letters) points for each pair of letters. The spaces before the first and after the last letter in a word are considered part of a letter pair. Scoring words using the $N + 1$ formula now can be achieved directly on a microcomputer. (See chapter 8 for more information.) The five scoring procedures and an example of each are presented in Table 6.2.

TABLE 6.2. Five Scoring Procedures for Spelling

Procedure	Sample Word	Student Spelling	Teacher Scoring	Number Correct/Total
1. Whole word	ready	redy	(redy)*	0/1 points
2. Syllables	along	alone	a-(lone)	1/2 points
3. Sound cluster	followed	folled	f-o-ll-( )-ed	4/5 points
4. Letters-in-place	away	awey	a-w-(e)-y	3/4 points
5. Letter sequencing	heard	hurd	h-(he)-(ea)-(ar)-rd-d	3/6 points

*( ) = errors or 0 points.

Once the errors are identified, the teacher enters the word or makes a tally to correspond with the appropriate word type, error type and error tendency shown in Figure 6.1. After you tally each word from the sample of spelling errors (Table 6.1) on the Error Analysis Chart (Figure 6.1), different error patterns begin to appear. The Spelling Error Analysis Chart is designed to accommodate any of the five scoring conventions presented in Table 6.2. A tally is made for each error in the "cell" corresponding to one of three word *parts*. The part of a word in which the error occurred is classified as being either regular, predictable, or irregular. A regular word is one which has exact phoneme-grapheme correspondence (e.g., pal, top and dig). A predictable word contains orthographic patterns that do not necessarily follow strict phoneme-grapheme correspondence, yet may be spelled correctly because of the application of rules. Words such as r*o*pe, hit*t*ing and stop*p*ed have sounds that are based on letter patterns. Irregular words, on the other hand, do not conform to sound-letter or orthographic regularities. Irregular words such as "melon," "through," and "laughing" might feasibly be spelled several ways.

Error *types* on the Error Analysis Chart are grouped according to errors that involve rules or patterns of consonants and vowels. The bottom section of the chart is used to record error *tendencies* and includes errors of order, substitution, insertion, and omission (DeMaster et al., 1986; Hasselbring & Owens, 1981). The entire word is written in the cells on the top half of the chart. Tally marks are used to indicate the frequency of error tendencies on the bottom half of the chart. Some words (e.g., manecail for mainsail) may have more than one type of error (e.g., a rule error and a regular consonant error). In such cases the teacher may enter both errors onto the chart.

Mr. Wiltry used the Error Analysis Chart to assess the types of errors and error tendencies observed in Albert's spelling sample. He entered each erred word in the section for error types and placed a slash mark in each cell to correspond with Albert's error tendencies. In Albert's case, the greatest number of error types are in words with predictable and irregular spellings. For the most part, Albert's error tendency is to make substitutions. Before finalizing his instructional priorities for Albert, Mr. Wiltry reflects upon his understanding that information derived from analyzing student errors can be organized according to: (1) prevalence of error types and tendencies (which he has done), (2) errors which have the greatest potential to generalize, and (3) errors that best lend themselves to easy correction (Ganschow, 1981). Mr. Wiltry is aware that some research indicates that the majority of spelling errors occur in vowels in midsyllables (e.g., folled) while two-thirds are substitutions or omissions (e.g., waz, stoped) (Burns, 1980). Also, he is familiar with the fact that as few as 100 words may account for 50 percent of all children's writing (e.g., the, was, on, for, and) Graham & Miller, 1979). To Mr. Wiltry this means that initially Albert may only need to learn to spell a few hundred words. Thus, Mr. Wiltry decides to examine available lists of words students write with high frequency.

Mr. Wiltry knows that a substantial percentage of English words do follow phoneme-grapheme correspondence, and he observes that Albert has some difficulty in this area. He feels that reteaching these relationships will give Albert a basic strategy for approaching any word (e.g., wint for went). Since no English words end in *v*, he will teach Albert this simple rule. In all, Mr. Wiltry decides to focus on teaching Albert (a) sound-symbol correspondence, (b) the rule that no words end in *v*, (c) the rule for adding endings to c-v-c words, and (d) the rules that are associated with the long vowel

Student	albert		Date	January 15

Material/level _The Dog Next Door, Ginn, Gr. 2, p. 187_

Word List ( )   Paragraph (✓)   Other: _plus 1 sentence_

TYPE OF ANALYSIS

Scoring: Word (✓)   Syllables ( )   Clusters ( )   Letters (✓)

PART OF WORD ERRED .... Prioritized

Type / Tendency		Regular	Predictable	Irregular	Comments
Type	Rules/Patterns		trale stoped kniv	too, four their fined	homonyms ⑦ phonics
	Consonants	were forresst	unkle 2x alone waz treez wen	ov	⑨ combine linguistic approach
	Vowels	wint chipmnk beelow ⑤	fined awey ⑪	hurd, redy folled cood 2x sumwhere ⑪	& rules
Tendency	Order			⑪	
	Substitution	/	╫ ///	╫ ///	⑱ Teach albert "intrinsic" approach
	Insertion	///	/		④ i.e. trial ⑤ & error
	Omission	/ ⑤	// ⑪	// ⑪	

Beginning time _____   Ending time _____   Number minutes __2__

Corrects __190 or 95/min.__   Errors __36 or 18/min.__
response scored = letters

Figure 6.1. Spelling Error Analysis Chart

SOURCE: Adapted from, "Consistency of Learning Disabled Students' Spelling," by V. De Master, C. Crossland, and T. S. Hasselbring, 1986, *Learning Disabled Quarterly, 9,* 89–96; and *A Microcomputer-based System for the Analysis of Student Spelling Errors,* manuscript, T. S. Hasselbring and S. Owens, 1981, Nashville, TN: Peabody College of Vanderbilt. Reprinted by permission.

sounds. Albert made four errors involving homonyms, so Mr. Wiltry decides to teach these homonyms.

Step 4: Select a Corrective Strategy

Instructional approaches may be based on knowledge of a student's error patterns in relation to whether words are regular, predictable or irregular. Words with phoneme-grapheme correspondence, for instance, may be remediated through a phonics or linguistic approach since correspondence between phonemes and graphemes is consistent more than 80 percent of the time (P. Hanna, J. Hanna, Hodges, & Peterson, 1971). For predictable words that lack strict sound-letter correspondence, learning rules and/or strategies for recalling the correct spelling often are advocated. However, as Lovitt (1973) notes, students seldom generalize rule usage without cues. Specific instruction on how and when to use spelling rules is recommended. In contrast, for errors in spelling of irregular or unpredictable words, a multisensory approach, flash cards, and look-copy-compare strategies have been shown to be effective (Hansen, 1978; Marino, 1981; Starlin, 1982). Whatever types of errors are made, research clearly supports the use of direct, systematic instruction coupled with your teaching the students study techniques. For example, valuable study strategies include the test-study-test method (e.g., Gates, 1931), studying from a word list (Graham & Miller, 1983), imitating the student's errors and providing a correct model (Kauffman, Hallahan, Haas, Brame, & Boren, 1978), and correcting spelling tests under the teacher's direction (Christine & Hollingsworth, 1966).

Another useful strategy involves creating a pool of misspelled words and using this pool to replenish a "flow list" of test-teach-test items (Hansen, 1978). That is, 5–10 words can be taught routinely in lists or in context. Once a word is mastered, it is placed in a word bank for intermittent review and another word is added. List or column word presentation is efficient for initial assessment (Graham & Miller, 1979) and may be most desirable for the student experiencing substantial difficulty. Several authors recommend instruction at the sentence rather than word list level (Starlin, 1982). Regardless of the specific strategy employed, instruction should be geared toward written (rather than oral) spelling.

Functional spelling is written spelling. It is essential that generalization to written expression be targeted across subject areas. One procedure for promoting generalization is teaching the student to proofread all writing. A student does not necessarily need to know how to spell a word to recognize that it is misspelled. Proofreading should be adjusted to the competency level of the student.

Once Albert has achieved an acceptable level of correct spelling on his written assignments, Mr. Wiltry is going to teach him the COPS proofreading procedure (Schumaker et al., 1981). Mr. Wiltry believes COPS will help Albert in his regular classroom assignments. Using the COPS procedure, Albert will proofread for Capitalization, Overall appearance, Punctuation, and Spelling. Mr. Wiltry plans to coordinate usage of this technique with Albert's social studies and science teachers.

Overall, Mr. Wiltry and all teachers must be mindful of basic learning principles when selecting and implementing corrective strategies: (a) Correct responses should be reinforced immediately during skill acquisition and concept formation, (b) strategies which ensure initial success (e.g., antecedent modeling) (Hendrickson & Gable, 1981) should be used to promote word mastery before faulty spelling habits are established, and (c) mastery learning and generalization training should be an integral part of every instructional plan.

Step 5: Implement Strategy and Evaluate Its Impact

Repeated measurement enables teachers to: (a) evaluate the validity of their initial error analysis and (b) make modifications in instruction based on objective data. Daily or frequently scheduled spelling tests—word lists or ''free flow'' dictation—should be administered in a standardized manner. Hold constant administration procedures, the time given for testing, the number and type of student responses, and the materials. In this way, the effect of an intervention strategy can be assessed with confidence.

S. Evans and her colleagues suggest that both the extent and frequency of evaluation should be determined according to the student's learning stage and to the severity of the learning problem (S. Evans, W. Evans, & Mercer, 1986). [The reader is referred to Deno and Mirkin (1977) and White and Haring (1980) for more detailed suggestions pertaining to direct-measurement evaluation. For additional consideration of the advantages and disadvantages of rate and percentage, Hendrickson, Gable, and Stowitschek (1985) is suggested].

To evaluate a student's performance (and the effectiveness of a given remedial strategy), the teacher must establish a performance standard or criterion level. To identify valid proficiency aims teachers may obtain performance rates of students whose spelling in written assignments is acceptable. By obtaining spelling samples of several high and several low achieving students (all of whom are passing in all classes) a band of scores within which a so-called successful speller must perform can be established (Hendrickson et al., 1985).

To assist Albert in his social studies and science classes, Mr. Wiltry asked his teachers to identify three students who consistently received grades of C. Mr. Wiltry examined each of these students' assignments for one week. He collected timed samples of their written language. Next, he analyzed the quantity and quality of their efforts. Based on these data, he established an initial criterion level for Albert with regard to his written products.

Guidelines for Selecting and Implementing Instructional Strategies

1. Word lists of five to eight words are one of the most effective means of teaching new or difficult words. Tutors, independent practice on a computer or language master, and self-instruction using flash cards can be employed. It is important that the student be given the correct spelling prior to attempting to spell the word on his/her own. Feedback should be immediate, and words that are mastered should be replaced with new words. Mastered words should be kept in a word bank for review and integrated into the curriculum of the classroom teacher.

2. When teaching phonics or spelling rules, teach one rule at a time. Spelling

rules of high utility include: the *final-e* rule, *plural* rules, the *q-u* rule, the *i-e* rule, the *contraction* rule, the rule for *possession* and the *y-to-i* rule. First introduce the phoneme-grapheme example or spelling rule. Then provide multiple examples. Give the learner opportunity to discriminate when to use the grapheme or the rule, and when not to use these. Next, provide novel situations in which the grapheme or rule might apply. Finally, have the student generate written assignments using words which illustrate the rule.

3. Students with learning problems, and those with spelling difficulties in particular, often do not proofread their work well. Reinforce the student for simply circling misspelled words (as an initial step in teaching proofreading). Later require identification and correction of misspellings. Students also can be taught specific guidelines for editing each other's written assignments.

4. Mnemonic devices and other memory techniques may assist students in learning correct spellings. Teaching that a principal is your *pal* and that a principle is a ru*le,* links spelling and meaning and is a handy memory device. Mnemonic strategies such as COPS (discussed earlier) can be taught to integrate spelling with other written language skills.

5. All students should be taught to use external resources to promote their spelling. Dictionaries, glossaries, and ''demon word'' lists, as well as other people are possible sources for getting the correct spelling of a word. Introduce the utilization of external sources early in the instruction of spelling.

6. Students need to be taught techniques for studying. For young and exceptional students, a multisensory approach may be useful, particularly during acquisition of new spelling words. The Gillingham and Stillman (1970) approach known as the visual-auditory-kinesthetic-tactile (VAKT) approach is well known. These authors recommend first teaching phoneme-grapheme associations, then visual letter patterns, and then the teaching of word patterns. Students can practice with the teacher in a group and on their own.

    Graham and Miller (1979) recommend many repeated writings of the word. The student looks at the word while saying it. Then the student writes the word twice, covers the word, and writes it again. Afterward, the student checks the word. This sequence is repeated. Finally, the student writes the word three times, covers it, and writes it one last time. After each independent writing students should always check their work. This approach combines use of a permanent model, of repetition, and of independent practice.

7. Motivation and relevance are important to correct spelling. While there are a multitude of ways to motivate students to become better spellers, the teacher's attitude about spelling is equally important to or more important than any individual technique. Effort should be made to design all teaching techniques to ensure that each student will succeed. Student progress should be emphasized and any demonstration of increasing competence pointed out. By designing games (e.g., spelling bingo, concentration, hangman) and other high interest instructional activities, spelling can be associated with fun. Effort should be taken to tie the importance of spelling to real life situations of the student. The computer can be used to promote spelling skill and a spelling consciousness.

The computer is appealing to most students. Today, numerous drill and practice tutorial programs are available for spelling practice. In addition, classroom experience shows that students using the computer develop increased pride in their written products.

8. Since practice and feedback are central to success, teachers must allocate time each day to spelling instruction. Instructional approaches should include group and individual teaching arrangements. Immediately after any spelling test, students' work should be corrected. Students may exchange papers or correct their own work. A station for correcting work can be created with different students working as spelling checkers. If possible, students should have an immediate opportunity to practice the correct spelling of words they misspelled. Kauffman and his colleagues (1978) suggest that it helps the student discriminate correct from incorrect spelling if you first imitate the student's misspelling and then write the correct spelling next to it.

9. Students need intrinsic problem-solving approaches. One such approach is to teach students to spell the word in question phonemically. They slowly sound out the word and write it down applying any correct phonemic rule. Knowledge of morphemes (e.g., prefixes, suffixes) also is employed. Next, they generate different spellings of the word, and through the process of elimination choose the best or most likely spelling.

In summary, there are numerous strategies teachers can use to promote the acquisition, fluency, and generalization of spelling competence. Once initial strategies are selected and implemented, it is important to collect data on student performance. Mastery for the learner with spelling difficulty will be achieved through individual assessment, remediation, and generalization training.

SUMMARY

Traditionally, spelling performance has been measured infrequently through the administration of various standardized, norm-referenced tests or dictated weekly word lists. A five-step procedure for gathering, analyzing, classifying, and remediating student mistakes in spelling has been presented. The content of this chapter is based on the premise that students engage in systematic, nonrandom attempts at spelling; and that by isolating and identifying error patterns we have a much greater chance of selecting appropriate remedial techniques. The information in this chapter should be viewed as a guide for improving the effectiveness of spelling assessment and instruction rather than as a set of rigid standards.

DISCUSSION QUESTIONS AND ACTIVITIES

1. List and describe the five steps of error analysis in spelling.
2. Give three examples of errors students might make on regular, predictable, and irregular parts of words.

3. Score each of these words using the whole-word, syllable, sound-cluster, letter-in-place and letter-sequencing approaches: moorning for morning, bake for bait, tru for through, hansum for handsome, and liter for letter.
4. Give a free flow dictation test to a child with poor spelling. Implement each of the five steps of the suggested error-analysis process.
5. Give the same free flow dictation test to three students with different reading abilities. Analyze their errors using the Error Analysis Chart. Describe any differences. Hypothesize about their reading skills in relation to their spelling skills.

CHAPTER 7

Errors in Written Language

Marilyn K. Rousseau

The City College of the City University of New York

CHAPTER OBJECTIVES

After reading this chapter you should be able to:

1. Perform an error analysis on a sample of a student's writing.
2. Perform an oral edit analysis of the sample.
3. Pinpoint probable causes of errors in written language.
4. Identify appropriate remediation techniques.

KEY TERMS

descriptive assessment   oral edit
diagnostic assessment   syntactic complexity
error analysis   T-unit

INTRODUCTION

Written language skills are different in important ways from other basic literacy skills such as mathematics, oral language, or reading. Mathematics follows set logical rules; oral language may be learned largely through imitation; and in reading, the language symbols remain printed on the page in their entirety. Writing, however, requires the writer to focus on the objective (story, plot, description, argument, explanation, and so forth) while also focusing on the techniques of writing. These involve such diverse skills as handwriting or typing, spelling, punctuation, and the correct use of grammar and style. Time and again students protest, "But *I* know what I mean. I just can't write it." Indeed, by the time they figure out the mechanics of writing a sentence, many students have lost sight of the objective. The resulting writing is often fraught with deficits and errors.

Deficits and errors in writing are distinctively different problems. A deficit exists when the writer fails to meet certain standards set by an evaluator (e.g., a twelfth-grade student who consistently writes short, simple sentences). By contrast, an error exists when the writer fails to follow commonly-accepted rules ". . . whose violation unequivocally brands you as a writer of nonstandard English" (Williams, 1989, p. 176).

The purpose of this chapter is to present a means of identifying errors in writing and to facilitate the planning of intervention strategies. The chapter includes a brief overview of descriptive assessment, excluding standardized tests, and a more in-depth discussion of diagnostic assessment. Descriptive assessment includes tests and informal measures used to compare achievement levels, to sort people into groups, to identify skill deficits, and to measure growth in written language development. By contrast, diagnostic assessment often consists of simple checklists designed to pinpoint writing errors. Finally, the chapter includes a detailed description of an error analysis procedure and a procedure for determining the writer's intent.

DESCRIPTIVE ASSESSMENT OF WRITTEN LANGUAGE

Informal tests usually involve scoring a student's writing sample on several measures. Syntactic complexity, also called fluency or maturity (Hunt, 1965), is, for example, a frequently measured aspect of writing skill (Hunt, 1977; Isaacson, 1988; Loban, 1976; Mellon, 1969; O'Donnell, Griffin, & Norris, 1967; O'Hare, 1973; Rousseau, Poulson, Bottge, & Dy, 1988). Writing samples also may be ranked according to a "holistic" procedure (Cooper, 1977) based on the reader's impressions. Whereas measures of syntactic complexity identify specific writing structures (e.g., the use of dependent clauses, phrases, and appositives), holistic scoring is concerned with the overall quality of the writing.

Syntactic complexity in writing refers to the ability to express a large number of ideas in relatively few words (Weaver, 1979). Skilled writers use complex syntactic structures to consolidate sentences and to expand meaning within sentences, whereas unskilled or beginning writers tend to write simple sentences with little embellishment (Hunt, 1965).

A conventional measure of syntactic complexity is the minimal terminable unit, or T-unit (Bartholomae, 1980). A T-unit is an independent clause including any dependent clauses attached to or embedded in it (Hunt, 1977). As writers gain command of the language, they expand their T-units by increasing their use of complex structures.

The T-unit is a useful measure for scoring writing for several reasons. First, the T-unit is the smallest unit of writing that can stand alone grammatically (Hunt, 1965), and unlike the sentence, it provides an easy-to-score measure for analysis. Second, the use of the T-unit as the common denominator against which to measure deficits, errors, and growth enables practitioners and researchers to compare changes in writing both within and across students, schools, and specific writing skills. Third, use of the T-unit avoids the problems inherent in depending on the capitalization and punctuation of unskilled writers in determining sentence boundaries. Fourth, consistently high reliability (inter-

TABLE 7.1. Measures of Syntactic Complexity in Writing for Normally Achieving Students at Ten Grade Levels

Measure and Author	Grade									
	3	4	5	6	7	8	9	10	11	12
Words/T-Unit					✓					
Loban	7.60	8.02	8.76	9.04	8.94	10.37	10.05	11.79	10.69	13.27
O'Donnell	7.76		9.34		9.99					
Hunt		8.60				11.50				14.40
O'Hare					9.69					
Rousseau et al.				9.23	9.28	9.52				
Nodine et al.				8.20						
Dependent clauses/T-Unit										
Loban		.19	.21	.29	.28	.50	.47	.52	.45	.60
O'Donnell et al.	.18		.27		.30					
Hunt		.30				.42				.68
O'Hare					.37					
Rousseau et al.				.28	.27	.29				

observer agreement) scores for T-units can be obtained (Rousseau et al., 1988; Rousseau, Krantz, Poulson, & McClannahan, 1989).

Although no standardized results are available to help teachers set specific criterion levels for student performance, a number of studies document the developmental nature of syntactic complexity. Table 7.1 presents a summary of selected measures of syntactic complexity in writing as reported by various researchers.

DIAGNOSTIC ASSESSMENT OF WRITTEN LANGUAGE

No clear distinction exists in the literature between assessing errors in writing and assessing development or achievement in writing. Most of the literature focuses on assessing written-language development (see reviews by Moran, 1987 and Poplin, 1983). Nevertheless, it is errors, that is, those rules that when broken unequivocally mark the writer as a user of nonstandard English (Williams, 1989), that hinder the unskilled writer's academic progress.

Shaughnessy (1977) identified and analyzed the causes of recurring errors made by unskilled writers. She argues that many errors are the result of the writer's trying to follow rules of grammar in situations in which the rules do not apply. Therefore, she advocates the use of error analysis to diagnose writing problems.

Bartholomae (1980) points out that instruction in writing is not based on a systematic analysis of the ways writing skills develop or how unskilled writers write, and proposes that errors ". . . can only be understood as evidence of intention" (p. 255). The only way to determine the writer's intentions is to analyze discrepancies between the written passage and the writer's oral reading of it.

In contrast to standardized tests, error analysis is a more useful measure for planning individualized instruction because an error analysis enables the teacher to identify problems unique to individual students. Standardized tests, although useful for administrative purposes such as measuring overall achievement levels, do not diagnose specific errors. Indeed, Hammill and Larsen (1988) caution teachers against trying to plan instructional programs for individual students based on the results of the Test of Written Language-2 *(TOWL-2)* because it does not diagnose specific errors. A limitation shared by standardized tests and error analyses is that they represent only one sample of a student's performance at a given time. However, unlike standardized tests, error analyses can be administered repeatedly throughout the school year to pinpoint specific skills in need of remediation and to provide continuous, direct measures of writing progress. In addition, error analysis is probably a more valid measure of an individual student's performance than a standardized test because it directly measures the student's writing (Guerin & Maier, 1983).

ERROR ANALYSIS OF WRITTEN LANGUAGE

The analysis of writing errors is divided into two major activities: (1) assessment of errors based on examination of a written product, and (2) the use of an oral edit to gain understanding of the student's intent. In the error analysis process, you will identify eight categories of errors made by students. Definitions/Descriptions of error types are presented in alphabetical order in the lower section of Table 7.2. These categories of errors are subdivided further into specific skill areas for more discrete analysis. Spelling error types are not included here, but are addressed in a separate chapter. Table 7.2 also contains the definitions of terms required to conduct an error analysis and to complete the Error Analysis Form (Figure 7.1).

The T-unit is recommended as the standard for reporting errors because it provides a constant measurement factor that will allow you to make comparisons within and among writing samples regardless of composition length or time allowed for writing. Establishing the number of each error category per T-unit is the first step in the error analysis of writing.

The second step of error analysis, the oral edit, addresses the question of intent (Bartholomae, 1980). By examining discrepancies between the written product and the writer's oral reading of it, the teacher is able to determine the sequence of skills to be taught. Finally, the teacher selects an intervention or teaching strategy based on the error analysis data and the types of oral edits used by the student. The following section provides general information on collecting and scoring writing samples.

GENERAL INSTRUCTIONS FOR COLLECTING
AND SCORING WRITING SAMPLES

Collecting the Sample

In collecting writing samples, the teacher may wish to prompt student writing by using story starters such as incomplete sentences, pictures, objects, or anything that provides a catalyst for beginning the writing activity. The teacher should allocate the same amount

Error Analysis Form

Student ___Tony___ Age __11-3__ Grade __6__ Date __9/20/89__

Writing time (Min.) ___30___ Picture ___#4___ Topic ___#3___

Total words	83	No. T-units	8
Garbled words	16	Average words/T-units	8.38
Readable words	67	Scorer	

Error Category	Error Type	Number per T-unit	Prior
Careless	Omitted words	$0/8 = 0$	
	Substituted words	$3/8 = 0.38$	
Excessive Usage (and/so/but/or)	Beginning of T-unit	$7/8 = 0.88$	
	Within T-unit	$1/8 = 0.13$	
Verbs	Inflections	$1/8 = 0.13$	
	Subject-verb	$0/8 = 0$	
	Verb tense changes	$3/8 = 0.38$	
Nouns	Number	$0/8 = 0$	
	Possession	$0/8 = 0$	
Pronouns	Possession	$0/8 = 0$	
	Agreement/antecedent	$0/8 = 0$	
Punctuation	End	$8/8 = 1.00$	
	Within T-unit	$0/8 = 0$	
Capitalization	Beginning	$6/8 = 0.75$	
	Proper nouns	$6/8 = 0.75$	
	Inapprop. capital.	$4/8 = 0.50$	
Paragraphs	Extraneous T-units	$\# = 0$	
	New line/ea. T-unit	Yes No	

Figure 7.1. Error Analysis of Tony's Writing Sample

TABLE 7.2. Definitions for Use with Error Analysis Form

	Definition/Description
T-unit	*T-unit:* An independent clause including any dependent clauses attached to or embedded in it. Two independent clauses joined by a conjunction (and, but, or, so) count as two T-units. The conjunction is counted as being at the beginning of the second T-unit. For example, "The cat climbed the tree/ and the girl went after him/." A direct quotation in dialogue is the direct object of the verb *said* if it is attributed to a speaker and is considered part of the same T-unit. For example, " 'Go get him,' he said./"
Average words/T-unit	The total words, excluding garbles, divided by the number of T-units rounded off to the nearest hundredth.

	Definition/Description
Capitalization Errors	
Beginning	Failure to begin each T-unit with a capital letter, except when two T-units are joined by a conjunction (see *T-unit* above).
Proper Nouns	Failure to capitalize the name of a specific person, place, or thing.
Inappropriate	Capitalizing words other than proper nouns or sentence beginnings.
Careless Errors	
Omitted Words	Words the writer has omitted.
Substituted Words	Words similar in spelling or pronunciation used in place of the correct word.
Excessive Usage	
Beginning of T-Unit	Beginning almost every T-unit with *and, so,* or *but.*
Within T-unit	Use of *and* to string together verbs or nouns. For example, "She ran and ran and ran.
Garbled Words (Garbles)	Words the reader cannot decipher within 60 seconds ("The spaceship sotst landed on the earth") including extraneous words ("He ran to the the park.") and sentence fragments ("Because they were going."). Sometimes one or more key words in a T-unit are garbled making the entire T-unit unreadable.
Noun Errors:	
Number	(a) No change or incorrect change in inflections (endings) to show number and possession of nouns that end in *-f, -fe,* or *-y.* For example, *calfs* instead of *calves, pennys* instead of *pennies.* (b) Failure to change vowel stems for some nouns. For example, *woman-women.* (c) Adding plural endings for nouns that do not require any change to show plural. For example, *sheeps* for *sheep.* (d) Incorrect use of *-s* or *-es.* For example, *bushs* for *bushes.*
Possession	Failure to add *-s* or *-es.*
Paragraph Errors:	
Extraneous T-units	T-units that do not fit into the context of the narrative. For example, "Captain America threw his shield at the robot. *He wouldn't know.* Then Captain America chased him."
New Line Each T-unit	The writer begins each new T-unit or sentence on a separate line.

Pronoun Errors:	
Possession	Failure to use correct forms of possession for pronouns. Correct forms are: I-my, we-our, he-his, she-her, it-its, they-their. For example, "They did not understand *they* problem."
Agreement with Antecedent	Failure to use a singular pronoun with a singular antecedent or a plural pronoun like a plural antecedent. For example, "If *a person* walks to work, *they* will get some exercise."
Punctuation Errors	
End	Failure to end each T-unit with a period, question mark, or exclamation mark (unless it is two T-units joined by a conjunction).
Within T-units	Failure to use, or incorrect use of, punctuation marks such as commas, colons, semicolons, apostrophes, quotation marks, parentheses, and hyphens.
Readable Words	The number of words written in prose form, excluding garbled words, omitted words, story title, sound effects (Zoom!, and so forth), and end markers such as *The End*. Include substituted words and additional words as readable words.
Total Words	Same as readable words, but including garbles.
Verb Errors	
Inflections	Failure to add verb endings or adding incorrect verb endings (*-s, -es, -ed, -ing*). For example, "When he *finish* his work, he *walking* home."
Subject-Verb Agreement	Failure to use singular subjects with singular verbs, and plural subjects with plural verbs. For example, "She *don't* want to go."
Verb Tense Change	A change in verb tense (present to past, past to future, and so forth) within T-units or between T-units. For example, "He *went* to the game and *pays* for his ticket."

of writing time each day, usually 20 to 30 minutes. Be sure the directions clearly state the purpose of the writing exercise and how much time will be allowed. Tell the students to spell the words like they sound if they are unsure of the spelling. If a student stops writing before the end of the writing time, encourage the student to write more by asking questions such as, "What do you think might happen next?" At the end of the writing session allow time for editing and correcting spelling.

When the students have completed their writing assignments, make two copies of each paper. Save the originals for the students to read from during the oral edit and for making extra copies as needed. The first copy will be marked by the teacher for error analysis and the second copy will be marked for the oral edit.

Step 1: Scoring the Error Analysis

To complete the first step, the analysis of errors, use the Definitions for Use with Error Analysis Form (Table 7.2), the Error Analysis Scoring Instructions (Table 7.3), and the sample Error Analysis Form (Figure 7.1).

Step 2: Scoring the Oral Edit

To complete the oral edit, use the Oral Edit Definitions and Scoring Instructions (Table 7.4) and the Oral Edit Form (Figure 7.2).

TABLE 7.3. Error Analysis Scoring Instructions

Enter the name of the *Student, Age,* (years and months), *Grade,* and the *Date* the student wrote the sample.
Writing Time: Record the total number of minutes allowed for writing, and the actual number of minutes the student wrote.
Picture # or *Topic #:* List the picture or topic number used for the writing stimulus.

1. *Total Words:* Draw a line through the title, sound effects, and end markers such as "The End." Count the total words written. Exclude words marked out.
2. *Garbled Words:* Circle garbled words. Enter the total in the space provided.
3. *Readable Words:* Subtract the number of garbled words from the total words and enter in the space provided.
4. *T-unit:* Mark the end of each T-unit with a slash mark (/) and number the T-unit. Enter the number of T-units.
5. *Average Number of Words per T-Unit:* Divide the total readable words by the number of T-Units. Round off to the nearest hundredth.
6. *Scorer:* Sign your name.

Note: FOR ALL ERROR TYPES BEGINNING WITH *OMITTED WORDS* THROUGH *INAPPRO-PRIATE CAPITALS* COUNT THE TOTAL ERRORS AND DIVIDE BY THE TOTAL T-UNITS TO FIND THE NUMBER PER T-UNIT.

1. *Careless Errors:*
   Omitted Words: Write omitted words in pencil above the appropriate space. Write only words that are obvious (such as *and, he, the*) and that do not change the meaning of the T-Unit.
   Substituted Words: Write *sub* above substituted words.
2. *Excessive Usage:*
   Beginning of T-Unit: Count the number of T-Units that begin with conjunctions.
   Within T-unit: Underline each use of conjunctions if they appear more than once for coordination within the T-Unit. Do not count conjunctions at the beginning of the T-Unit in this count.
3. *Verbs:*
   Inflections: Write in the correct verb ending.
   Subject-Verb Agreement: Write *s-v* above the verb for every subject-verb error.
   Verb Tense Changes: Place a check mark (√) at the end of each T-Unit in which the verb tense is different from the verb tense in the previous T-Unit. If there are tense changes within a T-Unit, place a check mark in the margin for each change. An exception is if the verb tense change occurs with a change from narrative to direct quotation.
4. *Nouns:*
   Number: Underline nouns that show incorrect form for number.
   Possession: Write *NP* above the error.
5. *Pronouns:* Write the correct pronoun above each incorrect use.
6. *Punctuation:*
   End: Write in the correct form for the omitted or incorrect punctuation and circle it.
   Within T-units: Using a red pencil, write in the correct form for the omitted or incorrect punctuation.
7. *Capitalization:*
   Beginning: Write correct upper-case letters over lower-case letters used at the beginning of T-Units.
   Proper Nouns: Write correct upper-case letters over lower-case letters used for proper nouns.
   Inappropriate: Draw an X through the incorrectly capitalized letter.
8. *Paragraphs:*
   Extraneous T-units: Underline extraneous T-Units.
   New Line for Each T-unit: Circle *Yes* or *No.*

Summary: Count the number of each type of error and enter in the appropriate row under "# per T-unit" on the Error Analysis Form. Divide the number of each error type by the number of T-units, and enter the result in the space provided.

Student _____ Picture/Topic _____ Date _____

Scorer _____

Error Category	Error Type	Oral Edit Type					
		1	2	3	4	5	6
Careless	Omitted words						
	Substituted words						
Excessive Usage	Beginning of T-unit						
	Within T-unit						
Verbs	Inflections						
	Subject-verb						
	Verb tense change						
Nouns	Number						
	Possession						
Pronouns	Possession						
	Agreement/antec.						
Paragraphs	Extraneous T-units						
Garbles	Single words						
	Word groups						

Oral Edit Type

1 Acknowledges and corrects error
2 Corrects error without acknowledgement
3 Acknowledges error but does not correct
4 Reads correct form incorrectly
5 Substitutes incorrect oral form for incorrect written form
6 Reads error as written

Figure 7.2. Oral Edit Form

TABLE 7.4. Oral Edit Definitions and Scoring Instructions

You will need two copies of the student's writing sample for the oral edit. Save the original for the student to read from and for making additional copies. Use a copy to record corrections the student makes when reading. Have the student read his or her story into a tape recorder so you can check your scoring. The tape will provide a permanent product of the student's effort. Below are listed the responses you will score while the student reads aloud.

1. *Acknowledges and Corrects Error:* The student acknowledges the error and corrects it.
   Example: "The boy run—no, ran—to the barn."
   Scoring: Circle the word or words the student spontaneously acknowledges and corrects. Write an *a* above the circled word(s).

   Example for Scoring: "The boy (run) to the barn."

2. *Corrects Error without Acknowledgement:* The student corrects the error orally, but does not show that he or she has noticed that it is an error.
   Example: The passage is written like this: "Alice spelled the tea on her dress." The student reads the T-Unit as, "Alice spilled the tea on her dress."
   Scoring: Circle the word(s) written incorrectly but read correctly.

   Example for Scoring: "Alice (spelled) the tea on her dress."

3. *Acknowledges Error and Does Not Correct:* The student acknowledges the incorrect word(s), but does not correct it.
   Example: The passage is written as follows: "He weren't going to the game." The student reads and comments, "He weren't—that's wrong—going to the game."
   Scoring: Circle the word(s) the student acknowledged as incorrect. Write an *a* with an X through it above the word.

   Example for Scoring: "He (weren't) going to the game."

4. *Reads Correct Form Incorrectly:* The student does not read what was written. He or she substitutes an incorrect form for a correct form.
   Example: The student wrote, "The boy rested before he ate," but read it as, "The boy rests before he ate."
   Scoring: Write the word the student read incorrectly above the correct word.

   Example for Scoring: "The boy rested before he ate."

5. *Substitution of Incorrect Form for Incorrect Form:* The student misreads an incorrect form.
   Example: The student wrote, "She don't want to go," but read, "She can't want to go."
   Scoring: Circle the word(s) read incorrectly and draw a line through it.

   Example for Scoring: "She (don't) want to go."

6. *Errors Read as Written:* The student reads the error exactly as written without acknowledging the error.

   Example: The student wrote, "It weren't nothing wrong with it," and read, "It weren't nothing wrong with it."
   Scoring: Underline the incorrect word(s) the student read as written.

   Example for Scoring: "It weren't nothing wrong with it."

7. *Cannot Read the Errors:* The student is unable to read what he or she wrote, and acknowledges this.

Example: The student wrote, "The whog sa tegin now," and says something like, "I can't read it."
Scoring: Draw a line through the passage the student cannot read.

Example for Scoring: "~~The whog sa tegin now~~."

Tally the number of oral edits for each error type and enter the number in the appropriate box on the Oral Edit Form.

Practice Scoring

Begin by placing a copy of the student's writing assignment and an Error Analysis Form in front of you. Go through each step of the instructions in Table 7.3. Next, carefully read and edit the sample of the student's work. Figures 7.1 and 7.3 contain a completed Error Analysis Form and a scored sample of a student's written work. After you have completed an analysis of one of your own students' work, it is time to conduct an oral edit. Together the error analysis and oral edit should provide a clear picture of where to begin remediation.

INTERPRETING THE ORAL EDIT AND SETTING PRIORITIES FOR TEACHING

The types of oral edits made by the writer allow the teacher to determine appropriate intervention strategies. The first priority for teaching includes Oral Edit Types 1 and 2 because they already exist in the writer's repertoire, as evidenced by corrections made by the writer during the oral reading. For these errors the least intrusive and most easily implemented intervention is reinforcement for correct responding. The teacher should prepare performance graphs (Deno & Mirkin, 1977) for recording correct and incorrect uses of the writing components pinpointed by the Error Analysis and Oral Edit. Thereafter, the teacher should closely monitor the student's writing and reinforce correct responding to those components. There is probably no need for further intervention in the form of teaching or curricular changes.

The second priority for teaching are those errors designated Oral Edit Types 3 and 4. The writer either acknowledges errors but fails to correct them, or reads the correct form incorrectly. It is unclear whether the responses are in the writer's repertoire; therefore, the teacher should reinforce and record correct responding as described above. If reinforcement alone does not correct the problem, the correct response is probably not in the writer's repertoire and the teacher must devise an additional intervention strategy as described below.

The third priority for teaching includes errors designated Oral Edit Types 5 and 6. The writer substitutes incorrect oral forms for incorrect written forms or reads errors as they are written. Errors in these categories will probably require a detailed intervention plan, because the writer does not recognize his or her errors. The teacher should set up performance graphs (Deno & Mirkin, 1977) to record the student's progress during intervention. Intervention will depend, of course, on the nature of the problem. Some errors, such as those with plural nouns, might be remediated by having the student complete worksheets in which he or she must identify and use the correct noun endings.

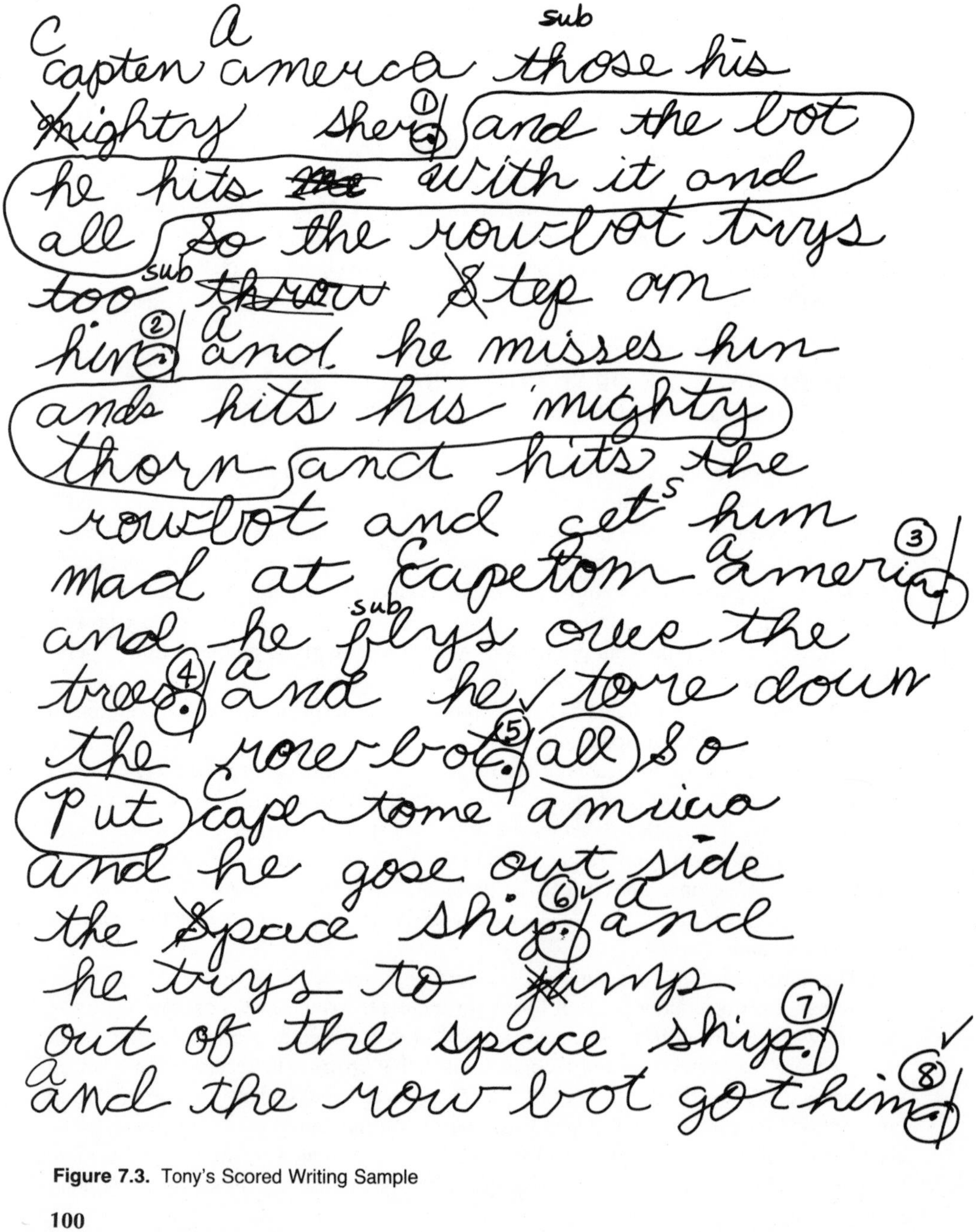

Capten a america those his
mighty sher① and the bot
he hits ~~me~~ with it and
all① so the rowlbot trys
too sub ~~throw~~ step on
him② and he misses him
ands hits his mighty
thorn and hits the
rowlbot and set^s him
mad at capetom america③
and he sub flys over the
tree④ a and he / tore down
the rowerbot all⑤ so
Put cape tome amiica
and he gose out side
the space ship⑥ and
he trys to ~~jump~~
out of the space ship⑦
and the row bot got him⑧

Figure 7.3. Tony's Scored Writing Sample

100

When the student reaches proficiency level on the practice exercises (e.g., 80 percent correct on the worksheet), the teacher should begin teaching the student to generalize from the practice worksheets to other forms of writing (Stokes & Baer, 1977). Correct responding in other writing assignments should be systematically reinforced and recorded on the graph.

Another type of intervention that can be effective is sentence-combining (Cooper, 1977; O'Hare, 1973; Schuster, 1980). Sentence-combining requires the student to consolidate two or more short sentences into a single, more complex sentence. Visual prompts assist the writer during the initial stages. The prompts are faded as the student gains proficiency in the targeted skill through repeated practice on the exercises. Following is an example of a sentence-combining item for teaching compound predicates and remediating problems with verb inflections.

Joan walked to the exit. She *opened* the door. (and)

In the above example the student should create one sentence with a compound predicate joined by *and* (Joan walked to the exit and opened the door.) The student must also use the correct verb endings or lose points accordingly. Schuster (1980) provides excellent guidelines for scoring sentence-combining exercises.

An important point for teachers to keep in mind is that when the student reaches mastery on the practice exercises, he or she will not necessarily generalize the skill to other writing assignments. The teacher must reinforce use of the skill in a variety of settings and with a variety of writing assignments (Stokes & Baer, 1977).

SUMMARY

An error analysis performed on a student's written composition is the most useful of all assessment methods because it provides information necessary for setting teaching priorities and determining curricular content. Teachers should analyze student writing using a two-step process: (1) the analysis of the writing sample and (2) an oral edit. Thus, teachers may gain objective data on student writing skills and on the conceptual knowledge students possess unavailable by other means. A thorough error analysis of students' writing allows teachers to set teaching priorities, plan curricular content, and select effective intervention techniques.

DISCUSSION QUESTIONS

1. What are the purposes of descriptive and diagnostic assessment?
2. How is a writing deficit different from a writing error? Give examples of each.
3. Why is the T-unit a useful measure for reporting both writing deficits and writing errors?
4. What information does the oral edit provide that cannot be obtained from the error analysis alone?

CHAPTER 8

Computer-based Assessment and Error Analysis

Ted S. Hasselbring
Prisca Moore
Peabody College of Vanderbilt University

CHAPTER OBJECTIVES

After reading this chapter you should be able to:

1. State four different types of computer-based assessment and error-analysis programs.
2. Describe how a test-generation program is used in the assessment process.
3. Describe how a test scoring and interpretation program is used in the assessment process.
4. Describe the use of an interactive administration and error analysis program in the assessment process.
5. Describe the process of curriculum-based assessment and the role that technology can play in this process.
6. Describe what is meant by an expert system, and the role of expert systems in assessment and error analysis.

KEY TERMS

aim star
AIMSTAR
artificial intelligence
CAMS (Chronometric Analysis of Math Strategies)
CBA (Computer Based Assessment)
chronometric analysis
expert system
faulty algorithms

fluency
interactive assessment
knowledge engineer
line of progress
minimum 'celeration line
response latency
tailored assessment
test generation programs
test scoring and reporting programs

OVERVIEW OF COMPUTER-BASED ASSESSMENT AND ERROR ANALYSIS

Throughout this book, the contributing authors have discussed a number of useful strategies for the assessment and analysis of student learning problems. In their discussions, several of the authors have pointed out that the assessment and analysis of error patterns, when carried out consistently and conscientiously, lead to improved student learning. Given that this is true, one must ask why student learning problems are not analyzed more frequently by classroom teachers? Bennett (1983) provides several possible reasons why error analysis is seldom carried out in the classroom. First, he suggests that too often teachers have not been trained to carry out the assessment and error analysis process, so even if they want to analyze student error patterns they often don't have the technical skills necessary to do so. Second, Bennett points out that the assessment and analysis of error patterns can often be a very labor-intensive process requiring a significant amount of time and effort. When asked, most educators report that they don't have the time that is required to conduct error analysis procedures on their students even when they know it is important. As a result, assessment and error analysis becomes a low priority in most classrooms.

The problems associated with assessing and analyzing errors are not easily solved. Although this book should help people to develop the technical skills necessary for conducting error analyses, the problem of "too little time" is not as easily overcome. Recently, however, a number of educators have begun to exploit the power of microcomputer technology to reduce the time required to assess and analyze student learning problems. Although computer-based assessment is only in its infancy, it has already shown potential for saving time as well as for improving the accuracy of the error-analysis process (Hasselbring, 1986a).

The purpose of this chapter is to provide a general discussion of how microcomputers can be used in the assessment and error-analysis process. When appropriate, we will provide examples of specific software programs that can be used for assessing and analyzing student learning problems. Throughout this chapter, we classify computer-based assessment and error-analysis software into five different categories. These are: (a) test generation, (b) test scoring and reporting, (c) interactive assessment, (d) curriculum-based assessment, and (e) expert systems. What follows is a discussion of each of these software types.

TEST GENERATION

Often, the first part of conducting an analysis of student errors involves the selection or development of an appropriate assessment instrument. While the process of selecting an appropriate instrument can be tedious and time consuming, selecting an assessment instrument is not nearly as burdensome as developing one. Anyone who has gone through the process of developing an assessment instrument knows that it can take many hours. Further, the problem is compounded when parallel versions of an instrument are required. Recently, however, test-generation programs have been developed that can be used to remove much of the tedium and to reduce the amount of time it takes to create assessment instruments.

Using a test generation program, a teacher can quickly and easily create an assessment instrument that covers specific skills and objectives at a specified level of difficulty. Generally, these programs are designed to allow the teacher to build banks of test items that are classified by topic, question format, or objective. The computer can then select and print out specific assessment items based upon criteria provided by the teacher.

One such example of a test generation program is called *Exam*. Developed by the Brownstone Research Group, *Exam* can be used to create assessment instruments as well as keep computerized records of student performances on these tests. Before generating a test, the teacher must first use *Exam* to develop a bank of test items covering the topic or skills to be assessed. The test items can be written in a variety of formats which include: multiple choice, true/false, matching, or essay. In addition to categorizing assessment items by type, *Exam* allows the teacher to categorize items by topic or level of difficulty. Once the test items are developed, they can be stored on disks for future use. The stored item bank can be edited at any time by adding items, deleting items, or by changing the wording of any question.

Following the creation of an item bank, *Exam* can be used to select specific items from the bank and print an assessment instrument. The teacher enters the criteria to be used for selecting items from the bank, such as difficulty level and type of item, and the computer does the rest. A variety of instruments can be created using the same item bank by altering the type of questions, the order of questions, or the difficulty level. This gives the teacher an opportunity to individualize the evaluation of students by creating and administering different versions of an assessment instrument that covers the same information.

By allowing the computer to assist in the development of assessment instruments, teachers can quickly and easily generate a series of tests. If these instruments are carefully sequenced with regard to item difficulty, the teacher is able to determine at what point a child's skills break down or in what specific area. Not only is this information useful for developing remediation programs but this information is also useful for documenting when and what skills have been mastered.

TEST SCORING AND REPORTING

Test generation programs like the one described above are useful in as much as they allow teachers to create tests which serve as diagnostic tools. However, after generating the test and giving it to the student, the teacher must still score the student responses and analyze the results. Currently, there are computer programs that can score and summarize student responses on an assessment. The earliest of these programs were developed primarily for school psychologists to allow them to quickly score and summarize standardized tests such as the WISC-R, WAIS-R, PIAT, and Woodcock-Johnson Psycho-Educational Battery. These programs allowed psychologists to be more productive since they no longer had to spend hours scoring and summarizing the tests manually. The computer was able to do much of this for them.

When using a scoring program, the test is administered in its traditional form, usually a paper-and-pencil format. In some cases it is administered orally, which means that the examiner must record the student's response. In neither case does the student interact with the computer, only with the examiner. The examiner must enter a student's scores from the administration of the test into the computer. This is generally done in one of two ways. Either the examiner types the information through the keyboard or has the computer read the information from an optical scanning sheet. After entering the student's assessment information, the computer then summarizes and prints out the results in report form. The primary advantage of this type of program is that it saves time by freeing the examiner from such clerical tasks as adding raw scores, looking through conversion tables, and, in some cases, providing written summaries of performance information.

Recently, a number of scoring programs have been developed specifically for classroom teachers. One example is the PRO-SCORE Systems by Pro-Ed. In each of the PRO-SCORE programs, the examiner first administers the test to the student in the traditional manner and then enters the student's responses into the program. The computer then generates a multipage report that includes: raw scores, standard scores, percentiles, descriptors for each subtest, as well as a cognitive aptitude score. Although these programs do not provide the type of detailed error analyses described throughout this book, the information that is provided can be useful as part of the overall assessment process.

In summary, test scoring programs like the ones described above can be useful in that they are able to reduce the amount of time associated with the scoring and error analysis process. However, on the negative side, these programs still require that the teacher enter the assessment information into the computer. In the next section, we will focus on programs that allow testing to be done directly on the computer.

INTERACTIVE ASSESSMENT

In many respects the types of programs discussed thus far fail to take full advantage of the computer. An area of computer-based assessment that is gaining a great deal of attention and does take advantage of many of the powerful characteristics of the computer is interactive assessment.

Interactive assessment differs from the programs described above in that the computer plays the role of the examiner and carries out and analyzes the assessment data. The advantages of interactive assessment are obvious. For one, huge savings in examiner time can be accrued. This is especially important if teachers want to monitor student progress on a regular basis or if they want to monitor the progress of several students. Also, in some cases, examiner bias, administration errors, scoring errors, and invalid or erroneous analyses and interpretations can be more tightly controlled or eliminated. However, on the negative side, with interactive assessment the teacher is removed from the assessment process. In some cases this can create a black-box phenomenon where it is often unclear as to how the computer came up with the analysis. Nevertheless, we believe that interactive assessment programs can provide extremely useful data to the classroom teacher with very little effort. Thus, as these programs become more sophisticated and better designed they will become an important part of the assessment and error analysis process.

For the purpose of describing this new and exciting form of assessment, we have selected two interactive assessment programs in the area of mathematics. Although these programs are both math oriented, from the descriptions you will see that they provide very different data for the classroom teacher. It is for this reason that they were selected.

Chronometric Analysis of Math Strategies

Today, many teachers and parents are content when children with learning handicaps can compute answers to basic math facts using counting strategies (i.e. fingers and number lines) or electronic calculators. However, research by Resnick (1983) suggests that these procedures can interfere with the learning of higher-level math skills such as multiple-digit addition and subtraction, long division, and fractions. Most cognitive scientists today believe that as basic math skills become more highly practiced, their execution requires less cognitive processing capacity, or attention, and they become fluent. Since all people have a limited capacity for information processing, not having to use part of this limited capacity for performing basic skills means that there is more capacity left for executing higher-order processes. Thus, it appears that the ability to succeed in higher-order processes is directly related to the efficiency with which these lower-level skills are executed.

Recent studies have shown that by isolating nonfluent math facts and providing individualized computer-mediated training and practice on these facts, a teacher can succeed in having even children with learning problems learn to retrieve the facts from memory (Hasselbring, Goin, & Bransford, 1987). A key component of this training relies on the identification of each child's repertoire of fluent and nonfluent facts.

The best way to determine if a fact is fluent or not is to record how long it takes a student to answer a problem. For example, most adults answer basic facts under .6 seconds while some children may take up to 10 seconds or more because of the inefficient strategies they are using. Until recently, it has been virtually impossible to record accurately the response latencies for individual math facts outside of a laboratory setting. Further, it is impossible to tell from traditional paper and pencil forms of assessment which facts have been memorized and which have not. Thus teachers have been denied this valuable source of assessment data. However, provide teachers with a tool that allows them to easily assess and monitor response latencies and they will be better able to provide students with the fluency training that they need.

To make the classroom assessment of fluency feasible, an interactive computer program called CAMS (Hasselbring & Goin, 1985), was developed. CAMS is an acronym for the Chronometric Analysis of Math Strategies.

CAMS is designed to record and analyze student response latencies for all basic facts in the four operations. Basic addition facts are defined as all facts from $0 + 0$ to $12 + 12$. Basic subtraction facts are defined as all facts from $0 - 0$ to $24 - 12$ with the subtrahend always being between 0 and 12. Multiplication includes 0×0 to 12×12 and division $0/0$ to $144/12$ with the divisor always being between 0 and 12.

Prior to beginning the actual assessment, the student is given several days of keyboard practice on numbers. During the practice periods, the computer records the response latency for each number between 0 and 24. The response times for each set of numbers are used in the data analysis to factor out motor response time from actual computation time. In other words, the time required to find and press the number key is subtracted from the total time required to solve the problem.

The testing of the basic facts is done interactively; that is, the student takes the assessment on the computer. The assessments for each of the four operations are given independently. CAMS presents the problems to the student on the video display unit of the computer. Once the assessment begins, the student is presented with a discrete set of facts one at a time. The student responds by typing the answer to the problem using the number keys on the top row of the computer keyboard. Then, the student presses the space bar to have a new problem presented. The student's response is timed from the presentation of the problem to the pressing of the number key. If a two- or three-digit answer is required, the timing stops with the pressing of the second or third number key. Student response latencies are recorded to the nearest one hundredth of a second.

CAMS provides the child with a tailored assessment. That is, CAMS decides which problems the student receives based upon responses to past problems. So, for example, if a child has had difficulty with problems from the six and seven tables in multiplication, CAMS will not continue to give the student problems from these tables. CAMS attempts to predict the problems that the student is able to answer and avoid problems that are too difficult. Thus CAMS avoids being overly frustrating for the student yet provides extremely rich data with regard to the student's level of fluency. Upon completion of the assessment CAMS analyzes the data and provides a three-part printed summary which includes a: (a) chronometric analysis, (b) descriptive analysis, and (c) fluency matrix. An example of a CAMS Report is shown in Figure 8.1.

The first section of the CAMS Report is a chronometric-analysis profile. The computer plots a student's latency data so that a visual profile of the student's strategy for solving the basic facts becomes apparent. For example, the profile shown in Figure 8.1 represents a student who is using a counting strategy for solving basic addition facts. These data represent the typical profile in addition facts for a learning-handicapped student. Notice that as the minimum addend becomes larger, the response latency also increases. This information can provide insight as to a student's strategy for solving the problems. Similar profiles can be plotted for subtraction, multiplication, and division.

The second section of the CAMS Report provides descriptive data on the student's level of fluency. This analysis indicates the number of fluent facts, the total number of problems presented, the accuracy of responses, and the number of correct and incorrect responses.

The final section of the report shows a matrix of fluent facts. Using the factored computation speed for each fact, this graph provides a visual representation of the fluent and nonfluent facts for the student. The cells of the matrix that are shaded indicate a fluent fact. Unshaded cells indicate nonfluent facts. The primary purpose of this graph is to provide a visual representation of the student's level of fluency for a set of basic facts.

In sum, CAMS provides the teacher with extremely detailed information concerning a student's level of mathematical fluency at a very low cost in terms of both teacher time and effort. With CAMS, the true power of the computer is exploited. The assessment is presented interactively on the computer; test items are tailored to the student

Name: Ben Parsons
Date: January 15, 1989

Chronometric Analysis - Addition

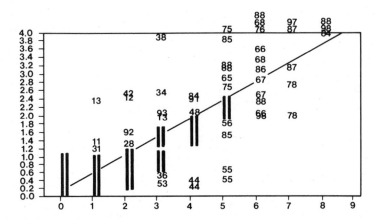

Fluency Report

Number of facts tested: 100
Number of fluent facts: 49
Total trials: 217
Correct responses: 198
Incorrect responses: 19
Response accuracy 91%

Fluency Matrix - Addition

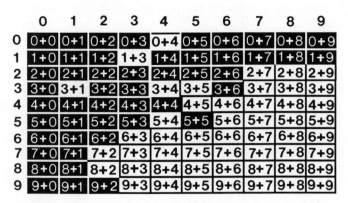

Figure 8.1. CAMS Report

and this is based upon decisions that the computer makes during the assessment process; scoring is done totally by the computer; and reports are generated that allow the teacher to quickly analyze the student's level of performance.

Error Analysis in Mathematical Computation

Although the importance of fluency in basic facts cannot be stressed too heavily, teachers are cautioned against the conclusion that if students have developed fluency in the basic math skills, they will naturally become better at higher-order computations. On the contrary, the development of the effortless recall of basic math facts simply permits the learner to allocate a greater proportion of attention resources to the higher-level processes. Systematic instruction in the higher-order skills is necessary if these students are to master these skills. Thus, an important part of this instruction is the identification and analysis of faulty algorithms students may develop.

Normally, faulty algorithms are analyzed by having a student complete a worksheet containing a variety of problems. For all problems incorrectly answered, try to determine why the student missed the problem. Often, the reasons are quite apparent, but at other times trying to determine where the student went wrong is time-consuming and difficult.

One solution is to have the computer analyze student responses and determine the cause of any errors. One set of programs that provide this type of analysis in addition, subtraction, multiplication, and division is the *Math Assistant* series by Scholastic. The *Math Assistant* series has several of the characteristics of the computer-based assessment programs described throughout this chapter. For example, *Math Assistant* can be used to create diagnostic tests at any level of difficulty because problems may be entered manually or the computer can generate them automatically; students can take tests at the computer or on printed material at their desks. When tests are taken on the computer, student responses are saved automatically and can be analyzed immediately by the computer. However, if students take the test on paper the students' answers must be typed into the computer manually for error analysis.

Error reports can be printed after the answers to student tests have been entered into the computer either by test-taking on the computer or by entering them manually. Either individual or group error reports are available. An example of an individual report is shown in Figure 8.2.

Individual Reports provide a summary of the number and percent of problems answered correctly; which problems were answered correctly; and the type of error made on problems answered incorrectly. Unfortunately, in order to see the problems that the student missed, the test must be printed out. Also, the error type is identified only by a number. In order to identify the error type one must go to the manual for a descriptor. For example, Error 1 represents a regrouping problem whereas Error 10 represents an error on basic facts. Further, when multiple errors occur on a single problem, only a single occurrence shows on Report A. Double errors are shown only on Report B.

Group Reports are virtually identical to Individual Reports except that error data are reported for multiple students. With this information, teachers can prioritize their instructional objectives for both group and individualized teaching formats.

Individual Report A   **Subtraction**

This is a record of student errors on all tests. The error number is listed for every incorrect answer. C shows a correct answer. * marks when no answer was given. # means that no answer was required because the test contained fewer than 20 problems).

Problem Number

1 2 3 4 5 6 7 8 9 10 11 12 13 14 15 16 17 18 19 20

Name: James Rose   Test: Level One/Sub   Score: 50%

16 1 10 C C C 1 12 C C # # # # # # # # # #

Individual Report B   **Subtraction**

This report shows the total number of times (in parentheses) each error was made on all tests.

Error 1   James Rose   (3)

Error 3   James Rose   (1)

Error 10   James Rose   (1)

Error 12   James Rose   (1)

Error 16   James Rose   (1)

Figure 8.2. Individual Student's Report

In sum, *Math Assistant* provides a useful error analysis of student computation errors in the four operations. Perhaps *Math Assistant* and other similar programs can be used most productively by having students take tests on a regular basis so that errors can be so monitored over time to determine if the instructional program is effective. Since it takes only a few minutes to prepare a test using *Math Assistant,* it provides an easy way to regularly monitor student performance. Ideally, these performance data should be used in conjunction with curriculum-based assessment software described in the next section in order to monitor student progress in a systematic manner.

CURRICULUM-BASED ASSESSMENT

In the past two decades, special education teachers have been trained to collect daily performance data to monitor the progress of their students. For example, consider an instructional program designed to teach a student place-value subtraction. Each day the teacher instructs on the rules of subtraction. Then the teacher probes the student on 40 problems to test the concepts of place-value subtraction. On each probe the teacher records the amount of time it takes the student to complete the 40 problems and records the number of correct and incorrect responses.

The purpose of collecting these data is to enable the teacher to determine whether the instructional program is working as planned. Specific techniques have been developed to enable teachers to use this type of classroom data to determine when an instructional strategy should be changed. Haring, Liberty, and White (1980) developed a set of guidelines, called data-based decision rules, to help teachers determine from classroom data not only *when* an instructional strategy should be changed, but also *what kind* of change would most likely produce favorable results for a particular student at a particular time. The decision rules are intended to help the teacher choose which kind of strategy has the highest probability of success.

In order to use these decision rules in the conventional manner, the teacher plots the data on semi-logarithmic graph paper. The initial three days of data are plotted as a baseline, and an "aim star" is shown at the intersection of the desired level of performance and the target data for achieving that level of performance. A "minimum 'celeration line" is then drawn from the midpoint of the baseline data to the aim star. It indicates the minimum level of acceleration or deceleration in the student's performance that is necessary to achieve the criterion level of performance by the target date.

As the teacher continues to conduct the instructional program, she collects and charts data. Three consecutive days of data falling below the " 'celeration line" indicate that the student is not learning satisfactorily and that a change should be made in the instructional strategy. In addition, a "line of progress" is drawn between the median of the most recent three days of data and the median of the three previous days of data to determine the trend of the student's performance. If the student is not progressing and/ or has fallen below the " 'celeration line," an additional flow chart is used to determine what type of change in the instructional strategy will likely be successful.

Research on the effectiveness of curriculum-based assessment has indicated that this methodology is quite promising for improving student achievement. For example, L. S. Fuchs and D. Fuchs (1986b) analyzed 21 research studies that evaluated CBA procedures. The results of this analysis indicated that the use of CBA procedures significantly increased the academic achievement of students whose teachers used these procedures. From these findings, one can conclude that when students' instructional programs are monitored using CBA procedures, such students will achieve much more than will students whose programs are not monitored using a CBA approach.

L. Fuchs and D. Fuchs concluded that the use of CBA procedures within special education increases student academic achievement, and, as well, that the greatest gains can be expected when teachers use specific data-based rules for making instructional decisions as well as graphed data displays. Despite the apparent effectiveness of CBA procedures, all indications are that teachers are reluctant to employ them. In a national survey of LD teachers, Wesson, King, and Deno (1984) found that, although teachers believe that CBA procedures are effective, they do not use the methodology because it is too time consuming.

Computer-based Monitoring and Decision Making

In an attempt to make curriculum-based assessment less time consuming and easier for teachers to implement, a number of developers have proposed the use of microcomputers for implementing CBA procedures (Fuchs, Deno, & Mirkin, 1984; Hasselbring & Hamlett, 1984; West, Young, & Johnson, 1984). Basically, these monitoring programs have been designed to assist teachers in storing, graphing, and analyzing student performance data. One such computer program that has been used successfully in special education is *AIMSTAR*.

AIMSTAR is an integrated set of computer programs that are designed assist teachers in storing, graphing, and analyzing student performance data. To use *AIMSTAR,* the teacher creates a student data file. Descriptive information about the student's instructional program, the program objectives, and teaching procedures are included. Following each teaching session, the teacher enters student performance data into the computer. For example, the teacher enters the number of correct and incorrect responses exhibited by the student and the amount of time required for the student to complete the trials. *AIMSTAR* then stores this information and allows the teacher to graph the student's data, apply data-based decision-rules, and produce a printout giving the status of the student's instructional program with recommended changes when appropriate. As shown in Figure 8.3, the advantage of this type of analysis and report is that it is immediately obvious when a student is having difficulty with a skill and when an instructional strategy is working.

It should be emphasized that monitoring and decision-making programs, such as *AIMSTAR,* do not eliminate the need for teacher intuition and judgement in planning instruction. Rather, these programs supplement teacher judgement by providing additional empirical data and analytic procedures. Using this technology, special education teachers are able to respond more flexibly and effectively to changing student needs and to produce greater student growth.

Expert Systems: The Future of Computer-based Assessment?

Thus far, we have discussed assessment and error analysis programs that are used primarily to reduce the tedium associated with the analysis of student learning problems. For the most part, however, these programs have in no way provided the same intelligent insight into the assessment and error analysis process that human diagnosticians can provide. But what does the future of computer-based assessment and error analysis hold? Consider the following scenario.

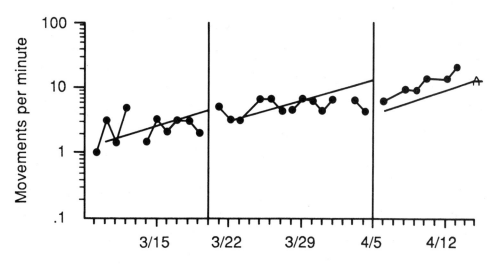

Figure 8.3. Ben Parsons
Match-to-Sample

A teacher in a rural area is perplexed by a learning problem exhibited by one of his students. The school is for too small to have the regular services of a school psychologist or diagnostician. However, with this student, the teacher feels the need for an expert's advice to help with an analysis of the student's problem and to recommend an effective instructional program. So the teacher goes to the computer at his desk and enters into a dialogue with it. Through the program, the teacher has access to the knowledge, judgement, and intuition of the country's best educational diagnosticians. The program queries the teacher concerning the student's problems; it requests information from the teacher that will help the system come up with an analysis and prescription that will have a high probability for success. The computer serves the role of an expert consultant that the teacher can call upon at any time and discuss problems that students are having in the classroom.

Unfortunately, the gap between the scenario above and reality is large. Nevertheless, both computer and cognitive scientists are making great strides in producing intelligent consultants, called *expert systems*. Expert systems have evolved over the past 25 years from the field of artificial intelligence and can be defined as computer programs capable of reaching a level of performance comparable to that of a human expert in some specialized problem domain (Nau, 1983). Expert systems are unlike conventional application programs in that they are the first systems designed to help humans solve complex problems in a common sense way. These systems use the methods and information acquired and developed by a human expert to solve problems, make predictions, suggest possible treatments, and offer advice that is as accurate as its human counterpart.

While expert systems in the field of education are only in the early phases of development, expert systems are being used more widely in other fields. Some of the expert systems currently in use include: *Caduceus,* which helps doctors diagnose medical problems; *CATCH,* which can scan 250,000 photographs to assist New York City policy in identifying criminal suspects; and *Prospector,* which sifts geological data to predict the location of mineral deposits. The practical applications for expert systems abound. Whenever human experts are in great demand and short supply, a computer-based consultant can help to amplify and disseminate the needed expertise.

Current expert-systems technology seems best suited to diagnosis or classification problems whose solutions depend primarily on the possession of a large amount of specialized, factual, and empirical knowledge (Duda & Shortliff, 1983). Thus, it is only logical that expert systems be developed in education for assessing and diagnosing error patterns and learning problems. Although *Math Assistant,* discussed earlier in this chapter, was designed to provide the teacher with expert-like information, by definition, *Math Assistant* is not a true expert system.

To date, several expert systems have been developed that are designed to assist in the diagnosis and analysis of student learning problems. One such prototypic system developed by Colbourn and McLeod (1983) assists teachers in the diagnosis and analysis of reading problems. This system guides the teacher through reading diagnosis from the initial suspicion that a reading problem exists to the point at which sufficient information has been gathered to plan an appropriate remedial program.

With this system, a dialogue is conducted between the user and the computer. The system poses questions or makes appropriate suggestions. If desired information is not available, the system provides the diagnostician the option of stopping the dialogue in order to obtain the needed data. In some cases where it is impossible to obtain the desired information, the system is capable of handling incomplete data. However, when the system must have further input in order to continue the diagnosis, the system reiterates what data are required and then terminates the session.

This expert system does not test the student directly, nor does it manage the testing activities. Instead, the teacher or diagnostician performs the tasks suggested by the system—such as administering a specific test—and enters this information into the system. After these new data have been entered, the system analyzes this information and proposes the next step in the assessment process. When a sufficient amount of information has been gathered and entered, the system provides a report of its diagnostic findings. The teacher can then plan a remedial program based on these results. An obvious extension of this system is to have it prescribe appropriate remedial strategies and instructional techniques based upon the diagnostic findings.

The performance of this expert diagnostic system has been evaluated by comparing it against human diagnosticians. When subjected to a number of test cases, it was found that the expert system's diagnostic reports were consistently good. In contrast, the diagnostic reports prepared by the human experts varied dramatically in terms of style, format, readability, relevance, and accuracy. Of course, some of the reports of the human diagnosticians were judged better than the reports of the expert system while many others were judged as inferior.

It appears that the development of expert systems for assessing learning problems shows great promise. However, one must view the emergence of expert systems with mixed emotion. If expert systems are developed with pedagogical soundness then these systems will no doubt benefit teachers and students. On the other hand, it is very likely that a number of systems that are pedagogically unsound will find their way to the educational market. Thus, educators must be cautious and evaluate very carefully any computer program that proposes to diagnose and analyze student learning problems.

SUMMARY

Computer-based assessment and error analysis, while only beginning to be used in school environments, appears to offer great promise for overcoming many of the problems associated with the assessment of children with learning difficulties. When programmed appropriately, microcomputers can remove much of the tedium associated with the administration and scoring of diagnostic instruments. With assessment programs becoming more sophisticated, the computer is playing a larger role in the analysis of learning problems. For example, in the case of the CAMS program described earlier in this chapter, the computer presents the student with appropriate assessment items, monitors student responses, scores, summarizes, and prints out a report on the student's performance. CAMS and other analysis programs are relatively simple in comparison to the expert systems being developed currently. Nevertheless, they have been shown to be extremely successful for saving examiner time, reducing scoring errors, and providing teachers with information that would be difficult to obtain without the use of a computer.

The assessment and analysis programs currently in use are only precursors to the more elaborate and powerful intelligent systems that will be available in the next five to ten years. These systems will be able to guide the teacher through the necessary steps for the analysis of learning problems, test the student directly where appropriate, analyze the student performance data, and prescribe appropriate instructional strategies for remediating the student's problems. Although it is unlikely that the use of computers will eliminate all of the difficulties involved in assessing and analyzing learning problems, existing research suggests that the process can be enhanced through the responsible use of this technology.

DISCUSSION QUESTIONS AND ACTIVITIES

1. List four different types of computer-based assessment and error analysis programs.
2. Describe how a test generation program might be used for assessment and error analysis.
3. Describe how a test scoring and interpretation program could be used to assist in conducting an assessment and analysis of student errors.
4. List advantages and disadvantages of using an interactive administration and error analysis program.
5. Describe the process of curriculum-based assessment and the role that technology can play in this process.
6. Describe what is meant by an expert system. Further, discuss how expert systems could change the role of error analysis for the classroom teacher.

7. Use a test generation program to create an assessment instrument that can be used to analyze student errors in math, reading or language arts.
8. Use an interactive test administration program with a student to conduct an assessment and analysis of student errors in math, reading, or language arts.
9. Use a curriculum-based assessment program to monitor student performance data to determine if your instructional programs are having an effect on reducing student errors.

CHAPTER 9

Content Area Skill Assessment

B. Keith Lenz
Daryl Mellard
University of Kansas

CHAPTER OBJECTIVES

After reading this chapter you should be able to:

1. Distinguish between assessment of basic skills and content skills.
2. Discuss factors that contribute to the design of content area assessment.
3. Devise a content area skill assessment program.
4. Discuss ways of involving students in content area skill assessment.

KEY TERMS

content demands
content demonstrations
content drivers
formative test

situation-specific strategy
summative test
task-specific strategy

INTRODUCTION

An assessment model with a dual orientation—basic skills and academic content—has not been the focus of the assessment process in special and remedial education. Instead, the primary emphasis has been on evaluation and remediation in the basic academic skill areas. There has been little or no attention to the application of these basic academic skills to content area learning. However, because of increased attention to the failure of students to generalize basic academic skills to content area learning and a growing concern over the lack of scientific and cultural literacy of students, assessment systems are needed that take into consideration content area learning. The implementation of an assessment system that has both a skill and a content orientation requires the teacher to continue assessing achievement and error patterns in the basic academic areas (as described elsewhere in this textbook). However, it must also focus on how the student integrates and applies these skills across content area subjects.

Skill versus Content Assessment

During the beginning years of schooling, instruction focuses on learning skills. In pre-school and in kindergarten, these skills are frequently referred to as readiness skills. In the primary grades, they are called basic academic skills. First readiness then basic skills are considered to be the tools a student needs for learning both in the academic environment and in settings outside of school. The primary basic skill areas for which skill mastery is assumed as a student moves into higher levels of content mastery include the following: the basic academic skills of reading (e.g., decoding and comprehension), written expression (sentences, paragraphs, spelling, and so forth), arithmetic (addition, subtraction, multiplication, division, fractions, decimals, and so forth), and study skills (e.g., notetaking, textbook usage, outlining, test preparation, and so forth.)

As a student begins to become proficient in many of the basic academic skill areas, the student is expected to apply these skills to acquire content in broader domains. Indeed, as students move from the elementary grades, through the middle school grades, and into secondary school coursework, the criteria for success become increasingly more dependent on the students' ability to demonstrate mastery of the content required for scientific and cultural literacy. Simultaneously, success becomes less dependent on students' abilities to demonstrate mastery only on isolated basic academic skills. However, beyond the elementary school grades, it is often assumed that as a result of continued exposure to increasingly difficult content learning experiences, basic academic skill proficiency will increase and develop without special attention. In addition, we often draw distinct lines between the academic disciplines in the upper-middle and secondary-school curriculum. Attention to the development, integration, and application of skills that will promote content area learning is rarely given. Yet, most educators argue that it is the lack of basic academic skills and strategies that contribute most to secondary school failure, and that greater curricular and instructional attention should be given to this area. Therefore, in conceptualizing an appropriate and responsive assessment model, the standards that should be applied to evaluate student progress and achievement should be based on this: the successful application of basic academic skills and strategies in the context of the demonstration of required levels of mastery in content knowledge areas.

Content mastery is expected in a number of different domains. Generally, these content areas are associated with specific academic subjects. These primary content areas include social studies (e.g., American history, world history, civics, state history, and sociology), science (e.g., health, physical science, biology, physics, and chemistry), language arts (e.g., literature, speech, drama, and foreign language), mathematics (e.g., consumer math, algebra, geometry, and calculus), and vocational or industrial education (e.g., home economics, mechanics, business, and agriculture). In addition, a variety of other instructional areas, such as physical education, music, and art, may demand that students demonstrate content mastery. These domains comprise the content curriculum of the regular middle- and secondary-school program. Similarly, content mastery is evaluated and student success is determined across these knowledge domains.

However, because eligibility criteria for admission to special and remedial services is based on a skill-deficit model, the assessment process has focused primarily on measures of how basic academic skills are acquired. As a result, the focus of on-going classroom assessment and intervention has been on the attainment of basic academic skills. It is important to consider as well the impact of skill attainment on content area learning. Nevertheless, the primary purpose for teaching students basic academic skills is to facilitate their content application(s). Thus, while continued efforts to promote skill acquisition and application in the upper grade levels are appropriate, the teacher must also implement assessment systems that relate to the application of skills to content domains. Such an assessment system must have a dual orientation—skills and content. Implementing this type of assessment system will require the teacher to continue assessing error patterns in the basic academic areas. At the same time, the teacher should also assess how the student integrates and applies these skills across the content areas.

Review of Traditional Content Area Assessment

Assessment of content knowledge is most frequently accomplished with teacher-made or textbook-based tests, for example, chapter tests. Performance on such tests has been the basis for assigning class ranks and grades and for judging students' levels of proficiency. Levels of proficiency address such questions as: Is the student adequately prepared for learning new, advanced material? Or, how well did the student learn following a particular instructional method (e.g., use of pretests, advance organizers, chapter outlines, and peer grouping)? Thus, the assessment has both formative and summative purposes. However, these measures provide little information regarding the student's learning methods or processes.

Another traditional measure of content knowledge is the use of group administered, norm-referenced, standardized achievement tests. The Stanford Achievement Test, Scholastic Aptitude Test, and Metropolitan Achievement Test are examples of this type of achievement index. The use of these tests, or any other measure for that matter, assumes that they are selected for specified purposes and that the tests have demonstrated their utility for those purposes. These tests are not intended as formative measures to help direct lesson planning or choice among instructional methods, but rather to provide more global measures on which normative comparisons of students' proficiencies could be made. While teacher-made tests or textbook tests typically sample content from a particular curriculum, these broad measures are less curricular specific. That is, the test items are likely representative of information presented in a number of curricula. However, as with teacher-made or textbook tests, these measures have typically focused solely on sampling students' content knowledge. They have ignored students' learning patterns and how their learning might best be demonstrated.

These traditional approaches have emphasized assessment of content knowledge at the expense of providing information about the learning characteristics of the students. Information presented through lectures, filmstrips, simulations, or textbooks is not information on how students learn. During the process of acquiring, integrating, and expressing information, the information presented initially is actively processed by the student and is transformed. This transformation might occur in any phase of the learning—acquisition or integration. The implications of these information-processing constructs for instructional and assessment methods are evidenced in recent work in cognitive psychology (e.g., Gagne, 1985; Mayer, 1987).

Previous chapters contain information on the analysis of students' error patterns in basic skills—reading, spelling, arithmetic, handwriting, and written language. In contrast, this chapter is aimed at providing guidance in developing valid and reliable assessment of a student's (a) academic content knowledge and (b) learning behaviors (i.e., his/her characteristics of information processing). This attention to the student's learning behaviors helps distinguish the proposed assessment model from traditional assessment. The dual focus of the assessment model not only indicates the student's knowledge of content, but also the repertoire of skills the student used in learning and expressing himself or herself. As a result the teacher has information about the student's breadth and depth of content knowledge as well as information about how the content material was acquired and, perhaps, best demonstrated. Concurrently, the student's test performances also show the teacher the content not learned and the skill deficits which the student has in expressing information. By inference, the teacher then has sufficient information on which to judge the potential efficacy of instructional methods.

Validity Issues in Content Area Skills Assessment

This model was developed with attention to the psychometric standards (American Psychological Association, 1985) recommended for tests. Reliability and validity standards for measures of specific academic content are no different than they are for other measures, such as the curriculum-based measurement a teacher might use in assessing basic skills. In each instance, the teacher wants to feel confident that the inference made about the student's behavior is accurate and that the student's performance is stable. That is, the performance is representative of consistent performance.

Validity is a construct with many different facets (American Psychological Association, 1985) and does not have a singular standard or numerical index. However, even in this situation the questions can be stated: What are the appropriate standards for judging validity? How does one know if the assessment is valid? We propose a very fundamental specific standard for judging the validity of content-area skill assessment as described here. The validity of the content-area skill assessment is evaluated against the student's academic success as the student performs in the class. If the performance reflected on the content-area skills assessment leads to adequate and appropriate interpretations or actions, the assessment is valid. This standard will be developed in the following paragraphs by referencing district-level standards of proficiency and four types of validity evidence. (See Messick, 1989, for an extended treatment of the many aspects of validity.)

Frequently, school districts, and in some instances even state departments of education and specific academic departments, have specified goals, objectives, or desired outcomes for students. These specifications become the ultimate standards against which classroom test performance is evaluated. Thus, they should be used in evaluating the validity of the assessment model proposed here. The proposed assessment model is valid to the extent that its results are comparable to the results of other measures which assess student proficiency on the district's goals and objectives. For example, assume that a school district has a curriculum guide in which the basic skills and content knowledge expected of its students are specified. This district-level specification then becomes the standard for evaluating the accuracy of the content-area skills assessment. We do not specify the numerical data which might be used to quantify these constructs or the criterion against which one would judge differences between the measures. However, we believe that several alternative data elements and criteria are worthy of consideration because of the different perspectives each lends. One's values, perhaps expressed in school district policies, should guide the decision-making.

For our purposes, we have selected four dimensions of validity constructs which are particularly appropriate to any measure of academic achievement. Thus, validity, that is the accuracy of a test score, should be interpreted with consideration to at least these four dimensions. Note that a different issue is considered in each dimension. Therefore, different approaches and information are needed in judging validity. The first validity dimension is that the test should be evaluated for the extent to which it matches the emphasis given the content in the course of actual instruction. This evaluation provides evidence of instructional validity. Content which is not included in instruction has no instructional validity. Second, the measure should be evaluated for the extent to which a match exists between the test items and the content emphasis provided by the curriculum. This dimension is considered curricular validity. A third concept is the degree to which the measure has value for planning efficacious instructional methods. This concept is a shift from the first concept concerning instructional validity. In the latter, one predicts an outcome of modifying instructional methods. In this validity dimension one asks the question: What instructional methods do the test results suggest are most appropriate? Last, one should discern the extent to which the required test response format (e.g., multiple choice, fill-in-the-blank, matching, and short answer) matches the likely application of the information. In this dimension we are concerned with the generalization of the content knowledge, which particularly in light of district and state level testing procedures, is important information. These four validity constructs provide an alternative base for evaluating the validity of a test item or many such items.

As these alternative concepts suggest, validity is not an all or nothing concept. Similarly, validity has more dimensions than those dimensions represented by these four constructs. Ideally, one should be able to rank order individual test items on the basis of each of the constructs offered above. On the basis of the rank ordering, one would know which items are most valid for a particular purpose and thus could be grouped to form a multiple-item test. The content-area skill assessment model is intended to have high instructional and curricular validity. The model should provide information regarding instructional planning—not only about the scope and sequencing of content but also about instructional methods. Finally, the model provides variable response formats from which a teacher can choose those most appropriate.

This content-area skills assessment model is in the developmental phase at the University of Kansas's Institute for Research in Learning Disabilities. Many components of the model have been implemented in a variety of high-school settings over the past ten years. However, at the time of this writing, the model has not been fully implemented in any one setting. This chapter represents the latest conceptual developments and applications for integrating content assessment within the framework of students' cognitive processing skills. These developments are reported in the following section which includes the step-to-step sequence that comprises a content-area skills assessment.

STEPS TO CONTENT AREA SKILL ASSESSMENT

Three basic assumptions are related to content acquisition-assessment. Together, they will set the stage for understanding our discussion of the subject. The first assumption is that in order for assessment to be effective, the assessment process must be driven by the content that teachers wish students to master in content courses. The teacher's specification of instructional content provides the relevance and validity parameters of the assessment. Second, the assessment process must include measures of two criteria: (a) the efficiency of content learning, and (b) the effectiveness of content learning. Separating the content and the skill criteria will permit greater opportunity to pinpoint a student's strengths and weaknesses. Third, since, as the student moves through the school system, content acquisition becomes the primary measure of academic success, content acquisition must eventually be used as the criterion for the success of skill acquisition. Viewed together, these three assumptions are the framework of the Content Area Skill Assessment (CASA) process that we present in this chapter. The steps involved in the CASA process are described from the perspective of a teacher who is usually concerned with teaching students about the application of skills to content domains and with measuring the effectiveness of such instruction by content mastery. These content domains are primarily represented by common mainstream middle- and secondary-school social studies and science courses.

Step 1: Define Content Demands

A "content demand" refers to the type of information a student is expected to master for a given class. These various types of information might be broadly considered as (a) verbatim recall, (b) paraphrased recall, and (c) the application of information. "Content demands" must be examined in three areas. First, the teacher must determine what drives what is covered in the content class. Second, the teacher must determine how the student is expected to demonstrate content mastery. And third, the teacher must determine the evaluation criteria used to judge the degree and quality of students' acquisition of content. In conceptualizing these demands, the teacher must also be cognizant of distinguishing content from skill mastery and of how the assessment will be evaluated on these two criteria.

Content Drivers.   Content drivers are those forces that determine which content is important for students to master and how the information should be organized for learning. As you know, the teacher does not always have control over what information must be covered in a particular class. For example, curriculum objectives adopted by a state or district may specify what each course will cover and govern what will be in a particular course. Content-specific minimum competency tests, textbook adoptions and achievement tests also play a part in determining the selection of content. For instance, it is not uncommon for textbook adoption to represent content specifications in a subject area. Still, the content teacher often plays a major role in selecting the content actually covered in the course. In schools where specific curriculum content has been mandated, the teacher often is responsible for interpreting and determining the specificity of coverage. In those schools where specific curriculum content has not been mandated, the selection of content is absolutely up to the teacher.

Assessment depends on a clear understanding of what is to be known or learned by the student. However, identification of what is to be learned across the content areas is quite different from what is to be learned in the skill areas. In basic skill assessment, the behavior measured is generally agreed upon and often quite narrow in focus (e.g., comprehension, word recognition, addition). However, in the content areas, the knowledge base is open to various interpretations and to considerable change, and is often very broad in focus (e.g., the rise and fall of nations; the life cycle of an organism). Therefore, in content-area assessment, the task is to determine what content will actually be covered by a teacher. Figure 9.1 shows a content map that can be used to identify the major learning topics, subtopics and points of some segment of a content area. Each topic, subtopic, and learning point could be translated into a specific behavioral objective. However, the purpose of the content map is to briefly outline what is most critical in a body of knowledge. You can create a content map for an entire course, a unit, a chapter, or a specific lesson. Figure 9.2 shows a content map completed for a chapter on General Biology.

Regular classroom content teachers very often have difficulty specifying what drives the content that they teach. Therefore they are unable to construct such a map. In this case, the best approach is to collect the assignments and tests used in the course and match these with the organization of the textbook used in the course. For example, the main learning point of senses was included on the chapter test. Ear was covered in the chapter subtopic on sense organs. Therefore, the main learning points that pertain to the ear are placed on the content map under that subtopic. (See Figure 9.2.) An evaluation of all the information included in assignments and tests will help you create a content map. After the content map is created, reviewing it with the content teacher provides a check of its completeness, weight, and accuracy. However, in spite of a teacher's review comments, the information included on the classroom tests is ultimately the information used by the teacher for determining content mastery.

Content Demonstrations.   Once you have determined the relative importance of the content, the next step is to determine how the teacher wants the student to demonstrate content mastery. Content demonstrations can be categorized according to a number of dimensions. First, they can be categorized as being in-class or out-of-class: those performed during the class period, or those completed out of the classroom setting (e.g., homework). Demonstrations can consist of tests or assignments. While every product may be considered a test, generally two types of tests are identified: 1) formative, and 2) summative.

Summative tests usually denote the end of a segment or unit of study, for example, the traditional "chapter test." Formative tests are usually quizzes that provide checkpoints through a unit of study. There are three types of formative assignments:

Figure 9.1. Content Map

CONTENT MAP

CLASS: General Biology _____ TIME PERIOD: 9/12 - 9/18

TOPIC | Sense Organs - Chapter 14

SUBTOPIC	eye	tongue; nose	ear	skin
DETAILS	List and describe the four outside parts of the eye and five inside parts of the eye. Describe the four steps of how the eye sends messages to the brain through neurons	Explain how the tongue and nose work together. How do neurons make the tongue work? What are the four tastes? How do neurons make the nose work?	How do air molecules affect hearing? Describe the four steps of how the ear sends messages to the brain through neurons. What are the parts of the ear?	List and describe the four neurons in the skin and the conditions they detect.

Figure 9.2. Sample Completed Content Map

125

(1) studying, (2) daily homework, and (3) projects. Studying assignments require the student to prepare for a test or some type of class activity. Daily work consists of assignments that are routine follow-up activities of class content designed to promote practice and understanding. For example, the completion of chapter questions and worksheets are considered daily work. Projects are assignments that require several days to complete. They require student application of content in the form of a presentation, report, theme, visual, or product. Projects are frequently considered as summative activities. Depending on the expectations of the teacher, all three assignment types can be completed in or out of the classwork setting.

Identifying the systems that a content teacher requires for demonstration of content provides information on the type of mastery required and the types of skills involved. Figure 9.3 shows a form for listing the various content demonstration systems used in a classroom. Figure 9.4 shows how the form would be completed for a class in biology.

Content Evaluation Criteria. The final step in determining content demands is to identify the evaluation criteria a teacher uses to judge relative mastery of the content. These criteria can be adequately considered if you determine the quantity and weight of each type of content demonstration. This type of information must be collected by interviewing the content teacher about the grading system for the class. Figure 9.5 shows how such an evaluation is completed.

In summary, Step 1, "Define Content Demands," requires the teacher to identify the demands of content learning that define success in the primary content-acquisition setting—usually the regular classroom. Once the content demands have been defined, the information can be used for many students as well as over time.

Step 2: Evaluate the Content Demands

The next CASA step is to examine the content demands and begin to make decisions about the nature of the content. Therefore, this step builds on the content demands identified in Step 1. That is, the teacher must have identified the content over which the student will be tested or in which competence must be demonstrated. Once this identification step has been completed, the content must be evaluated to determine the type of information that is being targeted for learning.

Content Classification. Content can be classified meaningfully in three ways: (a) structural relationships, (b) thematic content, and (c) rules. First, content can be classified according to the structural or organizational relationships of the information to be learned. That is, the content can be organized according to its relationship with the information accompanying it in the text. Structural relationship is usually expressed by organizing the content into topics, subtopics, main ideas, and details. A content map constructed from a typical textbook can be used to illustrate these structural relationships (as in Figure 9.2). Social studies content can often be organized in this way. The second way of classifying content is according to its thematic content: concepts and facts. Concepts can be represented in the vocabulary of the content that the student is to learn. Facts are the contributing information that support the concepts. Rules are the third type of classification. Rules define the relationship between concepts and facts. Frequently,

CONTENT DEMONSTRATIONS

CLASS: _____ TIME PERIOD _____

TOPIC: _____

	DONE IN-CLASS	DONE OUT-OF-CLASS
FORMATIVE MEASURES		
SUMMATIVE MEASURES		

Figure 9.3. Content Demonstrations Form

CONTENT DEMONSTRATIONS

CLASS: *Biology*   TIME PERIOD *4/12 – 4/19*

TOPIC: *Carnivores*

	DONE IN-CLASS	DONE OUT-OF-CLASS
FORMATIVE MEASURES	*mid-chapter quiz*	*3 sets of questions on various sections of the chapter* *Define 20 key vocabulary words on a worksheet provided by the content teacher*
SUMMATIVE MEASURES	*chapter test*	*Write a report on a carnivore of your choice and turn in the day of your chapter test*

Figure 9.4. Sample of Completed Content Demonstrations Form

CONTENT EVALUATION CRITERIA

CLASS: _Biology_   TIME PERIOD: _4/12 - 4/19_

TOPIC: _Carnivores_

Content Demonstrations	Number Required	Percentage of Grade	Characteristics	Criteria for Passing
mid chapter quiz	1	20%	10 questions - multiple choice	6/10
answer questions on various sections of the chapter	3 sets	10%	total of 15 quest.- teacher will correct, but student gets full credit for completing assignment regardless of accuracy	15/15
Vocabulary definitions	1	10%	20 vocabulary definitions - based on text glossary	14/20
Chapter test	1	40%	40 multiple choice questions worth 2 pts each 2 essay questions worth 10 points each	70/100
Report on carnivores	1	20%	must meet 4 criteria - equally weighted at 25 points each 1.) specify type of carnivore 2.) habits 3.) predators 4.) 2 pages in length	70/100 (partial credit possible)

Figure 9.5. Content Evaluation Criteria Form

rules are general or specific declarative statements that describe the consequences of applying specific concepts. These relationships can often be represented using various forms of a general cause and effect statement (i.e., an "if . . ., then . . ." statement). A *general* rule statement can often be constructed using an "if . . ., then it is likely/ not likely that . . ." statement structure (e.g., *if* a presidential candidate is a member of a minority group, *then it is not likely* that he or she will be elected). A *specific* rule statement can be constructed using the more definite "if/when . . ., then . . ." statement structure (e.g., *if* an animal's heart stops, *then* it will die). However, the same relationships can also be expressed without the sometimes awkward "if . . . then . . ." jargon (e.g., The longer the war, the poorer the nation. Another example is: The Emancipation Proclamation declared all slaves in the United States to be free, however, it did not immediately free all the slaves from slavery.). Rules can also be procedural; procedural rules describe sequences of action or sequences in which concepts are applied. (e.g., the process of photosynthesis, the process of how a bill becomes a law). Science content is frequently organized in this fashion.

Most of the time, the content can be classified in more than one way, and many times the content can be classified according to all three classification systems (i.e., structural relationships, thematic content, and rules). For example, in content covering the events of the 1960s in American history, thematic concepts around which the content could be organized might be "civil rights," "generation gap," and "communist expansion." While the text might actually chronicle a history of events, the concepts listed above might cut across the various topics and subtopics of the text. On one hand, if the content map was focused on concepts and rules, the flow, sequence, or story qualities of the content might be lost. On the other hand, organizing the content according to topics, main ideas, and details might result in the lack of identification of themes and rules important to the generalization of content learning. Therefore, an effective approach to evaluating the content might be to construct the content map according to structural relationships (as in Figure 9.2), but then to return to the map and identify themes and rules that might cut across topics. Figure 9.6 shows how this might be accomplished. In summary, evaluation and categorization of content according to these three dimensions will enable you to develop an assessment system that is appropriate for a specific content area.

Step 3: Identify the Unit of Measure

Up to this point, the focus of the CASA process has been on the nature, organization, and delivery of the content to be learned and on how mastery of the content is determined from the perspective of the content teacher. Understanding this perspective is important, because this is the perspective that determines the basic academic skills and strategies that the student must select and utilize. Rarely are the needed academic skills identified for the student. The assumption is that the student has mastered the basic skills, recognizes the tasks involved, and can choose from his or her repertoire of skills those that are most appropriate and then apply them.

Traditional classroom content assessment practices usually have two major limitations. First, assessment usually focuses only on the content that the student has learned and provides little information on the success of the students' "learning processes" or

Important
Concepts: 1) 2) 3)

NAME: General Biology ——————— TIME PERIOD: 9/12 – 9/18

TOPIC	Sense (organs) – Chapter 14			
SUBTOPIC	eye	tongue & nose	ear	skin
DETAILS	List and describe the four outside parts of the eye and five inside parts of the eye	Explain how the tongue and nose work together	How do air (molecules) affect hearing?	List and describe the four (neurons) in the skin and the conditions they detect.
	Describe the four steps of how the eye sends messages to the brain through (neurons)	How do (neurons) make the tongue work?	Describe the four steps of how the ear sends messages to the brain through (neurons)	
		What are the four tastes?	What are the parts of the ear?	
		How do (neurons) make the nose work?		

Figure 9.6. Sample Completed Content Map Emphasizing Key Concepts

the "instructional processes" engaged in by the teacher. If the student does poorly, no information on the relative success or failure of the teacher or student in facilitating the learning process is provided. Second, traditional classroom content assessment has been primarily summative rather than formative in nature. That is, decisions and changes in what the student is doing to learn the content or what the teacher is doing to teach the content, are rarely linked to assessment information. Instead, assessment merely indicates whether the student can demonstrate knowledge of the content in the way prescribed by the teacher.

In CASA, the traditional content measure (e.g., the "chapter" test) remains in place. However, in addition to the traditional summative measure, formative measures are included. Smaller or different units of measure are used to determine how learning and instruction are best organized to enhance the mastery of content on those measures typically used by a content teacher. This smaller or different unit of measure we will call a CASA unit. The CASA unit includes any chunk of content information which must be acquired, stored, expressed, or demonstrated. Figure 9.7 shows a number of different types of units often associated with acquisition, storage, expression, and demonstration demands. In general, the smaller the content unit, the easier it is for the teacher to assess and make intervention decisions. However, this consequence is not all positive. The larger the unit, the more content relevant it becomes (i.e., like what the student has to face in the regular classroom) and the more the unit yields information related to the effect of the intervention decision.

Unit size is an important issue because the teacher may have to adjust the CASA unit. For example, Craig is faced with learning the information in a science chapter on the five senses. The teacher plans to complete instruction on the chapter in two weeks. The traditional content assessment used by the regular content teacher is composed of several different measures, each of which requires the application of different basic academic skills and each of which provides different information. Consider the following list of traditional classroom measures: chapter test, completion of the study questions at the end of the chapter, writing the definitions of a set of vocabulary words found in the chapter, and completing a chapter study guide the night before the test.

In an attempt to identify the appropriate CASA unit, the teacher first asks, "Am I primarily concerned with the acquisition, storage, expression, or demonstration of content information?" In Craig's case, the teacher decides that acquisition is the primary concern: "I think that Craig just can't get the information." The next question the teacher asks is, "What types of acquisition demands are placed on Craig in this class?" Examining the content delivery systems for the science class, the teacher sees that the content of the class is primarily based on the book, and the lectures serve to reinforce the content presented by the text. At this point the teacher decides that the CASA unit must be based on the textbook, and in this case, the chapter on the five senses. Opening the book, the teacher sees that there are sixteen pages in the chapter. Craig's teacher examines the content map and sees that the chapter is organized into six sections; an introductory discussion on the five senses is the first content section and is then followed by a section on each of the five senses. In selecting the CASA unit, the teacher must consider the basic academic skills required in mastering the content and Craig's proficiency with those skills. If Craig has trouble with basic paragraph comprehension, then the CASA unit will need to be at the paragraph level. If Craig appears to have difficulty

IDENTIFYING THE UNIT OF MEASURE

CLASS: *American History*   TIME PERIOD: *all year*
TOPIC: *across the course*

	SAMPLE DEMANDS	SAMPLE UNITS OF MEASURE
ACQUISITION	Read textbook	paragraph multiple paragraphs chapter section whole chapter
STORAGE	Memorize information	Lists Lists and definitions
	note taking from text	paragraph chapter section whole chapter
	note taking from lecture	1 min lecture 5 min lecture 10 min lecture 30 min lecture
EXPRESSION	Writing reports	sentences paragraphs themes
	Taking tests	1 page tests 2 page tests 3 page tests
	Group discussion	1 min topic discussion 2 min topic discussion 3 min topic discussion

Figure 9.7. Form for Identifying the Unit of Measure

integrating information across paragraphs, then the CASA unit may need to be based on the sections of the chapter. However, if Craig's difficulty appears to be at the level of integrating a great deal of information throughout the chapter, then the unit of measure might need to be on the level of information organization throughout the chapter.

Selection of the most appropriate CASA unit is initially based on the failure of the student to process the task that most closely approximates the desired behavior. For example, the decision to focus on how Craig acquired information was based on the fact that he had failed all tests and assignments on the content of the previous chapter. Combined with the information on the content demands of the class, it was easy to focus on the acquisition of information from the text. However, to pinpoint where the intervention and content assessment process will be most beneficial, the teacher must start by assessing several informal CASA units. If the student demonstrates skill and content mastery at each unit check, then the teacher can proceed to the next larger CASA unit (e.g., paragraph level to section level).

An informal CASA unit check might consist of a task that approximates what the student is expected to do for that particular content-learning task. For example, if the student is expected to read and remember what he has read, a paragraph level check in which the student reads silently and then explains the content of the paragraph in an oral fashion may best approximate the demand. Writing the information remembered from the paragraph may also be part of the task. Yet requiring the student to write, significantly changes the demand that was originally of interest (i.e., reading and remembering). If the student writes about what he has read in a paragraph, the teacher moves further away from the *demand* of fluent reading. A simple verbal response, although not part of the natural reading process, more closely approximates what the student might say to himself or herself as he or she reads.

If the student successfully generates the appropriate content from the paragraph-level check, then the teacher may move to a section- or topic-level check. Here, a writing or notetaking task may be more appropriate. Processing a section of a text will require the integration of information across paragraphs and, thus, reflection and decision making related to the relative importance of information.

Step 4: Construct the CASA Measure

Once the type of CASA unit has been identified, the next step is to construct a measure that you can apply on a consistent basis. We have found that there are two primary dimensions that must be included in the CASA measure. The first measure is a direct measure of content that indicates how effective the student is in meeting the content-acquisition demand. The second measure is a measure of the process that the student is using to meet the demand of content learning. This second measure is an efficiency measure of the student's application of a basic academic skill. Together, the two measures provide a comprehensive assessment of the student's knowledge, skills, and abilities. Figure 9.8 shows these two dimensions of the CASA measurement system.

To determine the effectiveness of content acquisition, the teacher must evaluate the quantity and quality of information demonstrated by the student. These terms are used in a slightly different way here than elsewhere in this book. Quantity is a measure of how much information is generated by the student for a given CASA Unit. For example,

CONTENT MEASUREMENT DIMENSIONS

DIMENSIONS	DEFINITIONS
EFFECTIVENESS MEASURES	
QUANTITY	The amount of information demonstrated on the measure
QUALITY	The accuracy and nature of the information demonstrated on the measure
EFFICIENCY MEASURES	
SPEED OF RESPONSE	The amount of time required to correctly respond to the demand
RESPONSE TO CUES	The degree to which a correct response is provided when importance cues are provided (e.g., color, bold print, verbal cues, etc.)
PHYSICAL ACTIONS	The degree to which the student can be observed correctly responding to a demand
INDICATORS OF MENTAL ACTION	The degree to which the student correctly explains how a demand is being met as the task is performed

Figure 9.8. Content Measurement Dimensions

a student may learn 16 out of 20 pieces of content information from a five-paragraph CASA unit. Another dimension of the effectiveness of content acquisition is a measure of quality. Distinguishing accuracy from quantity permits a more comprehensive representation of what the student has learned. For example, a section of a text may contain 100 pieces of information that are judged by the teacher as being important. A quantity score will tell you that the student demonstrated mastery of 70 out of 100 pieces of information. However, if the teacher wants to evaluate the structure and relationship of the information that has been learned, then the teacher might want to represent this performance through a quality measure. A quality measure indicates knowledge of the number of main ideas and details or concepts, facts, and rules that were demonstrated by the student. Figure 9.9 shows how the 80/100 quality score can give more direction to the teacher on the type of feedback to provide a particular student on the task.

Efficiency represents the second important dimension that should be a part of the CASA measure. Efficiency is evaluated through the student's (a) speed of response, (b) response to specific cues, (c) physical actions, and (d) indications of mental action. *Speed of response* is a simple measure of the rate at which the student responds to the content demand. A slow response or too speedy a response in relation to quantity and quality may indicate that the students' strategy (i.e., approach to the task) is not efficient. The students' *response to cues* is a measure of how well the student responds to cues presented in the content-learning demand. For example, if in a lecture the teacher cued the student 10 times that specific information was to be on a test, the student's notes should be checked to see if the cues in textbooks such as highlighted words, visuals, and study questions may also be included in the CASA measure. These responses can provide the basis for excellent feedback and intervention decisions. The student's *physical actions* can also be a source of valuable assessment information. If a task requires a specific observable action, then this can be part of the CASA unit. For example, if the task requires the student to skip every other line in writing, this may have little effect on the quantity, quality, accuracy, or speed of response, but may be part of the strategy that contributes to the *process* of editing and producing a written product that is better overall. The final area of assessment relates to the *mental actions* in which a student might be engaging. While it may be impossible to observe mental action, indicators of mental action can be assessed. The common way of assessing a student's strategies for learning is to have the student "think aloud" during the task. For example, the teacher may want to coach the student to ask himself or herself questions at specific points in the process. The teacher can then require that these questions be asked orally. This permits the teacher to monitor the student's questions and responses. Unless specifically required as a part of the task, this type of measure is often used as part of the intervention process. The measure may not be useful for ongoing assessment because it places great debriefing and listening demands on the teacher's time. However, it may *have* to be included in the assessment process if the student does not respond to initial intervention efforts. This type of assessment is particularly valuable when a teacher needs to investigate why a particular intervention is not working.

Figure 9.10 shows how a CASA measurement system is applied to a number of content-learning demands. The CASA measurement system must reflect variables that are critical indicators of success on the content-learning task. In general, the more dif-

Which type of score provides more information for feedback to the student?

Quantity Score		Quality Score	
Number of items on the test	Number of items correct	Number of main idea items on the test	Number of main idea items correct
		25	1
100	70	Number of detail items on the test	Number of detail items correct
		75	69

Figure 9.9. Sample Scoring Procedures

ficulty the student has with a task, the greater the need will be for corrective feedback—thus the greater the need for pinpointing the most appropriate types of assessment information.

STEP 5: Implement the CASA Measurement System

There are four guidelines for implementing CASA. First, the CASA measurement system must be implemented in conjunction with ongoing content instruction. Second, the frequency of assessment must be based on the *cost* of the measure. Third, the CASA

CONTENT AREA SKILL ASSESSMENT PLAN

STUDENT'S NAME: _Craig_   CONTENT AREA: _American History_

UNIT	EFFECTIVENESS MEASURES		EFFICIENCY MEASURES			
	QUANTITY	QUALITY	SPEED OF RESPONSE	RESPONSE TO CUES	PHYSICAL ACTIONS	INDICATORS OF MENTAL ACTION
Read 5 paragraphs and paraphrase their content into a tape recorder	3 pieces of information from each paragraph	1 main idea and at least 2 details paraphrased	Record actual time	X	X	X
Read a chapter section and take notes	Count the number of pieces of info in notes	Correct segregation of main ideas from details	Amount of time divided by # of words	% age of noted info cued by bolded and italicized print	X	Indicates use of paragraph & chapter structure to organize notes
Take notes on a one minute lecture	Count the number of pieces of info in notes	Correct segregation of main ideas from details	X	% age of noted words cued by teacher use of organizers (e.g. "1st, 2nd, 3rd" "this is important")	X	X
memorize the lists of information on 2 pages of text	% age of information correctly identified	accuracy of information in lists	amount of time divided by the number of list items possible	X	X	X

Figure 9.10. Sample Content Area Skill Assessment Plan

implementation must lead to student feedback as well as specific and positive intervention decisions. Fourth, students must be taught to be responsible for the implementation of the CASA system. Each of these guidelines will now be discussed.

Implement in Conjunction with Ongoing Content Instruction.   The primary purpose of CASA is to evaluate content learning in relation to the strategies that either the teacher or the student applies to facilitate learning. Accordingly, the units of measure and the material used for assessment should be based on actual content material that the student must face in regular content-learning circumstances.

Using a different set of materials and content does not accurately assess the student's ability to respond to actual content-learning demands. However, in some circumstances, the assessment can be separated from ongoing content-learning demands. These circumstances will be addressed later, but for the most part this should be avoided.

The Frequency of Assessment Is Contingent on Cost.   While many assessment models do not directly address the "cost" of assessment, "cost" is usually a top concern of teachers. In general, "cost" refers to the resources as measured in effort, time, and material to obtain the essential information for the measure. Cost will be different for each teacher. For example, a teacher who has 15 students in a class may not be able to *afford* to give two students a five-minute CASA unit lecture every single day. A teacher with 5 students may be able to *afford* this type of measure. The teacher with 15 students may be able to implement the assessment procedure only three times a week.

Assessment costs must also be balanced against the benefits associated with assessment. The benefits are more accurately measured in terms of student effects. That is, the assessment should be frequent enough to guide teachers in decision making that leads to student progress. Let us assume that a teacher decides that the five-minute lecture-type CASA measure can only be given once a week. The teacher collects the assessment information and begins to intervene. The effects of the intervention are then measured by implementing assessment based on the five-minute lecture-type CASA unit once a week. If the student improves on the CASA measure *and* notetaking in the regular class improves, then the frequency of once a week might be judged as a cost effective choice. However, if the student does not improve, the teacher probably cannot continue with the once a week check because it does not provide enough information on which to provide feedback and make effective intervention decisions. If the teacher does not increase the frequency of assessment, then instructional time and learning time is wasted. In effect, infrequent assessment costs more in the long run because it is useless.

Implementation of the CASA Unit Must Lead to Intervention Decisions.   Once the CASA measure is implemented, the teacher must use the assessment information to make specific remedial instruction decisions. If the student has not shown improvement after consecutive, consistent implementation of the CASA unit, then the teacher needs to revise instruction to bring about improved performance. The types of interventions that might be selected will be discussed later, but as part of the assessment process the teacher may need to evaluate whether the CASA unit is *sensitive* to the intervention.

For example, a comprehension measure may not be sensitive to an intervention focused on improving a student's word identification performance.

The Student Needs to Be Involved in the CASA Process.   Students should play a major role in the assessment process. In general, students need to:

1.   be given a rationale for the CASA process;
2.   be given an explanation of the relationship between skills and content acquisition;
3.   have the results of the CASA process and their implications explained;
4.   be involved in identifying the types of intervention that will be implemented for success with content learning;
5.   have the assessment charting process explained;
6.   be responsible for following the assessment schedule, obtaining feedback on performance from the teacher, and charting progress on a graph; and,
7.   be responsible for monitoring progress and, if appropriate, informing the teacher for the need for a change in the intervention.

We should point out that these assessment activities do not take place in the absence of teacher supervision. The teacher must check all the activities that the student is expected to complete independently, and give the student feedback on his or her attention to the assessment responsibilities.

STEP 6: Select an Intervention

Content acquisition decisions can focus on either the student or on the teacher. Interventions that focus on the student depend on the teacher's ability to change the delivery of content in a manner that will result in *specific* content learning.

Selecting Student-centered Interventions.   Student-centered interventions are selected according to the type of content-learning demands to be met. Therefore, interventions will focus on assisting students to master strategies that will enable them to acquire, store, and express information and demonstrate competence. Regardless of their focus, strategies define how an individual should approach a task, and include how a person thinks and acts when planning, executing, and evaluating performance on a task and its outcomes. A student is taught a strategy in order to make the student a more effective and efficient learner. Generally speaking, a strategy consists of critical guidelines and rules for selecting the best procedure related to meeting a specific demand and making decisions about its use. A procedure is simply a set of steps related to a component analysis of a basic academic skill (e.g., long division procedure, changing a word into the plural form using the "add s" rule, and so forth). Therefore, strategies *guide* the section and application of basic academic skills already mastered by the student.

Usually, strategy instruction focuses on teaching general task-specific strategies that will address a set of learning demands that the student might experience across a number of settings (e.g., listening to lectures, reading textbooks, taking a test). However, situation-specific strategies can also be taught for addressing a very narrow task demand (e.g., passing the drivers education test, reading the biology text, and so forth). These interventions can generally lead to content gains in a specific area, but rarely have an impact on similar content-learning tasks in other courses. Therefore, situation-specific strategies can be used to assist a student to meet a demand that must be faced immediately, while instruction in task-specific strategies is used to assist students to meet demands across settings and over time.

Probably the most fully researched set of task-specific strategy interventions are those that have been included in the Strategies Intervention Model (Deshler & Schumaker, 1986, 1988) developed by the staff and their colleagues at the University of Kansas Institute for Research in Learning Disabilities. Although the model was initially developed for use primarily with students with learning disabilities, the strategies have been found to be successful with other low-achieving students, and with others who are academically and behaviorally at-risk. This model includes a set of strategy interventions that have been matched to specific demands that students must frequently face in content-area classes encountered beginning in about the fifth grade. Although strategies related to assisting students to meet social and motivational demands related to school success have also been developed, the Learning Strategies Curriculum of the Strategies Intervention Model was specifically designed to improve students' academic performance in content area learning. A list of the strategies that have been included in this curriculum are provided in Figure 9.11. Each of these strategy interventions contains an assessment system that matches the CASA dimensions that have been described in this chapter.

Teacher-centered Interventions.   Teacher-centered interventions are also selected according to the content-learning demands that must be met. However, the interventions selected here focus on a teacher's ability to change the delivery of content in a manner that will result in specific content learning. Delivery refers to all activities engaged in by the teacher to promote content acquisition. It includes the selection and use of texts, classroom presentation, organization of information, classroom learning activities, assignments, and tests. Therefore, a teacher-centered intervention places no demands on the student to change how he or she processes information. Rather it places demands on how the teacher can compensate for the students' *lack* of strategies to attack the task of learning the content.

Teacher-centered interventions can be implemented by the content teacher or by the remedial or special education teacher. If a regular content teacher implements the interventions, the intervention would be infused into the routine activities of the regular class. Such interventions might include: cooperative learning groups, lecture routines, advance organizers, or concept mapping. Each of these is designed to increase the student's learning activities which in turn promote understanding and retention (see Bulgren, Schumaker, & Deshler, 1988; Deshler & Schumaker, 1988; Lenz, Alley, Schumaker, 1987; Lovitt, Rudsit, Jenkins, Pious & Benedetti, 1986; Stowitschek, Gable, & Hendrickson, 1980).

A model for enhancing the delivery of content has also been developed by the staff of the University of Kansas Institute for Research in Learning Disabilities and their colleagues. The Content Enhancement Model (Lenz, Bulgren, & Hudson, 1989) consists of three major components designed to enhance the delivery of content acquisition

LEARNING STRATEGIES CURRICULUM
The University of Kansas
Institute for Research in Learning Disabilities

ACQUISITION STRAND

Word Identification Strategy: teaches students a problem-solving procedure for quickly attacking and decoding unknown words in reading materials allowing them to move on quickly for the purpose of comprehending the passage.

Paraphrasing Strategy: directs students to read a limited section of material, ask themselves the main idea and the details of the section, and put that information in their own words. This strategy is designed to improve comprehension by focusing attention on the important information of a passage and by stimulating active involvement with the passage.

Self-questioning Strategy: aids reading comprehension by having students actively ask questions about key pieces of information in a passage and then read to find the answers for these questions.

Visual Imagery Strategy: designed to improve students' acquisition, storage, and recall of prose material. Students improve reading comprehension by reading short passages and visualizing the scene which is described, incorporating actors, action, and details.

Interpreting Visuals Strategy: designed to aid students in the use and interpretation of visuals such as maps, graphs, pictures, and tables to increase their ability to extract needed information from written materials.

Multipass Strategy: involves making three passes through a passage for the purpose of focusing attention on key details and main ideas. Students survey a chapter or passage to get an overview, size up sections of the chapter by systematically scanning to locate relevant information which they note, and sort out important information in the chapter by locating answers to specific questions.

STORAGE STRAND

FIRST-Letter Mnemonic Strategy: designed to aid students in memorizing lists of information by teaching them to design mnemonics or memorization aids, and to find and make lists of crucial information.

Paired Associates Strategy: designed to aid students in memorizing pairs or small groups of information by using visual imagery, matching pertinent information with familiar objects, coding important dates, and a first-syllable technique.

Listening and Notetaking Strategy: designed to teach students to develop skills which will enhance their ability to learn from listening experiences by identifying the speaker's verbal cues or mannerisms which signal that important information is about to be given, noting key words, and organizing their notes into an outline for future reference or study.

EXPRESSION AND DEMONSTRATION OF COMPETENCE STRAND

Sentence Writing Strategy: designed to teach students how to recognize and generate four types of sentences: simple, compound, complex, and compound-complex.

Paragraph Writing Strategy: designed to teach students how to write well-organized, complete paragraphs by outlining ideas, selecting a point-of-view and tense for the paragraph, sequencing ideas, and checking their work.

Error Monitoring Strategy: designed to teach students a process for detecting and correcting errors in their writing and for producing a neater written product. Students are taught to locate errors in paragraph organization, sentence structure, capitalization, overall editing and appearance, punctuation, and spelling by asking themselves a series of questions. Students correct their errors and rewrite the passage before submitting it to their teacher.

Theme Writing Strategy: teaches students to write a five-paragraph theme. They learn how to generate ideas for themes and how to organize these ideas into a logical sequence. Then the student learns how to write the paragraphs, monitor errors, and rewrite the theme.

Assignment Completion Strategy: teaches students to monitor their assignments from the time an assignment is given until it is completed and turned in to the teacher. Students write down assignments; analyze the assignments; schedule various subtasks; complete the subtasks and, ultimately, the entire task; and submit the completed assignment.

Test Taking Strategy: designed to be used by the student during a test. The student is taught to allocate time and read instructions and questions carefully. A question is either answered or abandoned for later consideration. The obviously wrong answers are eliminated from the abandoned questions and a reasonable guess is made. The last step is to survey the entire test for unanswered questions.

The University of Kansas Institute for Research in Learning Disabilities, 2-89

Figure 9.11. Learning Strategies Curriculum

SOURCE: Figure 11, *Learning Strategies: A Curriculum Framework,* by J. B. Schumaker, F. L. Clark, D. D. Deshler, and B. K. Lenz, 1989, The University of Kansas Institute for Research in Learning Disabilities, 2-89. Reprinted by permission.

of low-achieving students. The first component consists of Content Enhancement Planning that focuses on the instructional planning process; it includes how a teacher selects, plans, and evaluates information for content delivery and acquisition. The second component consists of Content Enhancement Routines that focus on how a teacher organizes the lesson to achieve teaching objectives; it includes how a teacher infuses concept teaching, advance organizers, and other active learning activities into content instruction. The third component consists of Content Enhancement Devices that focus on the infusion of learning techniques throughout the lesson. These are aimed at student understanding and remembering of specific content elements.

Content Enhancement Planning is primarily concerned with teacher thinking and decision making about the what and how of teaching content. However, the Content Enhancement Routines and Devices are concerned with the direct delivery of content.

In general, there are four phases which are important to the implementation of these enhancements. First, the teacher must teach students about the enhancement. For example, if the teacher is to use a lecture outline as an enhancement, then the teacher must teach the students about the purpose and structure of the outline, and explain and model how it is to be completed. Students must be taught to a specified mastery level in the use of the outline. Second, the teacher must cue students when the enhancement is being used and must facilitate positive applications of the enhancement. For example, if the teacher is going to provide a mnemonic device to students to help them remember a difficult list of information, the teacher should specifically tell students that a mnemonic device will be constructed. Third, enlisting the aid of students, the teacher should present the enhancement. For example, if the teacher is going to provide an advance organizer to students, the teacher must teach the students about advance organizers, cue students when the advance organizer is being generated, then actively engage students in the process of constructing the advance organizer. Fourth, the teacher should reach closure on the enhancement by reviewing the enhancement process. For example, after a concept teaching routine has been implemented, the teacher should review the concept and check to determine whether the desired enhancement has been achieved.

MAKING DECISIONS ABOUT INTERVENTION

Evaluating the relative merits of student-centered versus teacher-centered interventions is difficult. In general, student-centered interventions can provide the student with skills and strategies for meeting content-learning demands that must be faced over a lifetime. In contrast, teacher-centered interventions can assist the student in meeting content-learning demands that must be faced immediately. Accordingly, a combination of interventions may need to be selected to promote both the short-term and long-term success of the student in meeting content-learning demands. However, the more teacher-centered the intervention, the more important it becomes to determine how efficient the teacher is in compensating for a student's lack of skills and strategies.

SUMMARY

Success in the middle and secondary grades is often dependent upon the student's ability to demonstrate mastery of not only basic applications but also knowledge that comprises the content areas. As a result, the assessment process used by middle and secondary teachers needs to go beyond the simple evaluation of either basic academic skills or content knowledge. Rather, it should become more sensitive to the learning demands of the content that exist across both of those dimensions. The CASA process that we have discussed provides a model for evaluating skill and strategy acquisition and the effect of both student-centered and teacher-centered interventions on content learning. The combination of aspects of the error analysis presented in other chapters with content-area assessment should yield a more full and more complete picture of a student's instructional needs.

DISCUSSION QUESTIONS AND ACTIVITIES

1. Interview a secondary-school teacher to learn more about classroom assessment in the content area.
2. Interview a secondary-school psychologist to learn about the relationship between formal assessment and classroom planning for instruction.
3. Review an achievement test that covers content areas to learn more about information that can be obtained from standardized test administration.
4. Select one or more of the strategies discussed and adapt it to your teaching situation.

CHAPTER 10

Making Error Analysis Work

Robert A. Gable
Old Dominion University

Jo M. Hendrickson
University of Iowa

CHAPTER OBJECTIVES

After reading this chapter you should be able to:

1. Discuss ways of determining assessment priorities according to individual student needs.
2. Discuss ways of using available resources to make assessment more practical.
3. Identify the steps necessary to increase the validity and reliability of teacher-made tests.

KEY TERMS

audiotutorial assessment reliable
ecological influences   valid

INTRODUCTION

As we have been emphasizing throughout the book, when the goal is instruction, direct, repeated measurement and analysis of a student's academic responses is the most useful form of assessment. Even so, many teachers are reluctant to replace the occasional use of standardized, norm-referenced tests with more content-specific procedures. Few teachers have been trained in the technical skills necessary to analyze student error patterns (Bennett, 1983). A common fear is that the time spent evaluating student performance will become so excessive that little time will remain for carrying out instruction. We acknowledge that introduction of error analysis into an already demanding schedule requires special planning. To many teachers, it may seem that nothing less than sorcery will satisfy the demands of establishing and maintaining an effective plan for assessment *and* instruction. This final chapter, therefore, is aimed at making error analysis work for you. To do so, we will discuss five strategies for integrating assessment and instruction.

STRATEGY 1: ADMINISTER VALID AND RELIABLE TESTS

As we discussed in previous chapters, questions surrounding the validity and reliability of norm-referenced, standardized tests are equally applicable to teacher-made tests. One way to make classroom assessment more content valid is to select test items from the curriculum of daily instruction—this will ensure that your test measures what you intend it to measure. In devising a technically sound test, you must recognize that some subject areas and their content will be more functional or meaningful to students than others (Howell & Morehead, 1987). Teacher decision-making also relates to the selection of the criteria used to distinguish acceptable from unacceptable performance. Various authorities have sought to establish criterion validity in informal assessment of basic curricular areas (e.g., Deno, Mirkin, & Chiang, 1982; Lovitt & Hansen, 1976a; Starlin, 1982). It has also been suggested that the performance of other competent learners can serve as a standard (Choate et al., 1987). Even so, some standards may not fit every student or every instructional situation.

Another issue regarding test construction is more easily resolved. This is the number of actual test items. The general rule-of-thumb is that curriculum-based tests used for error analysis should contain no fewer than five items that correspond to a specific skill (Bennett, 1982).

The second major aspect of informal assessment pertains to standard administration procedures. To increase the likelihood that you will have a reliable assessment program and can repeatedly test what you intend to test, you must control certain variables. Variables to control when conducting an error analysis include:

1. The number of test items (e.g., anywhere from 5 to 50 items);
2. The way in which the student responds to each item (e.g., orally or in writing);
3. The location of the test's administration (e.g., student's desk, teacher's desk, test center);
4. The time allotted for completing the test (e.g., one minute, five minutes);
5. The material used in the test (e.g., flash cards, skill sheets, weekly readers);
6. The person administering the test (e.g., a teacher with whom the student(s) feels comfortable);
7. The administration and scoring procedures (e.g., group versus individual, whole-versus partial-response credit) (e.g., spelling scored by word or syllable).
8. The test items that you analyze (e.g., the student's first responses may be regarded as ''warm-up'' and last as ''wind down'').

STRATEGY 2: MAKE ASSESSMENT DECISIONS ON A CONTENT-SPECIFIC AND STUDENT-SPECIFIC BASIS

Generally, the required level of specificity, from math worksheets completed to the number of digits/operations correct, and the frequency of assessment, from once a week to every lesson, depend on several interrelated factors. These include the curricular content and the discrepancy between the student's current performance and what you hold as a reasonable performance expectation. In analyzing student error patterns, we are reminded of the expression, "If it isn't broken, don't fix it." In error analysis, this means that if a student is progressing satisfactorily in reading and arithmetic but evidencing persistent problems in spelling, you would then concentrate on conducting a thorough analysis of the spelling difficulties. To measure progress, you would administer only periodic assessment in reading or arithmetic.

Whereas some students may evidence learning problems in every curricular area, others may have difficulty in only one or two subjects. We concur with those who recommend that the basic or core curriculum areas of reading, arithmetic and written language are generally the most significant academic subjects (e.g., Choate et al., 1987). The responsibility rests with the teacher to set assessment and instruction priorities for individual students. It is important to recognize the objective *and* subjective aspects of these decisions.

Choate and her colleagues (Choate et al., 1987) categorize academics according to core curriculum, collateral curriculum, and support curriculum. As we mentioned, the core curriculum is comprised of reading, mathematics, and written expression. Collateral curriculum pertains to content areas such as science and social studies. The support curriculum consists of spelling, handwriting and study skills. The use of these three general categories helps guide us in singling out areas for in-depth assessment.

In the primary grades, it may be useful to begin with the above sequence—first, reading, then arithmetic, and finally, written language. As students advance through grades the success in *all* subject areas hinges on a student's skills in the three basic or core curricular areas. Unfortunately, as students are promoted to higher grades less attention is given to the assessment and instruction of these basic skills. Rather than abandoning assessment of the core areas subject areas, we recommend that teachers use various content areas to monitor student progress (e.g., edit a science essay for spelling, grammar, and handwriting). In all, the decisions you make regarding *what* content to assess and *how* intensely to do so should be governed by individual student need.

As a first step, we suggest that you select one student and one subject area to apply error analysis. It is advisable to not attempt to integrate a new assessment practice with an entire class. To do so would likely result in both mistakes and teacher frustration. By comparison, initiating the procedure with one student and in one subject area affords you the opportunity to try out, refine, and gain confidence in the use of error analysis in the classroom. Ordinarily, this sequence of events takes about three to five weeks. After this you should be ready to expand evaluation efforts, first to other students and then to new curricular areas. Teachers who have used error analysis procedures view the process as a series of steps. They make time to reward themselves for accomplishing each of the steps that together comprise the procedure.

STRATEGY 3: MAKE QUALITY
PLACEMENT DECISIONS

In the past, decisions regarding grouping students for instruction usually were linked to information gleaned from norm-referenced, standardized test scores. As intuitively appealing as this practice may be, it has some major flaws. For example, a group test may yield grade equivalent scores that indicate ten students are performing at the 3.4 level in word recognition and word analysis. Although unlikely, it is possible that no two students answered any of the test questions exactly the same way. While their overall scores make it appear that these students are well-matched for instruction, a closer look may reveal that they share few common strengths or weaknesses. Accordingly, the teacher might temporarily group together only those students who answered the same questions incorrectly. It then becomes useful to discover if they made the same kind of mistakes—error analysis! As you can see, it is still possible to carry out initial steps of assessment in a group while curricular placement is predicated on the identification of common error types and common learning objectives. Once the teacher has taught these objectives, a new instructional group can be established. Some students may remain in the group because they continue to share learning objectives; others will join in other groups. This process of "flow-grouping" in which students come together on a time-limited basis for instruction on common objectives is well-suited to individualized assessment practices.

STRATEGY 4: MAKE FULL USE
OF CURRICULUM
AND TECHNOLOGY OPTIONS

The use of audiotutorial assessment procedures is one way of incorporating available technology into classroom assessment and instruction. Audiotutorial assessment refers to use of audio equipment in carrying out the assessment process. The teacher usually prepares material and with a tape recorder, administers the test. Audiotutorial assessment offers a means for individualizing assessment, provides a bridge between group and one-to-one assessment, and is a practical way to connect assessment and instruction. Finally, audiotutorial assessment offsets the negative aspects of adult-controlled assessment for some students (Stowitschek, Gable, & Hendrickson, 1980).

For students to function independent of teacher direction, they should incorporate frequent self-checks into audiotutorial assessment. These self-checks might, for example, consist of paper-and-pencil exercises that accompany a taped program and call on the student to answer several short questions that deal with correct procedures for completing the program. To increase the likelihood of the success of an audiotutorial program, you may need a series of supervised practice exercises in which students are led step-by-step through a sample program (e.g., the "free dictation" format for spelling). During this training phase, students should be taught how to operate the tape recorder or other equipment as well as how and when to respond.

Steps to Develop an Audiotutorial Assessment Program

1. Establish educational objectives in relation to student ability and needs.
2. Prepare tests packets and material based on student skills and needs in the selected content area(s).
3. Develop administration procedures, either written or audiotaped, that include instructions for students on the use of answer sheets, record forms, and so on.
4. Place students in an assessment program according to information obtained from cumulative folders or preliminary test data (e.g., standardized achievement test).
5. Introduce the audiotutorial procedure; then, observe and evaluate student performance for purposes of program modification.

Equipment necessary for conducting audiotutorial assessment includes prerecorded tapes (e.g., math facts, spelling words), a cassette audiotape recorder, and earplugs or headphones. Subject areas that are particularly adaptive to audiotutorial assessment include arithmetic, spelling, punctuation, handwriting, and language development (Stowitschek et al., 1980).

As discussed in Chapter 8, using computers for assessment represents another major teaching resource. Like audiotutorial assessment, computer-assisted assessment, without detracting from instruction, allows for the analysis of student performance. Programs that are simple to operate—and this includes ones with a voice synthesizer (e.g., for repeatedly dictating spelling words in free dictation)—can save the teacher time, reduce mistakes in scoring work samples, and produce information relevant to instructional decisions. In summary, the future holds a wide range of technological innovations for linking assessment and remediation.

STRATEGY 5: MAKE FULL USE OF AVAILABLE RESOURCES

Students are one of the most reliable and useful classroom resources. Yet, they are one that is often times overlooked. Indeed, students are capable of carrying out fairly complex assessment programs accurately and enthusiastically. Classmates may serve as test monitors and be responsible for checking and rescoring other students' written work. Test monitors can be taught to maintain daily performance records on other students. In other instances, classmates have been taught to reliably administer paper-and-pencil tests and to audiotape the oral recitation of other students. Students function most successfully as an assessment resource if one section of the classroom is designated as the test center. This area should be used only for administering, scoring, and charting students' academic performance. (Answer keys or the teacher's manual can be distributed on a lesson-by-lesson basis or stored in an accessible location.)

SUMMARY AND CONCLUSION

It would be a mistake to fail to point out the fact that a student's academic performance is the product of a multitude of factors. Not understanding the concept of regrouping in arithmetic may be one of them. Student performance is also inextricably bound to contextual factors within the classroom and beyond. Commonly referred to as ecological variables, factors ranging from hunger, fatigue, and anxiety to family discord may influence student performance. So may instructional arrangement and the material used. The teacher must be alert to environmental factors that may negatively effect a student's behavior. While some of these influences are beyond your control, recognition of the larger context of performance and instruction can contribute to your better understanding each student. In sum, we must remember that a variety of reasons may explain mistakes students make in their work.

SOME FINAL THOUGHTS ON MAKING ERROR ANALYSIS WORK FOR YOU

1. Begin with one student and one subject area. Set a reasonable timeline, usually about three weeks, to initiate and refine the error-analysis procedure.
2. Collect error analysis data *only* on essential or priority academic skills and *only* on those students who are not performing satisfactorily. Chart student performance immediately (or as soon as possible) after collecting the work samples.
3. Establish an assessment station used only for administering, scoring, and providing students with feedback on their performance.
4. Teach volunteers, parents, and classmates to administer probes and to collect and chart data on student performance.
5. Teach yourself or obtain further training on how to become more efficient in assessment—specifically, learn error analysis and program revision(s).

By integrating error analysis, planning, and remedial instruction into a *cycle* that is repeated across time, you can make decisions on *what* and *how* to teach as well as *how well* it is being taught (Zigmond, Vallecorsa, & Silverman, 1983). As we have discussed in preceding chapters, however, some caution is suggested in the practice of error analysis. As McLoughlin and Lewis (1986) point out, decisions on what constitutes an error, how it should be categorized, how many mistakes constitute a problem, and what to do about it—these are not always clear cut. Finally, we recognize that you already have a difficult task completing the various instructional, organizational, and managerial responsibilities associated with teaching. Realistically, not every teacher will be able to make full use of every chart or procedure that we have discussed. In closing we urge you to select and to apply those procedures best suited to your particular needs. We hope that the book serves as a resource and a steppingstone to improved assessment and remediation.

Glossary

Aim star. The point plotted on a graph where the desired level of performance and the target date for achieving that level of performance intersect.

AIM STAR. An integrated set of computer programs used to implement curriculum-based assessment procedures.

Algorithm. A step-by-step procedure for solving an arithmetic problem.

Arithmetic operation. A solution to the computation of a problem (e.g., addition, subtraction).

Artificial intelligence. A branch of computer science devoted to researching ways to make the computer emulate those attributes we classify as human intelligence.

Audiotutorial assessment. The use of pretaped audiomaterial to obtain information on placement and instruction.

Automaticity. The immediacy of a student response to a stimulus (e.g., arithmetic problem, spelling word).

Basal reader. A sequentially graded series of instructional material (e.g., readers, workbooks), written specifically to develop students' basic reading skills.

Bias. Unfairness in testing. Bias may influence the interpretation of scores and test content, the view of the development process, or the organization of the procedures with which the test is administered.

CAMS (Chronometric Analysis of Math Strategies). An interactive computer program designed for classroom assessment of fluency of mathematics facts.

CBA (Computer Based Assessment). Specific techniques used to analyze instructional data, for example, the amount of time required to complete a task, or the number of correct and incorrect responses used to determine whether an instructional program is working and if any instructional strategies should be changed.

Chronometric analysis. An analysis of a student's response-latency data. It provides a profile of the student's strategy for solving the problems.

Cloze procedure. The systematic deletion of words from a printed passage for the purpose of determining the reader's ability to supply the deleted words. It is used to determine reading comprehension and the readability level of written material.

Computation skill. The arithmetic operations of addition, subtraction, multiplication, and division of whole numbers, fractions, and decimals.

Content demands. The type of information that a student needs to learn for a particular class.

Content demonstrations. The ways a student can show mastery of material.

Content drivers. The forces that singly and collectively determine what is important to teach.

Copy. To imitate or reproduce an original item or model.

Criterion-referenced test. An assessment device designed to measure the student's ability to reach a predetermined level of performance on a specific task.

Curriculum-based measurement. An assessment system within which testing materials are derived from curriculum content. In it, measurement is ongoing, and assessment information is used to develop instructional programs.

Cursive. Writing in which the letters are jointed and flow together.

DEBUGGY. One of the earliest expert systems designed for education. It is used for diagnosing student errors or "bugs" in the domain of place-value subtraction.

Derivational relationship. The relation of a word to another word or base (e.g., changing a word by adding a prefix).

Developmentally at risk. Students who are at risk of having substantial developmental delays if early intervention services are not provided.

Developmentally delayed. Students who have established delays in developmental area(s) according to a state's definition.

Developmental stage. A phase in the orderly progression of learning.

Diagnostic assessment. A measuring device used to determine causes of learning problems, and/or areas of specific strengths and weaknesses.

Ecological influences. Personal and environmental factors that may affect student performance (e.g., anger towards a peer; some special interest in the content of a lesson).

Error analysis. The analysis of a work sample to identify specific error types and set priorities for teaching.

Errorless learning. Procedures that prevent a student from performing an incorrect response.

Expert system. Computer software that emulates the functioning of a human expert in a particular field of knowledge.

Faulty algorithms. A skill or series of skills a student incorrectly has developed to solve specific types of problems.

Fluency. A measurement of response latency for a skill or set of skills.

Formative test. An assignment or test administered while learning is in progress.

Free-dictation format. A way of presenting spelling in which the words for the lesson are embedded in sentences comprised of "easy reading vocabulary."

Grapheme. A visual symbol used to represent units of sound (phonemes in written language).

Handwriting. The production of written symbols to convey information.

IFSP (Individual Family Service Plan). A component of PL 99-457 that requires a written plan for comprehensive services to handicapped infants, toddlers, and their families.

Informal Reading Inventory (IRI). An informal instrument consisting of sequentially graded reading selections. It is employed to indicate areas of instructional need.

Interactive assessment. Software programs in which the computer carrying out and analyzing the assessment data acts in the role of examiner.

Knowledge engineer. The person who develops a knowledge base and a set of decision rules that represent the thinking process of human expert (or group of experts) in a particular domain.

Legibility. readability; the degree to which the letters or words of a written product can be deciphered.

Line of progress. The trend of a student's progress. It is drawn from the median of the three most recent days of data, and the median of the three previous days of data.

Manuscript. Printed letters or numerals that are separated from each other.

Minimum 'celeration line. A line drawn from the student's current level of performance to the desired performance level (aim star). It indicates the minimum level of acceleration or decleration necessary to reach the criterion level of performance.

Miscue. An oral response to a printed test that does not conform to what is written. Rather, it involves the substitution of a similar or equivalent form which, however, does not interfere with the reader's comprehension.

Morpheme. The smallest, meaning-bearing unit of language. It is often a word or inflection.

Norm-referenced test. An evaluative instrument in which a person's performance is judged in comparison with the performance of those in a large reference group of students of similar age or educational level.

Oral edit. The second part of the error analysis in which the writer reads his or her writing sample into a tape recorder. Then, an evaluator scores discrepancies between the written and oral passages. The results determine priorities for teaching and teaching strategies.

Phoneme. The smallest unit of sound that distinguishes one utterance from another (e.g., *h*am and *P*am).

Phonetic approach. A basic decoding approach to reading that emphasizes the mastery of sound-symbol correspondence.

PL 99-457. The public law passed by Congress in 1986 that establishes new programs for handicapped infants, toddlers, and preschoolers.

Preacademics. Prerequisite skills and knowledge needed by preschoolers prior to and in preparation for traditional academic learning.

Precision teaching. A set of testing-teaching procedures in which the measurement and instructional processes are closely linked.

Prerequisite skills/concepts. Those abilities that a student must possess in order to succeed in learning a new skill/concept.

Previewing. A procedure in which students are exposed to material *before* instruction or recitation.

Production-response format. Test questions that require examinees to produce responses.

Psychometric characteristics. Features of tests. These include reliability, validity, and standardization procedures.

Raw score. The total number of correct responses.

Referral. A decision to seek further assistance or information on a student (e.g., referral for hearing test).

Reliable. (See reliability.)

Reliability. The consistency of test scores.

Response latency. A measure of the time it takes for a student to answer a question.

Screening. An initial assessment during which students who may evidence a particular problem are sorted out from the general population.

Selection-response format. Test questions that require examinees to select responses.

Self-analysis. Analysis procedures performed by the learners instead of the teacher.

Sight words. A whole word that a student recognizes in pronunciation and meaning without the aid of word analysis techniques.

Situation-specific strategy. A strategy that has narrow or limited application (e.g., passing a driver's test).

Summative test. A test that is administered at the end of a chapter or unit of instruction.

Syntactic complexity. The ability to express a large number of ideas in relatively few words as measured by the average words per T-unit (T-unit length). T-unit length is the total number of readable words in a writing sample divided by the number of T-units.

Systematic error. Some forms of inaccuracy in test scores. A given one always affects scores in the same way.

Tailored assessment. Assessment in which the problems represented to the student are based upon the student's responses to previous problems.

Task-specific strategy. A strategy that applies to task performance across time and situations.

Template overlay. Transparent pages containing model letters or numerals. For comparison purposes, they are superimposed over the letters or numerals produced by the learner.

Template underlay. Insert under semitransparent worksheets that contain the learner's letter or numeral production for comparison.

Test-procedure error. A form of test bias emanating from the procedures with which the test is administered.

Test-generation programs. Software programs designed to allow teachers to quickly and easily create an assessment instrument that covers specific skills and objectives and that does so at a specified level of difficulty.

Test scoring and reporting programs. Software programs designed to score and summarize student responses on an assessment instrument.

Tracing. The reproduction of a model or partial model directly on or over the model.

Transfer/Generalization. Skills acquired in a situation in which instruction is provided will be performed in situations in which no instruction is provided.

T-unit. An independent clause including any dependent clause attached to or embedded in it. If two or more independent clauses are joined by a conjunction (and, but, or so), they count as two T-units. The conjunction is counted as being at the beginning of the second T-unit. A quotation is the direct object of the verb *said* if it is attributed to a speaker. For example, "Go get him," he said. *Go get him* is the object of the verb *said*. Any other T-units in the quotation are separate T-units. For example, "Go get him," he said./ "I want to talk to him./ I think he knows where the secret papers are."

Valid. (See validity.)

Validity. The soundness with which test scores can be interpreted in relation to a particular skill or knowledge base.

Word analysis. The process of analyzing unknown words encountered in print.

Word recognition. The process of identifying the pronunciation and meaning of words encountered in print.

References

Addy, P., & Wylie, R.E. (1973). The 'right' way to write. *Childhood Education, 49*, 253–254.

Ainsworth, M. (1970). Object relations, dependency and attachment: A theoretical review of the infant-mother relationship. *Child Development, 40*, 969–1026.

American Psychological Association, American Educational Research Association, & National Council on Measurement in Education. (1985). *Standards for educational and psychological testing.* Washington, DC: American Psychological Association.

Anastasi, A. (1976). *Psychological testing.* (4th ed.). New York: Macmillan.

Anderson, R., Hiebert, E., Scott, H., & Wilkinson, I. (1985). *Becoming a nation of readers: The report of the commission on reading.* Washington, DC: National Institute of Education.

Ashlock, R.B. (1982). *Error patterns in computation* (3rd ed.). Columbus, OH: Merrill.

Askov, E.N., & Greff, K.N. (1975). Handwriting: Copying versus tracing as the most effective type of practice. *Journal of Educational Research, 64*, 96–98.

Axelrod, S., & Paluska, J. (1975). A component analysis of the effects of a classroom game on spelling performance. In E. Remp & G. Semb (Eds.), *Behavior analysis: Areas of research and application* (pp. 277–282). Englewood Cliffs, NJ: Prentice-Hall.

Ayres, L. (1912). *A scale for measuring the quality of handwriting of school children.* New York: Russell Sage Foundation.

Bachor, D. (1979). Using work samples as diagnostic information. *Learning Disability Quarterly, 2*, 45–53.

Bartholomae, D. (1980). The study of error. *College Composition and Communication, 31*, 253–269.

Bennett, R.E. (1982). Cautions for the use of informal measures in the educational assessment of exceptional children. *Journal of Learning Disabilities, 15*, 334–337.

Bennett, T.Z. (1983). Research and evaluation priorities for special education assessment. *Exceptional Children, 50*, 110–117.

Bereiter, C. (1968). *Arithmetic and mathematics.* San Rafael, CA: Dimensions.

Bijou, S.W., & Bear, D.M. (1978). *Behavior analysis of child development.* Englewood Cliffs, NJ: Prentice Hall.

Blankenship, C.S., & Lovitt, T. (1976). Story problems: Merely confusing or downright befuddling. *Journal of Research in Mathematics Education, 7*, 290–298.

Blurton-Jones, N. (1972). Characteristics of ethological studies of human behavior. In N. Burton-Jones (Ed.), *Ethological studies of child behavior.* London: Cambridge University Press.

Bricker, D.D. (1986). *Early education of at-risk and handicapped infants, toddlers, and pre-school children.* Glenview, IL: Scott, Foresman.

Brigance, A. (1977). *Brigance Diagnostic Inventory of Basic Skills®.* Woburn, MS: Curriculum Associates.

Brownstone Research Group. (1987). *Exam* [computer program]. Denver, CO: Brownstone Research Group.

Bulgren, J.A., Schumaker, J.B., & Deshler, D.D. (1988). Effectiveness of a concept teaching routine in enhancing and performance of LD students in secondary-level mainstream classes. *Learning Disability Quarterly, 11,* 3–17.

Burns, P. (1980). *Assessment and correction of language arts difficulties.* Columbus, OH: Merrill.

Buros, O.D. (Ed.). (1965). *Sixth mental measurement yearbook.* Highland Park, NJ: The Gryphon Press.

Burton, R. (1982). Diagnosing bugs in simple procedural skill. In D. Sleeman & J. Brown (Eds.), *Intelligent tutoring systems,* (pp. 157–183). New York: Academic Press.

Buswell, G.T., & John, L. (1925). *Fundamental processes in arithmetic.* Indianapolis: Bobbs-Merrill.

Cahen, I., Craun, M., & Johnson, S. (1971). Spelling difficulty: A survey of the research. *Review of Educational Research, 41,* 281–301.

Callahan, R.E. (1962). *Education and the cult of efficiency.* Chicago: University of Chicago.

Carnine, D., & Silbert, J. (1977). *Direct instruction reading.* Columbus, OH: Merrill.

Carpenter, D., & Miller, L. (1982). Spelling ability of reading disabled LD students and able readers. *Learning Disability Quarterly, 5,* 65–70.

Carroll, J.B., Davies, P., & Richman, B. (1971). *Word frequency book.* New York: Houghton Mifflin.

Cartwright, G. (1986). Written language abilities of educable mentally retarded and normal children. *American Journal of Mental Deficiency, 72,* 499–503.

Carver, R.P. (1974). Two dimensions of tests: Pschometric and edumetric. *American Psychologist, 29,* 512–518.

Cawley, J.F. (1978). An instructional design in mathematics. In L. Mann, L. Goodman, & L.L. Wiederholt (Eds.), *Teaching the learning-disabled adolescent* (pp. 201–234). Boston: Houghton Mifflin.

Chall, J. (1983). *Stages of reading development.* New York: McGraw-Hill.

———— (1987). A misinterpretation. *Phi Delta Kappan, 69,* 94.

Chan, L., & Cole, P. (1986). The effects of comprehension monitoring training on the reading competence of learning disabled and regular class students. *Remedial and Special Education, 1,* 33–39.

Choate, J.S. (1987). Synthesizing assessment and programming. In J.S. Choate, T.Z. Bennett, B.E. Enright, L.S. Miller, J.A. Poteet, & T.A. Rakes. *Assessment and programming basic curriculum skills* (pp. 231–238). Boston: Allyn and Bacon.

Choate, J.S., Bennett, T.Z., Enright, B.E., Miller, L.S., Poteet, J.A., & Rakes, T.A. (1987). *Assessment and programming basic curriculum skills.* Boston: Allyn and Bacon.

Christine, R., & Hollingsworth, P. (1966). An experiment in spelling. *Education, 86,* 565–567.

Clymer, T. & Martin, P. (1976). *The dog next door and other stories.* Lexington, MA: Ginn and Company.

Colbourn, M. & McLeod, J. (1983). Computer-guided educational diagnosis: A prototype expert system. *Journal of Special Education Technology, 6,* 30–39.

Compton, C. (1984). *Guide to 75 tests for special education.* Belmont, CA.: Fearon.

Cook, R.E., Tessier, A., & Armbruster, V.B. (1987). *Adapting early childhood curricula for children with special needs* (2nd ed.). Columbus: Merrill.

Cooper, C.R. (1977). Holistic evaluation of writing. In C.R. Cooper, & L. Odell (Eds.), *Evaluating writing: Describing, measuring, judging*. Urbana, IL: National Council of Teachers of English.

Cooper, C.R., & Odell, L. (Eds.). (1977). *Evaluating writing: Describing, measuring, judging*. Urbana, IL: National Council of Teachers of English.

Cox, L.S. (1975). Diagnosing and remediating systematic errors in addition and subtraction computations. *The Arithmetic Teacher, 22*, 151–157.

Cullinan, D., Lloyd, J., & Epstein, M.H. (1981). Strategy training: A structured approach to arithmetic instruction. *Exceptional Education Quarterly, 2*, 41–49.

de Lone, R.H. (1979). *Small futures*. New York: Harcourt Brace Jovanovich.

DeMaster, V., Crossland, C., & Hasselbring, T.S. (1986). Consistency of learning disabled students' spelling performance. *Learning Disability Quarterly, 9*, 89–96.

Deno, S.L. (1985). Curriculum-based measurement: The emerging alternative. *Exceptional Children, 52*, 219–232.

――― (1986). Formative evaluation of individual student programs: A new role for school psychologists. *School Psychology Review, 15*, 358–374.

――― (1987). Curriculum-based measurement. *Teaching Exceptional Children, 20*, 41–42.

Deno, S.L., & Fuchs, L.S. (1987). Developing curriculum-based measurement for special education problem solving. *Focus on Exceptional Children, 19*, 1–16.

Deno, S.L., & Mirkin, P. (1977). *Data-based program modification: A manual*. Reston, VA: Council for Exceptional Children.

Deno, S.L., Mirkin, P., & Chiang, B. (1982). Identifying valid measures of reading. *Exceptional Children, 49*, 36–45.

Deshler, D.D., & Schumaker, J.B. (1986). Learning strategies: An instructional alternative for low-achieving adolescents. *Exceptional Children, 52*, 583–590.

Deshler, D.D., & Schumaker, J.B. (1988). An instructional model for teaching students how to learn. In J.L. Garden, J.E. Zins & M.J. Curtis (Eds.). *Alternative educational delivery systems: Enhancing instructional options for all students*. Washington, DC: National Association of School Psychologists.

Dewitz, P., Carr, E., & Patberg, J. (1987). Effects of inference training on comprehension and comprehension monitoring. *Reading Research Quarterly, 22*, 99–121.

Duda, R., & Shortliff, E. (1983). Expert systems research. *Science, 220*, 261–268.

Elliott, S.N., & Piersel, W.C. (1982). Direct assessment of reading skills: An approach which links assessment to intervention. *School Psychology Review, 11*, 267–280.

Engelhardt, J. (1977). Analysis of children's computational errors: A qualitative approach. *British Journal of Educational Psychology, 47*, 149–154.

Enright, B.E. (1986). *Error analysis in assessment and remediation of the exceptional pupil*. Paper presented at 64th Annual Conference of the Council for Exceptional Children. New Orleans, LA.

Enright, B.E., Gable, R.A., & Hendrickson, J.M. (1987). *How do students get answers like these?* Unpublished manuscript, Old Dominion University, Norfolk, VA.

Evans, S.S., Evans, W.H., & Mercer, C. (1986). *Assessment for instruction*. New York: Allyn and Bacon.

Fennell, F. (1981). *Elementary mathematics diagnosis and correction kit*. West Nyack, NY: The Center for Applied Research in Education, Inc.

Ferster, C.B., Culbertson, S., & Perrot-Boren, M.C. (1975). *Behavior principles*. Englewood Cliffs, NJ: Prentice Hall.

Finn, P.J. (1977). Computer-aided description of mature word choices in writing. In C.R. Cooper & L. Odell (Eds.), *Evaluating writing: Describing, measuring, judging*. Urbana, IL: National Council of Teachers of English.

Flood, J., & Lapp, D. (1987). Forms of discourse in basal readers. *Elementary School Journal, 87*, 299–306.

Freeman, F.N. (1959). A new handwriting scale. *Elementary School Journal, 59*, 218–221.

Fuchs, D. (1981). Differential responses of preschool language-handicapped children and familiar and unfamiliar testers as a function of task complexity, length of acquaintanceship, and sex of child. In V. Shipman (Chair), *Client identification and issues of validity: The influence of situational variables on children's cognitive performance.* Symposium presented at the annual meeting of the American Educational Research Association, Los Angeles, CA, April 1981.

Fuchs, D., Featherstone, N., Garwick, D.R., & Fuchs, L.S. (1984). Effects of examiner familiarity and task characteristics on speech and language-impaired children's performance. *Measurement and Evaluation in Guidance, 56*, 243–262.

Fuchs, D., Fuchs, L.S., Benowitz, S.A., & Barringer, K. (1987). Norm-referenced tests: Are they valid for use with handicapped students? *Exceptional Children, 54*, 263–271.

Fuchs, D., Fuchs, L.S., Dailey, A.M., & Power, M.H. (1985). The effects of examiners' personal familiarity and professional experience on handicapped children's test performance. *Journal of Educational Research, 78*, 141–146.

Fuchs, D., Fuchs, L.S., Garwick, D.R., & Featherstone, N. (1983). Test performance of language handicapped children with familiar and unfamiliar examiners. *Journal of Psychology, 114*, 37–46.

Fuchs, D., Fuchs, L.S., & Power, M.H. (1987). Effects of examiner familiarity on LD and MR students' language performance. *Remedial and Special Education, 8*, 47–52.

Fuchs, D., Fuchs, L.S., Power, M.H., & Dailey, A.M. (1983). *Systematic bias on the assessment of handicapped children* (Research Report No. 134). Minneapolis: University of Minnesota Institute for Research on Learning Disabilities. (ERIC Document Reproduction Service No. ED 236 202)

――― (1985). Bias in the assessment of handicapped children. *American Educational Research Journal, 22*, 185–198.

Fuchs, L.S. (1986). Monitoring the performance of mildly handicapped pupils: Review of current research and practice. *Remedial and Special Education, 7*, 5–12.

Fuchs, L.S., Deno, S.L., & Marston, D. (1983). Improving the reliability of curriculum-based measures of academic achievement for psychoeducational decision making. *Diagnostique, 8*, 135–149.

Fuchs, L.S., Deno, S.L., & Mirkin, P. (1984). The effects of frequent curriculum-based measurement and evaluation on pedagogy, student achievement, and student awareness of learning. *American Educational Research Journal, 21*, 449–460.

Fuchs, L.S., & Fuchs, D. (1984). Examiner accuracy during protocol completion. *Journal of Psychoeducational Assessment, 2*, 101–108.

Fuchs, L.S., & Fuchs, D. (1986a). Curriculum-based assessment of progress toward long- and short-term goals. *Journal of Special Education, 20*, 69–82.

Fuchs, L.S., & Fuchs, D. (1986b). Effects of systematic formative evaluation: A meta-analysis. *Exceptional Children, 53*, 199–208.

Fuchs, L.S., & Fuchs, D. (1986c). Linking assessment to instructional intervention: An overview. *School Psychology Review, 15*, 318–323.

Fuchs, L.S., Fuchs, D., Hamlett, C.L., & Hasselbring, T.S. (1987). Using computers with curriculum-based monitoring: Effects on teacher efficiency and satisfaction. *Journal of Special Education Technology, 8*, 14–27.

Fuchs, L.S., Hamlett, C.L., Fuchs, D., Stecker, P.M., & Ferguson, C. (in press). Conducting curriculum-based measurement with computerized data collection: Effects on efficiency and teacher satisfaction. *Journal of Special Education Technology.*

Fuchs, L.S., Tindal, G., & Fuchs, D. (1986). Effects of mastery learning procedures on student achievement. *Journal of Educational Research, 79,* 286–291.

Fuchs, L.S., Wesson, C., Tindal, G., Mirkin, P.K., & Deno, S.L. (1982). *Instructional changes, student performance, and teacher preferences: The effects of specific measurement and evaluation procedures* (Research Report No. 64). Minneapolis: Institute for Research on Learning Disabilities. (ERIC Document Reproduction Service No. ED 218 849)

Gable, R.A., Fleming, E.C., & Smith, D.D. (1980). Teaching oral reading: A review with recommendations for improving instruction. *Journal of Special Education Technology, 3,* 17–24.

Gable, R.A., Hendrickson, J.M., Evans, S.S., & Evans, W.H. (1987). Data decisions for instructing behaviorally disordered students. In R. Rutherford, Jr., C.M. Nelson & S. Forness (Eds.). *Bases of severe behavioral disorders in children and youth* (pp. 75–88) San Diego, CA: College-Hill Press.

Gable, R.A., Hendrickson, J.M., & Meeks, J. (1987). *Error analysis for correcting problems in oral reading of special needs students.* Unpublished manuscript. Old Dominion University, Norfolk, VA.

Gable, R.A., Hendrickson, J.M., Tenenbaum, H., & Morsink, C.V. (1986). *Analysis of the academic errors of students with learning difficulties* (Monograph No. 14). Gainesville, FL: University of Florida Multidisciplinary Diagnostic and Training Program.

Gable, R.A., & Shores, R.E. (1980). Comparison of procedures for promoting reading proficiency of two children with learning and behavior disorders. *Behavioral Disorders, 5,* 102–107.

Gagne, E. (1985). *The cognitive psychology of school learning.* Boston: Little, Brown.

Ganschow, L. (1981). Discovering children's learning strategies for spelling through error pattern analysis. *The Reading Teacher, 36,* 676–680.

Gates, A. (1931). An experimental comparison of the study-test and test-study methods of spelling. *Journal of Educational Psychology, 22,* 1–19.

Gillingham, A., & Stillman, B. (1970). *Remedial training for children with specific disability in reading, spelling and penmanship.* Cambridge, MA: Educators Publishing Service.

Glaser, R. (1981). The future of testing: A research agenda for cognitive psychology and psychometrics. *American Psychologist, 12,* 696–706.

Glaser, R., & Nitko, A.J. (1971). Measurement in learning and instruction. In R.L. Thorndike (Ed.), *Educational measurement* (2nd ed.). Washington, DC: American Council on Education.

Goh, E.S., Tesler, C.J., & Fuller, G.B. (1981). The practice of psychological assessment among school psychologists. *Professional Psychology, 12,* 696–706.

Golub, L.S. (1973). *Syntactic density score with some aids for tabulating.* (ERIC Document Reproduction Service No. 091 741)

Goodman, K. (1965). A linguistic study of cues and miscues in reading. *Elementary English, 42,* 639–643.

Goodstein, H.A. (1981). Are the errors we see true errors? Error analysis in verbal problem solving. *Topics in Learning and Learning Disabilities, 1,* 31–45.

Graden, J.L., Christenson, S., Ysseldyke, J.E., Meyers, J., Grenshaft, J., & Reschly, D.J. (1984). A national survey on students' and practitioners' perceptions of training. *School Psychology Review, 13,* 397–407.

Graham, S. (1985). Evaluating spelling programs and materials. *Teaching Exceptional Children,* Summer, 299–303.

Graham, S., & Miller, L. (1979). Spelling research and practice: A unified approach. *Focus on Exceptional Children, 12,* 1–15.

——— (1983). Spelling research and practice: A unified approach. In E. Meyer, G. Vergason, & R. Whelan (Eds.), *Promising practices for exceptional children: Curriculum implications.* Denver: Love.

Graves, A. (1986). Effects of direct instruction and metacomprehension training on finding main ideas. *Learning Disability Quarterly, 1,* 90–100.

Gray, W. (1967). *Gray Oral Reading Test.* Indianapolis: Bobbs-Merrill.

Grossnickle, F., & Reckazch, J. (1973). *Discovering meanings in elementary school mathematics.* New York: Holt, Rinehart and Winston.

Guerin, G.R., & Maier, A.S. (1983). *Informal assessment in education.* Palo Alto, CA: Mayfield.

Hammill, D.D., & Bartel, N.R. (1982). *Teaching children with learning and behavior problems* (3rd ed). Boston: Allyn and Bacon.

Hammill, D.D., & Larsen, S. (1988). *Test of written language-2.* Austin, TX: PRO-ED.

Hammill, D.D., & McNutt, G. (1981). *Correlates of reading: The consensus of thirty years of correlational research.* (PRO-ED Monograph No. 1), Austin, TX: PRO-ED.

Hanna, P., Hanna, J., Hodges, R., & Peterson, H. (1971). *Power to spell.* Boston: Houghton-Mifflin.

Hanna, P., Hanna, J., Hodges, R., & Rudorf, E. (1966). *Phonemongrapheme correspondences as cues for spelling improvements.* Washington, D.C.: U.S. Department of Health, Education and Welfare.

Hanna, P., Hodges, R., & Hanna, J. (1971). *Spelling structure and strategies.* Boston: Houghton-Mifflin.

Hansen, C.L. (1978). Writing skills. In N.G. Haring, T.C. Lovitt, M.D. Eaton & C.L. Hansen (Eds.), *The 4th r: Research in the classroom* (pp. 93–126). Columbus, OH: Merrill.

Haring, N.G., & Gentry, N. (1976). Direct and individualized instructional procedures. In N. Haring & R. Schiefelbush (Eds.), *Teaching special children* (pp. 351–402). New York: McGraw-Hill.

Haring, N.G., Liberty, K., & White, O.R. (1980). Rules for data-based strategy decisions in instructional programs. In W. Sailor, B. Wilcox, & L. Brown (Eds.), *Methods for instruction for severely handicapped students* (pp. 159–192). Baltimore, MD: Paul H. Brookes.

Hart, B., & Risley, T. (1975). Incidental teaching of language in the preschool. *Journal of Applied Behavior Analysis, 8,* 411–420.

Hasselbring, T.S. (1984). Computer-based assessment of special-needs students. In R.E. Bennett & C.A. Maher (Eds.), *Microcomputer and exceptional children* (pp. 7–19). New York: Haworth Press.

——— (1986a). Toward the development of expert assessment systems. *Special Services in the Schools, 2,* 43–56.

——— (1986b). *Spelling scoring procedures.* Unpublished manuscript. Nashville, TN: George Peabody College of Vanderbilt University.

Hasselbring, T.S., & Goin, L.I. (1985). *Chronometric Analysis of Math Strategies* [computer program]. Nashville, TN: Expert Systems Software.

Hasselbring, T.S., Goin, L.I., & Bransford, J.D. (1987). Effective mathematics instruction: Developing automaticity. *Teaching Exceptional Children, 19,* 30–33.

Hasselbring, T.S., & Hamlett, C.L. (1984). Planning and managing instruction: Computer-based decision-making. *Teaching Exceptional Children, 16,* 248–252.

Hasselbring, T.S., & Owens, S. (1981). *A microcomputer-based system for the analysis of student spelling errors.* Unpublished manuscript, Nashville, TN: George Peabody College of Vanderbilt University.

Helwig, J.J., Johns, J.C., Norman, J.E., & Cooper, J.O. (1976). Technical report: Students' self recording of manuscript letter strokes. *Journal of Applied Behavior Analysis, 9,* 231–236.

Hendrick, I.G., & MacMillan, D.L. (1984). *The role of mental testing in shaping special classes for the retarded.* Paper presented at the annual meeting of the American Educational Research Association, New Orleans, LA, April 1984.

Hendrickson, J.M., & Gable, R.A. (1981). The use of modeling tactics to promote academic skill development of exceptional learners. *Journal of Special Education Technology, 4,* 20–29.

Hendrickson, J.M., Gable, R.A., & Hasselbring, T.S. (1988). "Pleez lit me pas splelin." *Education and Treatment of Children, 11,* 166–178.

Hendrickson, J., Gable, R., Hester, P., & Strain, P. (1985). Teaching social reciprocity: Social exchanges between young severely handicapped and non-handicapped children. *The Pointer, 29,* 17–21.

Hendrickson, J., Gable, R., & Shores, R.E. (1987). The ecological perspective: Setting events and behavior. *The Pointer, 31*(3), 40–44.

Hendrickson, J.M., Gable, R.A., & Stowitschek, C.E. (1985). Rate as a measure of academic success in mainstream settings. *Special Services in the Schools, 1,* 1–15.

Hendrix, J. (1988). *The whole child* (4th ed.). Columbus: Merrill.

Hillerich, R.L. (1978). *A writing vocabulary of elementary children.* Springfield, IL: Thomas.

Hirsch, E., & Niedermeyer, F.C. (1978). The effects of tracking prompts and discrimination training on kindergarten handwriting performance. *Journal of Educational Research, 67,* 81–85.

Hobbs, N. (1966). Helping disturbed children: Psychological and ecological strategies. *American Psychologist, 21,* 1105–1115.

Hoffman, J. (1987). Rethinking the role of oral reading in basal instruction. *Elementary School Journal, 87,* 367–373.

Hofmeister, A. (1969). *An investigation of academic skills in trainable mentally retarded adolescents and young adults.* Unpublished doctoral dissertation, Eugene: University of Oregon.

——— (1973). Let's get it write! *Teaching Exceptional Children, 6,* 30–33.

——— (1981). *DLM handwriting resource book.* Allen, TX: DLM Inc.

Hopkins, B.L., Schutte, R.C., & Gorton, K.L. (1971). The effects of access to a playground on the rate and quality of printing of first and second grade students. *Journal of Applied Behavior Analysis, 4,* 77–88.

Hopkins, M. (1986). *Teaching arithmetic: A diagnostic approach.* Unpublished manuscript. Ocala, FL.

——— (1987). Assessment for instruction in mathematics. *The Pointer, 30,* 31–36.

Hops, H. (1982). Behavioral assessment of exceptional children's social development. In P.S. Strain (Ed.), *Social development of exceptional children.* Rockville, MD: Aspen Systems Corporation.

Howell, K.W. (1986). Direct assessment of academic performance. *School Psychology Review, 15,* 324–335.

Howell, K.W., & Kaplan, J.J. (1980). *Diagnosing basic skills: A handbook for deciding what to teach.* Columbus, OH: Merrill.

Howell, K.W., & Morehead, M.K. (1987). *Curriculum-based evaluation for special and remedial education.* Columbus, OH: Merrill.

Hoyson, M., Jamieson, B., & Strain, P.S. (1984). Individualized group instruction of normally developing and autistic-like children: The LEAP curriculum model. *Journal of the Division for Early Childhood, 8,* 157–172.

Hunt, K.W. (1965). *Grammatical structures written at three grade levels.* Research Report No. 3. Urbana, IL: National Council of Teachers of English.

——— (1977). Early blooming and late blooming syntactic structures. In C.R. Cooper & L. Odell (Eds.), *Evaluating writing: Describing, measuring, judging.* Urbana, IL: National Council of Teachers of English.

Ingram, C.F. (1980). *Fundamentals of educational assessment.* New York: Van Nostrand.

Isaacson, S. (1988). Assessing the writing product: Qualitative and quantitative measures. *Exceptional Children, 54,* 528–542.

Jenkins, J.R., Deno, S.L., & Mirkin, P.K. (1979). *Measuring pupil progress toward the least restrictive environment* (Research Report No. 10). Minneapolis: University of Minnesota Institute for Research on Learning Disabilities. (ERIC Document Reproduction Service No. ED 185 767)

Jenkins, J.R., & Pany, D. (1978). Standardized achievement tests: How useful for special education? *Exceptional Children, 44,* 448–453.

Jensen, J.R. (1981). *Straight talk about mental tests.* New York: Macmillan.

Johnson, J.L. (1969). Special education and the inner city: A challenge for the future or another means for cooling the mark? *Journal of Special Education, 3,* 241–251.

Johnson, M., & Kress, R. (1965). *Informal reading inventories.* Newark, DE: IRA.

Jones, J.C., Trap, J.J., & Cooper, J.O. (1977). Students's self-recording of manuscript letter strokes. *Journal of Applied Behavior Analysis, 10,* 509–514.

Kaiser, A., Hendrickson, J., & Alpert, C. (in press). Milieu language teaching: A second look. In R.A. Gable (Ed.), *Advances in mental retardation and developmental disabilities* (Vol. 4). Greenwich, CT: JAI Press.

Kauffman, J., Hallahan, D., Haas, K., Brame, T., & Boren, R. (1978). Imitating children's errors to improve their spelling performance. *Journal of Learning Disabilities, 11,* 33–38.

Koenig, C.R., & Kunzelmann, H.P. (1980). *Classroom learning screening manual.* Columbus, OH: Merrill.

Lambert, C. (1964). *Seven-plus assessment: Spelling.* University of London Press.

Larsen, S., & Hammill, D.D., (1986). *Test of Written Spelling-2.* Austin, TX: PRO-ED.

Lessen, E. (1980). Scoring procedures for the evaluation of spelling performance. *Academic Therapy, 15,* 347–350.

Lenz, B.K., Alley, G.R., & Schumaker, J.B. (1987). Activating the inactive learner: Advance organizers in the secondary content classroom. *Learning Disability Quarterly, 10,* 53–67.

Lenz, B.K., Bulgren, J.A., & Hudson, P. (1989). Content enhancement: A model for promoting content acquisition. In T. Scruggs & B. Wong (Eds.), *Proceedings of the 1988 division for learning disabilities symposium on intervention research.* West Lafayette, IN: Purdue University.

Lewis, E.R., & Lewis, H.P. (1965). An analysis of errors in the formation of manuscript letters by first-grade children. *American Educational Research Journal, 2,* 25–35.

Loban, W.D. (1976). *Language development: Kindergarten through grade twelve.* Research Report No. 18. Urbana, IL: National Council of Teachers of English.

Lovitt, T.C. (1973). *Using applied behavior analysis procedures to evaluate spelling instructional techniques with learning disabled youngsters.* Unpublished manuscript, Seattle: University of Washington.

——— (1975). Applied behavior analysis and learning disabilities. *Journal of Learning Disabilities, 8,* 504–518.

Lovitt, T.C., & Curtiss, K. (1968). Effect of manipulating an antecedent event on mathematics response rate. *Journal of Applied Behavior Analysis, 1,* 329–333.

Lovitt, T.C., & Esveldt, K. (1970). The relative effects on math performance of single versus multiple-ratio schedules: A case study. *Journal of Applied Behavior Analysis, 3,* 261–270.

Lovitt, T.C., Guppy, T.E., & Blattner, J.E. (1969). The use of a free-time contingency with fourth-graders to increase spelling accuracy. *Behavioral Research and Therapy, 1,* 151–156.

Lovitt, T.C., & Hansen, C. (1976a). Round one—placing the child in the right reader. *Journal of Learning Disabilities, 9,* 347–353.

——— (1976b). The use of contingent skipping and drilling to improve oral reading and comprehension. *Journal of Learning Disabilities, 9,* 481–487.

Lovitt, T.C., Rudsit, J., Jenkins, J., Pious, C., & Benedetti, D. (1986). Adapting science materials for regular and learning disabled seventh graders. *Remedial and Special Education, 7,* 31–39.

Lydra, W.J., & Church, R.S., (1964). Direct, practical arithmetic experiences and success in solving realistic verbal "reasoning" problems in arithmetic. *Journal of Educational Research, 57,* 530–533.

MacDonald, J.D., & Gillette, Y. (1988). Communicating partners: A conversational model for building parent-child relationships with handicapped children. In K. Marfo (Ed.), *Parent-child interaction and developmental disabilities: Theory, research, and intervention.* (pp. 220–252). New York: Praeger.

Mahoney, G. (1988). Enhancing the developmental competence of handicapped infants. In K. Marfo (Ed.), *Parent-child interaction and developmental disabilities: theory, research, and intervention.* (pp. 209–219). New York: Praeger.

Mahoney, G., & Powell, A. (1986). *The transactional intervention program: A child-centered approach to developmental intervention with young handicapped children.* Farmington, CT: Pediatric Research and Training Center.

Marino, J. (1981). Spelling errors: From analysis to instruction. *Language Arts, 58,* 567–572.

Mayer, R.E. (1987). *Educational psychology: A cognitive approach.* Boston: Little, Brown.

McEvoy, M.A., & Odom, S.L. (1987). Social interaction training for preschool children with behavior disorders. *Behavioral Disorders, 12,* 242–251.

McLoughlin, J.A., & Lewis, R.B. (1986). *Assessing special students: Strategies and procedures* (2nd ed.). Columbus, OH: Merrill.

Mellon, J.C. (1969). *Transformational sentence-combining.* (Research Report No. 10). Urbana, IL: National Council of Teachers of English.

Mercer, C.D., & Mercer, A. (1985). *Teaching students with learning problems* (2nd ed.). New York: Merrill.

Messick, S. (1989). Validity. In R.L. Linn (Ed.), *Educational measurement.*(3rd ed.). New York: American Council on Education and Macmillan.

Millman, J. (1972). Criterion-referenced measurement. In W.J. Popham (Ed.), *Evaluation in education: Current applications.* Berkeley: McCutchan.

Milone, Jr., M.N., & Wasylyk,T.M. (1981). Handwriting in special education. *Teaching Exceptional Children, 14,* 58–61.

Moran, M.R. (1987). Options for written language assessment. *Focus on Exceptional Children, 19,* 1–12.

Mosenthal, P.B. (1988). Three approaches to progress: Understanding the writing of exceptional children. *Exceptional Children, 54,* 497–504.

Morsink, C.V. (1984). *Teaching special needs students in regular classrooms.* Boston: Little, Brown.

Mudd, J.M., & Wolery, M. (1987). Training Head Start teachers to use incidental teaching. *Journal of the Division for Early Childhood, 11,* 124–134.

Naisbett, J. (1982). *Megatrends: Ten new directions transforming our lives.* New York: Warner Books.

Nau, D. (1983). Expert computer systems. *IEEE Computer, 16,* 63–85.

Nitko, A.J. (1983). *Educational tests and measurement: An introduction.* New York: Harcourt Brace Jovanovich.

O'Donnell, R.C., Griffin, W.J., & Norris, R.C. (1967). *Syntax of kindergarten and elementary school children: A transformational analysis* (Research Report No. 8). Urbana, IL: National Council of Teachers of English.

O'Hare, F. (1973). *Improving student writing without formal grammar instruction* (Research Report No. 15). Urbana, IL: National Council of Teachers of English.

Osborn, W.J. (1925). Ten reasons why pupils fail in mathematics. *The Mathematics Teacher, 18,* 234–238.

Owens, S. (1982). *A comparison of students' written and microcomputer responses on a diagnostic test of spelling errors.* Unpublished master's thesis, North Carolina State University.

Personkee, G., & Lee, A. (1971). *Comprehensive spelling instruction: Theory, research and application.* Scranton, PA: Intext Educational Publications.

Petrosky, A.R. (1977). Grammar instruction: What we know. *English Journal, 66,* 86–88.

Piaget, J. (1952). *The origins of intelligence in children.* New York: Norton.

———— (1963). *Play, dreams, and imitation in childhood.* New York: Norton.

Pink, W., & Leibert, R. (1986). Reading instruction in the elementary school: A proposal for reform. *Elementary School Journal, 87,* 51–67.

Pomeroy, J.P. (1971). *The relationship between selected piagetian spatial concepts and legibility of manuscript handwriting.* Unpublished doctoral dissertation, Tempe: Arizona State University.

Poplin, M. (1983). Assessing developmental writing abilities. *Topics in Learning Disabilities, 3,* 63–75.

Powell, W. (1968). *Reappraising the criteria for interpreting informal reading inventories.* Paper presented at the International Conference of the IRA, Boston.

———— (1978). *Measuring reading performance informally.* Paper presented at the International Conference of the IRA, Houston.

Pro-ED. (1987). *PRO-SCORE Systems.* [computer program]. Austin: Pro-Ed.

Quant, L. (1946). Factors affecting the legibility of handwriting. *Journal of Experimental Education, 14,* 297–316.

Reisman, F.K. (1982). *A guide to diagnostic teaching of arithmetic* (3rd ed.). Columbus, OH: Merrill.

Resnick, L.B. (1983). A development theory of number understanding. In P. Ginsburg (ed.), *The development of mathematical thinking* (pp. 109–151). New York: Academic Press.

Roberts, G. (1968). The failure strategies of third grade arithmetic students. *Arithmetic Teacher, 15,* 442–446.

Rousseau, M.K., Frantz, P.J., Poulson, C.L., & McClannahan, L.E. (1989). *Teaching writing skills to adolescents with autism.* Unpublished raw data.

Rousseau, M.K., Poulson, C.L., Bottge, B.A., & Dy, E.B. (1988). *Syntactic complexity in the writing of children labeled academically retarded and nonretarded.* Unpublished manuscript, City College of New York.

Ruedy, L.R. (1983). Handwriting instruction: It can be part of the high school curriculum. *Academic Therapy, 18,* 421–429.

Rupley, W., & Blair, T. (1987). Assignment and supervision of reading seatwork: Looking in on 12 primary teachers. *The Reading Teacher, 41,* 391–393.

Salvia, S., & Ysseldyke, J.E. (1988). *Assessment in special and remedial education* (4th ed.). Boston: Houghton Mifflin.

Sameroff, A. (1981). Longitudinal studies of preterm infants: A review of chapters 17–20. In S. Friedman & M. Sigman (Eds.), *Preterm birth and psychological development.* New York: Academic Press.

Samuels, S.J. (1979). The method of repeated readings. *The Reading Teacher, 32,* 403–408.

———— (1980). The age old controversy between holistic and sub-skill approaches to beginning reading instruction revisited. In C.M. McCullough (Ed.), *Inchword, inchworm: Persistent problems in reading instruction.* Newark, NJ: IRA.

Schmitt, M.C., & O'Brien, D.G. (1986). Story grammars: Some cautions about the translation of research into practice. *Reading Research and Instruction, 26,* 1–8.

Scholastic, Inc. (1985). *Math Assistant* [computer program]. New York: Scholastic Inc.

Schreiner, R. (1983). Principles of diagnosis of reading disabilities. *Topics in Learning and Learning Disabilities,* January, 70–85.

Schumaker, J.B., Deshler, D.D., Nolan, S., Clark, F., Alley, G., & Warner, M. (1981). *Error monitoring: A learning strategy for improving academic performance of adolescents* (Research

Report No. 32). Lawrence: University of Kansas Institute for Research in Learning Disabilities.

Schuster, E.H. (1980). *Sentence mastery*. New York: McGraw-Hill.

Sedlak, R.A., & Cartwright, G.P. (1972). Written language abilities of EMR and nonretarded children with the same mental ages. *American Journal of Mental Deficiency, 77,* 95–99.

Shapiro, E.S., & Derr, T. (1987). An examination of overlap between reading curricula and standardized achievement tests. *Journal of Special Education, 21,* 59–68.

Shaughnessy, M.P. (1977). *Errors and Expectations*. New York: Oxford University Press.

Sindelar, P., Smith, M., Harriman, N., Hale, R., & Wilson, R. (1986). Teacher effectiveness in special education programs. *Journal of Special Education, 20,* 195–207.

Skougie, J. (1987). *The method of repeated readings revisited*. Unpublished manuscript. Bakersfield: California State College, Department of Special Education.

Smith, D.D. (1981). *Teaching the learning disabled*. Englewood Cliffs, NJ: Prentice-Hall.

Smith, D.D., & Lovitt, T.C. (1975). The use of modeling techniques to influence the acquisition of computational arithmetic skills in learning disabled children. In E. Ramp & G. Semb (Eds.), *Behavior analysis: Areas of research and application*. Englewood cliffs, NJ: Prentice-Hall.

Snider, V., & Tarver, S. (1987). The effect of early reading failure on acquisition of knowledge among students with learning disabilities. *Journal of Learning Disabilities, 20,* 351–373.

Spache, G. (1943). Validity and reliability of the proposed classification of spelling errors. *Journal of Educational Research, 31,* 204–314.

———— (1976). *Investigating the issues of reading disabilities*. Boston: Allyn and Bacon.

Spache, G., & Spache, E. (1986). *Reading in the elementary school* (5th ed.). Boston: Allyn & Bacon.

Spodek, B., Saracho, O.N., & Lee, R.C. (1984). *Mainstreaming young children*. Belmont, CA: Wadsworth.

Stanley, J.C. (1971). Reliability. In R. Thorndike (Ed.), *Educational measurement* (2nd ed.). Washington, DC: American Council on Education.

Starlin, C. (1982). *On reading and writing*. Des Moines, IA: Department of Public Instruction.

Stedman, L., & Kaestle, C. (1987). Literacy and reading performance in the U.S. from 1880 to the present. *Reading Research Quarterly, 22,* 8–46.

Stewart, K. (1973). Two approaches to handwriting instruction. *Slow Learning Child, 20,* 142–146.

Stokes, T.F., & Baer, D.M. (1977). An implicit technology of generalization. *Journal of Applied Behavior Analysis, 10,* 349–367.

Stowitschek, C.C., Hofmeister, A., & Stowitschek, J.J. (1981). *Manuscript kit. DLM Handwriting Program*. Allen, TX: Developmental Learning Materials.

Stowitschek, C.E., & Stowitschek, J.J. (1979). Evaluating handwriting performance: The student helps the teacher. *Journal of Learning Disabilities, 21,* 203–206.

Stowitschek, J. (1978). Applying programming principles to remedial handwriting practice. *Journal of Special Education Technology, 1,* 21–26.

Stowitschek, J.J., Gable, R.A., & Hendrickson, J.M. (1980). *Instructional materials for exceptional children: Selection, management, and adaptation*. Rockville, MD: Aspen Systems Corporation.

Stowitschek, J.J., Ghezzi, P.M., & Safely, K.V. (1987). "I'd rather do it myself:" Self-evaluation and correction of handwriting. *Education and Treatment of Children, 10,* 209–224.

Stowitschek, J.J., & Stowitschek, C.E. (1975). *Correcting handwriting difficulties*, Nashville, TN: George Peabody College of Teachers of Vanderbilt University.

Sundbye, N. (1987). Text explicitness and inferential questioning: Effects on story understanding and recall. *Reading Research Quarterly, 22,* 82–97.

Templeton, S. (1986). Synthesis of research on the learning and teaching of spelling. *Educational Leadership*, March, 73–78.

Thorndike, E.L. (1910). Handwriting. *Teacher's College Record, 11,* 386–389.

Tindal, G., Fuchs, L.S., Fuchs, D., Shinn, M.R., Deno, S.L., & Germann, G. (1985). Empirical validation of criterion-referenced test. *Journal of Educational Research, 78,* 203–209.

Trap, J.J., Milner-Davis, P., Joseph, S., & Cooper, J.O. (1978). The effects of feedback and consequences on transitional cursive letter formation. *Journal of Applied Behavior Analysis, 11,* 381–394.

Van Houten, R., Morrison, E., Barrow, B., & Wenaus, J. (1974). The effects of daily practice and feedback on the acquisition of elementary math skills. *School Applications of Learning Theory, 7,* 1–16.

Varnhagen, C.K., & Goldman, S.R. (1986). Improving comprehension: Causal relations instruction for learning handicapped learners. *The Reading Teacher,* (May), 896–904.

Waggoner, J., LaNunziata, L., Hill, D., & Cooper, J. (1981). Space, size and accuracy of kindergarten and first-grade student manuscript handwriting. *Journal of Educational Research, 74,* 182–184.

Watts, L. (1971). *Reliability of a rating system of handwriting improvement.* Unpublished master's thesis, Logan: Utah State University.

Weaver, C. (1979). *Grammar for teachers.* Urbana, IL: National Council of Teachers of English.

—— (1982). Welcoming errors as signs of growth. *Language Arts, 59,* 438–444.

Weinshank, A., & Vinsonhaler, J. (1983). On diagnostic reliability in reading: What's wrong and what can be done? *Topics in Learning and Learning Disabilities* (January), 43–52.

Wesson, C., King, R., & Deno, S.L. (1984). Direct and frequent measurement: If it's so good for us, why don't we use it? *Learning Disability Quarterly, 7,* 45–48.

West, R., Young, R., & Johnson, J. (1984). *Using microcomputers to summarize and analyze outcome based education.* Unpublished manuscript. Logan: Utah State University.

White, O.R., & Haring, N.G. (1980). *Exceptional teaching* (2nd ed.). Columbus, OH: Merrill.

Wigdor, A.K., & Garner, W.R. (Eds.). (1982). *Ability testing: Uses, consequences, and controversies (Part I).* Washington, DC: National Academic Press.

Williams, J.M. (1989). *Style: Ten lessons in clarity and grace* (3rd ed.). Glenview, IL: Scott, Foresman.

Winikur, D.W., & Daniels, R. (1982). Trends in the role and function of New Jersey school psychologists. *School Psychology Review, 11,* 438–441.

Wixson, K. (1979). Miscue analysis: A critical review. *Journal of Reading Behavior, 11,* 163–175.

Wolery, M., Bailey, D.B., & Sugai, G.M. (1988). *Effective teaching: Principles and procedures of applied behavioral analysis with exceptional students.* Boston: Allyn and Bacon.

Yalow, E., & Popham, J. (1983). Content validity at the crossroads. *Educational Researcher, 12,* 10–14, 21.

Zigmond, N., Vallecorsa, A., & Silverman, R. (1983). *Assessment for instructional planning in special education.* Englewood Cliffs, NJ: Prentice-Hall.

Index

Frame, T., 84
Frantz, P. J., 91
Freeman, F. N., 66
Fuchs, D., 3, 4, 5, 8, 10, 11, 12, 111, 112
Fuchs, L. S., 2, 3, 4, 5, 8, 10, 11, 12, 111, 112
Fuller, G. B., 3
Functional instructional groups, 2

Gable, R. A., 12, 17, 30, 32, 34, 37, 46, 49, 50, 55, 56, 67, 78, 81, 85, 146, 149
Gagne, E., 120
Games with rules, 19
Ganschow, L., 82
Garner, W. R., 4
Garwick, D. R., 4
Gates, A., 84
Generalization and test validity, 121
Gentry, N., 81
Germann, G., 4, 10
Ghezzi, P. M., 69
Gillette, Y., 27–28
Gillingham, A., 86
Glaser, R., 3, 9
Goh, E. S., 3
Goin, L. I., 106
Goldman, S. R., 61
Goodman, K., 48
Goodstein, H. A., 42
Gorton, K. L., 66
Graden, J. L., 3
Graham, S., 78, 82, 84, 86
Graves, A., 60
Gray, W., 49
Greff, K. N., 65
Grenshaft, J., 3
Griffin, W. J., 90
Grossnickle, F., 34
Grouping students, 149
Group reports on errors, 109
Guerin, G. R., 92

Hale, R., 60
Hallahan, D., 84
Hamlett, C. L., 11, 12, 112
Hammill, D. D., 35, 78, 92
Handwriting error analysis guide, 70
Handwriting instruction, 63–77
Hanna, J., 81, 84
Hanna, P., 81, 84
Hansen, C. L., 48, 50, 55, 84, 147
Haring, N. G., 6, 8, 81, 111
Harriman, N., 60
Hart, B., 21
Hasselbring, T. S., 12, 79, 81, 82, 102, 103, 106, 112

Helwig, J. J., 66
Hendrickson, J. M., 12, 14, 28, 32, 34, 37, 46, 50, 55, 56, 67, 78, 81, 85, 141, 146, 149
Hendrik, I. G., 2
Hiebert, E., 46
Hill, D., 69
Hirsch, E., 65
Hobbs, N., 17
Hodges, R., 81, 84
Hoffman, J., 60
Hofmeister, A., 66, 68, 69, 74
Hollingsworth, P., 84
Homonyms, errors in spelling, 84
Hopkins, B. L., 66
Hopkins, M., 34
Hops, H., 22
Howell, K. W., 31, 32, 49, 51, 79, 80, 147
Hoyson, M., 21
Hudson, P., 141
Hunt, K. W., 90

Identification process, 2
Implementation
    of CASA, 137–140
    of error analysis, 146–151
Informal Reading Inventory, 47
Information-processing constructs, 120
Ingram, C. F., 56
Institute for Research in Learning Disabilities, 121–122, 141
Instructional environment, focus on, 3
Instructional processes, 132
Instructional validity, 121
Interactional view, 17, 18–19
Interactive assessment, 102
Intervention strategies, 99–101, 139–140
Interview, 80–81
Isaacson, S., 90

Jamieson, B., 21
Jenkins, J. R., 6, 141
Jensen, J. R., 4
John, L., 32
Johns, J. C., 66
Johnson, J. L., 2, 112
Johnson, M., 47
Jones, J. E., 66
Joseph, S., 66

Kaestle, C., 47
Kaiser, A., 28
Kaplan, J. J., 32, 49, 51, 79, 80
Kauffman, J., 84
King, R., 112
Koening, C. R., 80